T0330425

Extreme Leadership

NEW HORIZONS IN LEADERSHIP STUDIES

Series Editor: Joanne B. Ciulla, *Professor and Coston Family Chair in Leadership and Ethics, Jepson School of Leadership Studies, University of Richmond, USA*

This important series is designed to make a significant contribution to the development of leadership studies. This field has expanded dramatically in recent years and the series provides an invaluable forum for the publication of high quality works of scholarship and shows the diversity of leadership issues and practices around the world.

The main emphasis of the series is on the development and application of new and original ideas in leadership studies. It pays particular attention to leadership in business, economics and public policy and incorporates the wide range of disciplines which are now part of the field. Global in its approach, it includes some of the best theoretical and empirical work with contributions to fundamental principles, rigorous evaluations of existing concepts and competing theories, historical surveys and future visions.

Titles in the series include:

Inventing Leadership
The Challenge of Democracy
J. Thomas Wren

Dissent and the Failure of Leadership
Edited by Stephen P. Banks

Corporate Governance and Ethics
An Aristotelian Perspective
Alejo José G. Sison

Rethinking Leadership
A New Look at Old Leadership Questions
Donna Ladkin

Leadership Studies
The Dialogue of Disciplines
Edited by Michael Harvey and Ronald E. Riggio

Poor Leadership and Bad Governance
Reassessing Presidents and Prime Ministers in North America, Europe and Japan
Edited by Ludger Helms

Leadership by Resentment
From *Ressentiment* to Redemption
Ruth Capriles

Critical Perspectives on Leadership
Emotion, Toxicity, and Dysfunction
Edited by Jeanette Lemmergaard and Sara Louise Muhr

Authentic Leadership
Clashes, Convergences and Coalescences
Edited by Donna Ladkin and Chellie Spiller

Leadership and Transformative Ambition in International Relations
Mark Menaldo

Extreme Leadership
Leaders, Teams and Situations Outside the Norm
Edited by Cristina M. Giannantonio and Amy E. Hurley-Hanson

Extreme Leadership

Leaders, Teams and Situations
Outside the Norm

Edited by

Cristina M. Giannantonio

Amy E. Hurley-Hanson

Associate Professors of Management, George L. Argyros School of Business and Economics, Chapman University, USA

NEW HORIZONS IN LEADERSHIP STUDIES

Edward Elgar

Cheltenham, UK • Northampton, MA, USA

Published by
Edward Elgar Publishing Limited
The Lypiatts
15 Lansdown Road
Cheltenham
Glos GL50 2JA
UK

Edward Elgar Publishing, Inc.
William Pratt House
9 Dewey Court
Northampton
Massachusetts 01060
USA

A catalogue record for this book
is available from the British Library

Library of Congress Control Number: 2013946802

This book is available electronically in the ElgarOnline.com Business Subject Collection, E-ISBN 978 1 78100 212 4

ISBN 978 1 78100 211 7 (cased)

Typeset by Columns Design XML Ltd, Reading
Printed and bound in Great Britain by T.J. International Ltd, Padstow

Dedication

Esse quam videri

To my parents Susie and Joseph Giannantonio, who taught me to be, rather than to seem to be.

Cristina M. Giannantonio

Dedicated to my mom Roberta, my son Amory and my fiancé Pete. One was here and taught me how to love before she left. The other two will undoubtedly teach me so much more about love now that they are here.

Amy E. Hurley-Hanson

Thank You

I would like to thank my friends and families for their love and support throughout the writing of this book. To my mother Susie. Thank you for your unconditional love and your unwavering faith that everything would be all right. I suspect you have heard more about Shackleton, Scott, and Amundsen than any mom should have to listen to! To my father, Joseph. I miss you very much. Thank you for finding everything that I wrote far more fascinating than it really was. To my Aunt Rose and my Uncle Frank. Thank you for showing me what family and generosity look like. To Dr Stephen J. Carroll. Thank you for being my mentor and for every piece of academic advice you shared with me. I love you all.

Cristina M. Giannantonio

It is impossible to thank and acknowledge here all those who have contributed to the writing of this book. Nonetheless, I will attempt to do so. I am lucky to have incredible friends and family who have not seen me for months and who have also listened to me go on for hours about how I'm too busy and that I have to work on the book.

To my mother Roberta, who I miss more and more each day. Here's looking at you kid. Her journey on earth was much too short. I still reach for the telephone to call her daily. She was the wind beneath my wings. She instilled in me the ability to believe in a place called hope. She has always believed in me and encouraged my endeavors.

To Amory who I will always love. Amory is on his own extreme journey. He has allowed me to share parts of this journey with him. He has shown me strength I didn't know existed when facing adversity. His strength is something I admire more and more every day. His ability to overcome every obstacle he faces is awe inspiring. He has truly shown there is no try, there is only do or do not. I would not change you for the world, but I would change the world for you. You are my hope, you are my chance, you are my child. I love you very much and I promise to do everything to make all your dreams come true. May the force be with you forever.

To Pete who I love with all my heart. 'The moon was made for the sky to hold, and I, for you.' Pete showed me where the place called hope is. Pete has given up endless nights, weekends and time with me to allow me to write this book. We must remember Love is the best part of any story and our journey is just beginning. Pete, You Make Me Smile.

Amy E. Hurley-Hanson

Contents

Contributors   ix
Preface   xi
Introduction   xiii
Acknowledgments   xvii

PART I   EXTREME EXPEDITION LEADERS

1   Extreme leadership: lessons from Ernest Shackleton and
    the *Endurance* expedition   3
    Cristina M. Giannantonio and Amy E. Hurley-Hanson
2   Extreme leadership and decision-making: Scott and Amundsen
    and the race to the South Pole   15
    Leon Mann
3   Leadership and organizational learning in extreme situations:
    lessons of a comparative study from two polar expeditions – one
    of the greatest disasters (Franklin, 1845) and one of the best
    achievements (Nansen, 1893)   34
    Pascal Lièvre and Géraldine Rix-Lièvre
4   Leaders in Antarctica: characteristics of an Antarctic station
    manager   47
    Ian Lovegrove
5   The Darwin mountaineering expedition in Patagonia: a case of
    successful leadership failure   62
    Linda Rouleau, Geneviève Musca, Marie Perez and
    Yvonne Giordano
6   Leadership at the edge of the summit   72
    Betty S. Coffey and Stella E. Anderson
7   The ghosts of shared leadership: on decision-making and
    subconscious followership in the 'death zone' of K2   83
    Markus Hällgren, Marcus Lindahl and Alf Rehn
8   Greenland: creating world-class teams   96
    James G. Clawson

PART II EXTREME WORK TEAMS

9 Dr Lehman: extreme healthcare leadership along the shores of
   Lake Tanganyika   107
   Robert O. Harris
10 Bringing up the Thirty-Three: emergent principles in multi-tiered
   leadership   117
   Michael Useem, Rodrigo Jordán and Matko Koljatic
11 Team leadership: the Chilean mine case   131
   Terri A. Scandura and Monica M. Sharif
12 Where pure leadership is revealed: our police in harm's way   141
   Mark D. Bowman and George B. Graen

PART III EXTREME INDIVIDUAL LEADERS

13 Glenn Miller: leadership lessons from a successful big band
   musician   165
   Michael J. Urick and Therese A. Sprinkle
14 Extreme leadership as creative leadership: reflections on
   Francis Ford Coppola in *The Godfather*   187
   Charalampos Mainemelis and Olga Epitropaki
15 Lost in a fog? Power comes from values   201
   Andrea Hornett, Peggy Daniels Lee and James G. Perkins
16 Jeanne's story: a leader and her team's journey through crisis   214
   Connie S. Fuller
17 The Sandy Hook Elementary School shootings   224
   Amy E. Hurley-Hanson and Cristina M. Giannantonio

Index   237

Contributors

Stella E. Anderson, Walker College of Business, Appalachian State University, USA

Mark D. Bowman, School of Public Affairs, Methodist University, USA

James G. Clawson, Darden School of Business, University of Virginia, USA

Betty S. Coffey, Walker College of Business, Appalachian State University, USA

Olga Epitropaki, ALBA Graduate Business School at The American College of Greece, Greece and Aston University, UK

Connie S. Fuller, Business Psychology Department, The Chicago School of Professional Psychology, USA

Cristina M. Giannantonio, George L. Argyros School of Business and Economics, Chapman University, USA

Yvonne Giordano, ISEM Université de Nice-Sophia Antipolis, France

George B. Graen, Center for Advanced Study, The University of Illinois at Urbana-Champaign, USA

Markus Hällgren, Umeå School of Business and Economics, Umeå University, Sweden and visiting researcher, Department of Sociology, Stanford University, USA

Robert O. Harris, Benedictine University, USA

Andrea Hornett, Fox School of Business, Temple University, USA

Amy E. Hurley-Hanson, George L. Argyros School of Business and Economics, Chapman University, USA

Rodrigo Jordán, Instituto Vertical, Chile

Matko Koljatic, School of Management, Pontificia Universidad Católica de Chile, Chile

Peggy Daniels Lee, Kelley School of Business, Indiana University, USA

Pascal Lièvre Université d'Auvergne and France Business School, CRCGM, Clermont University, France

Marcus Lindahl, Division of Industrial Engineering and Management, Uppsala University, Sweden

Ian Lovegrove, Global Leader Initiatives, UK

Charalampos Mainemelis, ALBA Graduate Business School at The American College of Greece, Greece

Leon Mann, Melbourne School of Psychological Sciences and Research Leadership Unit, University of Melbourne, Australia

Geneviève Musca, Université Paris Ouest Nanterre La Défense, France

Marie Perez, Université Paris Ouest Nanterre La Défense, France

James G. Perkins, Custom Medical Specialties, Inc., USA

Alf Rehn, Management and Organization, Åbo Akademi University, Finland

Géraldine Rix-Lièvre, Université Blaise Pascal, Acté Clermont University, France

Linda Rouleau, HEC Montréal, Canada

Terri A. Scandura, School of Business Administration, University of Miami, USA

Monica M. Sharif, School of Business Administration, University of Miami, USA

Therese A. Sprinkle, College of Business, University of Dallas, USA

Michael J. Urick, Alex G. McKenna School of Business, Economics, and Government, St. Vincent College, USA

Michael Useem, Wharton School, University of Pennsylvania, USA

Preface

Cristina M. Giannantonio and
Amy E. Hurley-Hanson

The idea for this book started with the goal of organizing a symposium for the Academy of Management (AOM) focusing on 'Extreme Leaders, Extreme Teams, and Extreme Situations'. Our interest in extreme leadership began several years ago. Like many others, we had been captivated by the story of Sir Ernest Shackleton's *Endurance* expedition. Shackleton's efforts to rescue his crew after their ship was crushed by pack ice in the Antarctic continues to be an inspiring example of successful leadership behavior under unfathomable circumstances. Closer to home, the heroic efforts of the first responders to the collapse of the World Trade Center buildings on 11 September 2001 provided another inspiring example of successful leadership in a situation that was far outside the scope of daily experience. From these two cases we became interested in studying additional examples of successful leadership behavior in extreme situations.

While much is known about leadership effectiveness in corporate and business settings (Bass and Bass, 2008), much less is known about the variables that explain how leaders behave when facing extreme situations. The purpose of this book is to analyze unique examples of leaders and teams that have been successful in extreme situations. The leaders, teams and situations described in this book include both contemporary and historic cases of extreme situations that occurred in both corporate and non-corporate settings.

We define an extreme situation as one that falls outside the norm; that is, the situation falls outside the scope of daily experience. While some of the cases described in this book describe corporate and non-corporate examples of work that is inherently dangerous and risky, it should be noted that the situations described are extreme for them. That is, they faced situations that were outside the norm of their daily experiences. For example, mining is an inherently dangerous job; being trapped under ground for several weeks is an extreme situation.

A call for participants was sent to several divisions of the AOM, yielding several dozen proposals describing extreme cases. The leaders, teams and situations that academy members were researching were drawn from a wide range of corporate and non-corporate settings. This book includes a composite of cases that will offer management scholars and researchers alternative lenses through which to view effective leadership in extreme situations. The goal of the book is to better understand the factors that explain successful leadership behavior in a variety of extreme situations including corporate and non-corporate settings. Each chapter includes a description of the extreme situation, an analysis of the leadership theories that might explain the behaviors exhibited in the case, and a list of leadership lessons that can be extrapolated from the case.

There are numerous historic and contemporary examples of leaders and followers that have survived extreme situations. Management professors have long used cases drawn from business and corporate settings to illustrate leadership lessons and management principles. However, vivid and dramatic cases can also be found in a variety of non-corporate settings, including polar and mountain climbing expeditions, first responders and rescue workers, and those whose work takes them deep inside the earth and far above the clouds. We believe that we can contribute to management practice if we expand our models and theories to understand leaders who survive, and thrive, in extreme situations. In the last few years, companies have faced global and economic environments that fall well beyond the scope of their daily experience. We hope that the cases presented in this book will offer managers inspirational lessons for surviving at the extreme.

Finally, while writing this book the bomb explosions at the 2013 Boston Marathon and the shootings at Sandy Hook Elementary School on 14 December 2012 occurred. In examining these recent events we came to realize that virtually any one of us may experience an extreme situation at work or at play. We hope that the lessons learned in writing this book may influence our own leadership behaviors.

Introduction

Cristina M. Giannantonio and
Amy E. Hurley-Hanson

The cases described in this book include both corporate and non-corporate examples of extreme situations. The chapters in Part I describe extreme situations from outside the world of work. They are the stories of extreme expedition leaders who set out to explore the far reaches of the globe. Three of the chapters are set in Antarctica, a continent whose weather and terrain is considered extreme by any measure. The other chapters involve mountaineering and cross-continental expeditions whose leaders and teams faced extreme situations.

The chapters in Parts II and III describe extreme situations from within the world of work. In Part II, four chapters describe extreme work teams whose members are involved in rescue work and saving lives. The work of these teams is accomplished in a high-performance, high-stress, team setting.

The chapters in Part III describe extreme individual leaders from several different industries and occupations. Each of these leaders experienced an extreme situation and took personal actions to change an industry, transform a company or help their co-workers. These cases are primarily focused on the behaviors exhibited by individual leaders in a variety of contexts including business, the arts and education.

EXTREME EXPEDITION LEADERS

Cristina M. Giannantonio and Amy E. Hurley-Hanson (Chapter 1) turn to the Heroic Age of polar exploration and Sir Ernest Shackleton's *Endurance* expedition to find examples of effective behaviors by leaders and followers under an extreme situation. Shackleton was unable to complete his Imperial Trans-Antarctic Expedition when his ship, the *Endurance*, became frozen in pack ice, was crushed by the ice, and sank to the bottom of the sea. Undaunted by these events, Shackleton successfully led his crew of 27 men home to safety after an inconceivable year and a half stuck on the polar ice.

Leon Mann (Chapter 2) compares the expeditions of Robert Falcon Scott and Roald Amundsen as they raced to be the first to reach the South Pole. Mann explores the factors that explain Amundsen's success in reaching the Pole first and surviving the return journey. He examines the factors that led to Scott and four of his crew starving and perishing on their return from the pole.

Looking north, Pascal Lièvre and Géraldine Rix-Lièvre (Chapter 3) present a comparative study of two polar expeditions, Nansen's 1893–1896 expedition to the North Pole and Franklin's 1845 expedition to the Northwest Passage. Franklin's expedition is considered one of the greatest disasters in Arctic exploration, while Nansen's expedition is one of its greatest achievements. Lievre examines the factors that led to one man's success and another's failure.

Ian Lovegrove (Chapter 4) presents empirical findings from a longitudinal study of Antarctic station managers and their followers to determine the leadership characteristics needed to operate effectively in an extreme and isolated environment.

Linda Rouleau, Geneviève Musca, Marie Perez and Yvonne Giordana (Chapter 5) examine the Darwin mountaineering expedition, Project Darwin, as an example of successful leadership failure. Rouleau and her co-authors describe how the expedition leader was successful in keeping the team together even though they were not able to achieve their primary goal of ascending the mountain.

In another example of a mountaineering team, Betty S. Coffey and Stella E. Anderson (Chapter 6) discuss the May 2006 ascent of Mount Everest. They discuss a climbing team that abandoned their own expedition goals in order to provide aid to a lone climber in distress.

Markus Hällgren, Marcus Lindahl and Alf Rehn (Chapter 7) focus on high-altitude mountaineering and the manner in which leadership behaviors emerge in the Death Zone, the area above 8000 meters where the lack of oxygen quickly takes a toll on the human body. Hällgren and his co-authors examine the August 2008 expedition on K2 when 11 people were killed.

James G. Clawson (Chapter 8) discusses the 1991 attempt by four Norwegian men to break the world record by cross-country skiing across Greenland. Clawson notes that more people have summited Mount Everest than have crossed Greenland unsupported, and details how this extreme case offers lessons for leading modern organizations in today's global business economy.

EXTREME WORK TEAMS

Robert O. Harris (Chapter 9) describes the work of Dr Amy Lehman, a medical doctor who runs a floating healthcare facility in the Lake Tanganyika region in Tanzania, East Africa. Dr Lehman's medical team provides healthcare to one of the remotest regions on Earth under extremely difficult conditions.

Michael Useem, Rodrigo Jordán and Matko Koljatic (Chapter 10) examine the 2010 Chilean cave-in trapping 33 miners 700 meters below the surface of the earth. Useem and his colleagues examine the rescue attempts of the miners using a multi-tiered leadership perspective.

Terri A. Scandura and Monica M. Sharif (Chapter 11) analyze the rescue of the Chilean miners utilizing a model of team leadership to examine the shared trust and cohesiveness that led to the men surviving their ordeal and being rescued.

Mark D. Bowen and George B. Graen (Chapter 12) discuss the unique experiences of police officers who perform their jobs in extremely dangerous situations, or what they define as 'harm's way'. Bowen and Graen note that first responders must both succeed in their mission and protect their team from collateral damage. They suggest that a radically different approach to team leadership is needed in these situations.

EXTREME INDIVIDUAL LEADERS

Michael J. Urick and Therese A. Sprinkle (Chapter 13) present an analysis of Glenn Miller, the famous big band leader, through the lens of transformational leadership theory and complexity theory. Urick and Sprinkle argue convincingly that Miller's effect on the music industry as well as his military service during the Second World War make him an excellent example of extreme leadership.

Charalampos Mainemelis and Olga Epitropaki (Chapter 14) discuss Francis Ford Coppola as an artist whose work required him to serve in a leadership role as well as a creative one. Mainemelis and Epitropaki focus on a form of leader-induced extreme collaboration that occurs when a leader is a creative artist pursuing a cherished artistic vision. They suggest that for artists, working in leadership roles in organizations is often a means to fulfilling their personal artistic vision. They posit that this may induce extreme collaborative tensions that, although rarely pleasant, may lead to positive organizational outcomes.

Andrea Hornett, Peggy Daniels Lee, and James G. Perkins (Chapter 15) recount the experiences that Perkins experienced as President and

Chief Executive Officer (CEO) of Custom Medical Specialties, a supplier of CT coils. Their case explores the role of power in leadership during an extreme crisis when a leader is forced to make decisions with limited information.

Connie S. Fuller (Chapter 16) relates her experiences in a telecommunications company that utilized self-directed work teams in a manufacturing facility. She attributes much of the success of the work teams to the leadership skills of one of the team supervisors. In the face of daily lay-offs, employees reporting to this supervisor were able to maintain productivity and sustain their work teams.

Amy E. Hurley-Hanson and Cristina M. Giannantonio (Chapter 17) discuss the selfless acts of leadership that were exhibited by the principal, teachers and staff at Sandy Hook Elementary School in Newtown, CT on 14 December 2012. They analyze the leadership behaviors of several individuals who were faced with an unthinkable extreme situation in their workplace.

In summary, we believe that this book offers insights into the behaviors of leaders and teams facing extreme situations in a variety of corporate and non-corporate settings. Studying situations that fall outside of the scope of daily experience offers management scholars and researchers alternative lenses for understanding how to survive in extreme situations. These lenses are developed by studying expedition leaders, rescue teams and individuals who rush into, and not away from, disasters. We hope this book will bring together a learning community of scholar-teachers who see the value of integrating cases from diverse settings into the classroom to illustrate management concepts with cases and stories that engage and inspire our students to become leaders who can survive, and even thrive, in extreme situations.

Acknowledgments

We would like to acknowledge the many colleagues who supported us during the writing of this book. We would like to thank the members of Chapman University's Faculty Personnel Council for granting each of us a sabbatical to work on this book; Dr Arthur Kraft, then Dean of the Argyros School of Business and Economics who supported our sabbatical requests; and Dean Reginald Gilyard, who generously supported our work and provided us with the time to focus on our writing. We would like to thank Jillian Ryan Wood, Rita Desjardins and Craig Williams of the Argyros School of Business and Economics for literally running to help us each time we had a crisis. They saved us hours of frustration. We would like to thank Jaclyn Witt for her conscientious work as the editorial assistant for the *Journal of Business and Management* as well as her hard work on this book. Jackie has formatted more references for us than anyone should ever have to in their lifetime. Jackie responded to our requests for help with timeliness, grace and professionalism. We would like to acknowledge the unwavering support of the late Dr Barbara Mulch, Vice Provost and Dean of Graduate Studies. Barbara briefly served as our Dean during difficult times, and through it all was our friend and champion.

The idea for this book arose out of an Academy of Management symposium we organized on Extreme Leaders and Teams. We appreciate the many management scholars who shared their interest in extreme leadership with us and who were willing to make an idea for a book on extreme leadership become a reality. We are indebted to our contributors. Your research on extreme leadership and the stories you shared in this book validated and shaped our definition of extreme leadership. Thank you for your patience with us, for the many revisions, and for putting our deadlines ahead of your own.

We would like to acknowledge the victims of Sandy Hook Elementary School. As was the rest of the country, we were shocked and shaken by this tragic event. We hope that our research on the leadership lessons learned from Newtown may contribute in a small way to preventing these types of tragedies. Writing this book reminded us why we try to teach our management students that, of all the resources their company has, they are entrusted with the most important.

Finally, neither of us could have written this book alone. We are fortunate to be friends as well as colleagues. This bond makes it a pleasure to write together even when the subject is heartbreaking.

Cristina M. Giannantonio
Amy E. Hurley-Hanson

PART I

Extreme expedition leaders

1. Extreme leadership: lessons from Ernest Shackleton and the *Endurance* expedition

Cristina M. Giannantonio and Amy E. Hurley-Hanson

In 1914 Sir Ernest Shackleton set sail from London for Antarctica aboard the HMS *Endurance*. Having lost the race to the South Pole, Shackleton planned a polar expedition which would be the first to cross the Antarctic continent. Well aware of the dangers of polar expeditions, even Shackleton could not have predicted the extreme events that befell the *Endurance* Expedition. He earned his place in history not because he was the first to discover the South Pole, nor the first to cross Antarctica. Instead, Shackleton is remembered as a courageous leader who faced unfathomable challenges with optimism and conviction. Equally important, he is remembered as a compassionate leader who cared for his crew and rescued all 27 men who embarked on a remarkable journey into the unknown.

THE RACE TO THE SOUTH POLE

The Heroic Age of Antarctic exploration encompasses a 25-year time span beginning in 1897 with Adrien de Gerlache's Belgian Antarctic Expedition and ending with Ernest Shackleton's Imperial Trans-Antarctic Expedition, of 1914–1917. During this time, 17 expeditions were commissioned from ten different countries. Nineteen explorers died on these expeditions, most from scurvy and malnutrition, but some froze to death, while others were swept overboard and lost at sea.

The most notable expeditions of this time were led by Roald Amundsen, Robert Falcon Scott and Ernest Shackleton. They were three very different men, and although they earned their spot in history for three very different reasons, they shared a common goal: to be the first to reach the South Pole.

The race was won by Amundsen. Amundsen and his men reached the South Pole on 14 December 1911: 'We proceeded to the greatest and most solemn act of the whole journey – the planting of our flag' (Amundsen, 1912, p. 445). Amundsen was an experienced polar explorer. He sailed aboard the *Belgica* under the leadership of Adrien de Gerlache. He is credited with being the first to traverse the Northwest Passage. Amundsen was planning an expedition to the North Pole when he learned that Frederick Cook and Robert Peary had preceded him. He changed his plans and launched the Norwegian Antarctic Expedition to the South Pole, sailing aboard the *Fram*, the Norwegian word for 'forward'. Amundsen's success in reaching the South Pole is credited to his excellent preparation skills (McCutcheon, 2008; Amundsen, 1927 [2008]). He understood the advantages of sled dogs and skis for traversing the ice (Amundsen, 1927 [2008]; Huntford, 2010); he used animal furs and skins for clothing instead of wool cloth; and he had no problem using the dogs to feed his crew (Amundsen, 1927 [2008]), having seen the dangers of malnutrition and scurvy on previous expeditions. Critics claim that unlike other polar expeditions, Amundsen devoted no time or efforts to scientific exploration or geographic surveying and mapping (Larson, 2011). These criticisms cannot detract from his accomplishments and he is the undisputed winner of the race to the South Pole (Huntford, 2010).

A little over a month behind Amundsen was Scott and the crew of the *Terra Nova*. The British Antarctic Expedition was Scott's second attempt to reach the South Pole. He first attempted to reach the South Pole in 1901 as leader of the British National Antarctic Expedition sailing aboard the *Discovery*. Scott, Shackleton and Edward Wilson came within 530 miles of the South Pole before they were forced to turn back. Each of the men suffered from cold, exhaustion, malnutrition and scurvy. Shackleton's health was severely compromised on the return journey and Scott ordered him sent back to England before the end of the expedition. His experiences on the *Discovery* expedition would later shape Shackleton's planning, leading and organizing of his own expeditions to Antarctica.

Scott's second attempt to reach the South Pole was the *Terra Nova* expedition of 1910–1913. Scott and his crew were well aware of Amundsen's efforts to reach the South Pole at the same time. They were disappointed to arrive at the South Pole on 17 January 1912 and find the flag of Norway planted in the snow along with a letter left by Amundsen documenting his achievement. Scott and the other four men faced a roughly 800-mile return march to the ship. In contrast to Amundsen,

Scott believed that man-hauling was the most efficient way to travel in the Antarctic (Landis, 2001; MacPhee, 2010). Man-hauling involved harnessing a heavily laden sled to a person who then walks or trudges through the snow and ice pulling the sled unassisted by sled dogs. Man-hauling burned thousands of calories a day. Scott had underestimated the necessary food rations and his team was weakened by hunger and malnutrition on the return journey. Scott's return journey was beset by a series of blizzards which forced the men to stop marching and shelter in a tent. Each delay further depleted their food rations and slowed their progress in reaching the supply depots that had been laid in preparation for the march to and from the South Pole. Edgar Evans was the first to perish on the return journey. He died about one month after reaching the South Pole. After taking shelter, the other four men became too weak to resume their march. Lawrence Oates sacrificed himself by leaving the tent and telling the men, 'I'm just going outside and may be some time' (from 'Scott's last expedition: the journals', in Willis, 1999, p. 115). The frozen bodies of Scott, Edward Wilson and Henry Bowers were discovered months later.

One hundred years after his death, Scott's legacy is still controversial. Considered a romantic tragic hero for decades, recent analyses suggest that Scott made several poor strategic decisions that led to his death and the deaths of his crew (Huntford, 2010). Despite having reached the South Pole, his insistence on man-hauling, using ponies instead of sled dogs and underestimating the caloric needs of the men contributed to their inability to face the extreme conditions they encountered in Antarctica.

Shackleton was the third polar explorer who wanted to be the first to reach the South Pole. His first expedition to Antarctica was under the direction of Scott on the *Discovery* expedition. Shackleton's experiences under Scott taught him important lessons about the physical and psychological demands of polar exploration. His experience with Scott's leadership style strongly influenced his views about leadership, morale, motivation and trust. Having been forced to turn back before reaching the South Pole on the *Discovery* expedition, Shackleton was eager to undertake his own expedition to Antarctica. The British Antarctic Expedition of 1907–1909, the *Nimrod* expedition, came within 100 miles of the South Pole. Aware that there were ample provisions for the journey to the pole, Shackleton recognized that the supplies were not enough to sustain the men on the return trip. Disappointed, but putting the lives of his crew first, Shackleton returned to the ship and began planning his next expedition.

With Amundsen's victory in 1911, Shackleton set a new goal for himself. If he could not be the first to arrive at the South Pole, he would be the first explorer to cross the Antarctic continent. In 1914 Shackleton led 27 men aboard the *Endurance* to undertake the Imperial Trans-Antarctic Expedition. Shackleton and his men would eventually spend three years in the Antarctic enduring extreme conditions and unimagined setbacks before he was able to rescue all 27 of his men in 1917.

THE *ENDURANCE* EXPEDITION

Shackleton's plan for the Imperial Trans-Antarctic Expedition was to send two ships to opposite sides of the Antarctic continent. The *Endurance* would land on the one side of the continent and the *Aurora* would land on the other side. Working toward the middle of Antarctica, the crew of the *Aurora* would lay the supply depots that would sustain Shackleton and his expedition team on the second half of their 1800-mile journey across the continent.

Shackleton carefully planned each element of the expedition. A skilled fund raiser, Shackleton raised private money to fund the expedition. The three lifeboats, the *James Caird*, the *Dudley Docker* and the *Stancomb-Wills*, were named after three of his largest donors. Shackleton carefully selected the crew. Over 5000 people applied for 56 positions as sailors and scientists, as well as a photographer, an artist, a cook, a carpenter and a doctor. Recognizing the importance of previous experience in polar exploration, Shackleton hired several men who had been with him on the *Nimrod* expedition. Others were hired because Shackleton felt their personality and temperament would contribute to the morale of the crew and sustain the men during the long, cold nights and many months without sunlight.

The *Endurance* departed London on 1 August 1914. Four months later, the *Endurance* departed the whaling station on South Georgia Island on 5 December 1914. She entered the pack ice a few days later on 7 December. By 18 January 1915, the *Endurance* had become trapped in the pack ice and Shackleton informed the men that they would remain on the ship and wait for the ice to crack and open so they could set out for land in the three salvaged lifeboats. The men carried out their scientific studies, attended to daily ship's duties, trained the sled dogs, and kept up their spirits with games on the ice and aboard ship.

During this time, the pack ice continued to move and solidify, exerting pressure on the wooden ship. The ice broke through the hull of the ship and the ship began to list dangerously. On 27 October 1915, Shackleton ordered the men to abandon ship and the crew prepared to live in tents on Antarctic ice floes in what became known as Ocean Camp. On 21 November 1915, the *Endurance* was crushed by the ice and sank into the sea. Shackleton turned to his men and said: 'Now we'll go home.' After unsuccessfully attempting to drag the three lifeboats across the ice, Shackleton established Patience Camp on 29 December 1915. The men were patiently waiting for the ice to break so that they could set sail for nearby islands where Shackleton had previously laid food supplies.

The decision of when to set sail involved accurate timing and an element of guesswork. Shackleton knew that he needed to get the men off the rapidly melting and breaking up pack ice, but he had to be sure that the ice would not refreeze and crush the three tiny wooden lifeboats. The crew took to the sea on 9 April 1916. 'They made a pitiable sight – three little boats, packed with the odd remnants of what had once been a proud expedition, bearing twenty-eight suffering men in one final, almost ludicrous bid for survival' (Lansing, 1959, p. 160). They landed on Elephant Island two weeks later on 16 April.

Elephant Island was a desolate, harsh place with a small beach, violent winds, a massive glacier and a limited supply of food. Shackleton knew that the island could not sustain the men through another harsh winter. Weighing heavily on the minds of Shackleton and his crew was the realization that no one in the world knew where they were. Shackleton quickly decided that their only hope of rescue was to sail 800 miles across some of the world's most dangerous waters and head for the whaling village on South Georgia Island. On 24 April 1916, Shackleton and a crew of five men set sail for South Georgia. He appointed Frank Wild, his second in command, as leader of the remaining crew who would await rescue on Elephant Island. Wild employed the same strategies that Shackleton had used earlier, assigning the men daily chores (Alexander, 1998), conducting scientific studies and practicing readiness drills. Wild maintained the men's spirits and their unwavering faith in Shackleton by having the men practice breaking camp each day with the rallying cry: 'Make haste! The boss may come today.'

The *James Caird* reached South Georgia on 10 May 1916. It was a harrowing and death-defying sea crossing that taxed the limits of Shackleton, his men and the lifeboat. Having landed on the opposite side of South Georgia from where the whaling village was located, Ernest Shackleton, Frank Worsley and Tom Crean climbed the glacier peaks and traversed the island to the opposite side. They arrived at Stromness whaling station on 20 May 1916. It would take three months and four attempts before Shackleton could break through the frozen pack ice and return to Elephant Island to rescue the other members of his crew. As his lifeboat approached the shore, he called, 'Are you all well?' and received an answering shout of 'We are all well, boss' (Shackleton, 1919, p. 241). Not one man was lost.

LEADERSHIP THEORIES

Biographies of Ernest Shackleton consistently describe him as a charismatic person. 'Shackleton, an Anglo-Irishman from the ranks of the merchant marine, was charismatic, mixing easily with both crew and officers' (Alexander, 1998, p. 6). As this analysis will show, there is little doubt that Shackleton exhibited the characteristics of a charismatic leader. Charismatic leaders were first defined by Max Weber as 'resting on devotion to the exceptional sanctity, heroism or exemplary character of an individual person, and of the normative patterns or order revealed or ordained by him' (Weber, 1947, pp. 358–359).

While there are many leaders who have charismatic personalities (Judge et al., 2006) this does not mean that they engage in charismatic leadership. House's (1977) theory of charismatic leadership included the attributions of the followers. House theorized that when leaders displayed certain behaviors their followers attributed extraordinary abilities to these leaders and were motivated to follow them. They are able to articulate their vision to their followers and set high expectations for their followers (Bullock, 2007).

In examining the *Endurance* expedition, it makes sense that Shackleton would emerge as a charismatic leader because many researchers theorize that crisis situations are when charismatic leadership tends to emerge (Rogelberg, 2007; Bass and Bass, 2008). The extreme situations Shackleton and his crew found themselves in were the right venue for charismatic leadership to emerge. Researchers have thoroughly explored the characteristics that charismatic leaders display. In this chapter the analysis is based on the framework provided by Conger and Kanungo (1998). Their research identified four distinct characteristics: articulating and possessing a vision; being willing to take risks to achieve their vision; exhibiting sensitivity to followers' needs; and demonstrating novel behavior.

Shackleton repeatedly displayed all four of these characteristics throughout the *Endurance* expedition. He had a very clear vision of what he wanted to accomplish. Prior to launching the *Endurance* expedition, Shackleton's goal was to be the first explorer to reach the South Pole. Once that race was lost, Shackleton turned his attention to being the first to cross the Antarctic continent. His previous experiences on Antarctic expeditions crystallized his focus and allowed him to articulate his vision in a clear manner that would allow for success instead of failure. Shackleton was never vague about the importance of the *Endurance* expedition, and he set clear goals for what the expedition would accomplish and how those goals would be accomplished. Shackleton's ability to articulate his vision and generate interest in the *Endurance* expedition is evidenced by his success in generating funds for the expedition and the astounding number of applicants who applied for the 56 positions aboard the two ships.

Shackleton took risks to achieve his mission since polar exploration, by its very nature, is a risky undertaking with much uncertainty. Expeditions to Antarctica were particularly risky and extreme. 'The coldest, stormiest and most remote area on the planet, the Antarctic can be an almost unimaginably hostile environment' (Mulvaney, 2003, p. 305). Shackleton was able to persuade his crew to take risks when their options were limited and their chances of survival were slim. His decision to sail to South Georgia in a wooden lifeboat to find help is one example of the risky behaviors he took to rescue his crew.

Shackleton exhibited sensitivity to his followers' needs throughout the *Endurance* expedition. Before the *Endurance* set sail for Antarctica, Shackleton planned for months to make sure that every need of his men would be taken care of. He carefully calculated caloric needs and provided ample food stores to prevent the men from becoming mal-nourished and developing scurvy. He outfitted the crew with the best equipment available at the time, one example being sleeping bags lined with reindeer fur (Landis, 2001). He also planned activities that would meet the crew's needs for relaxation and maintain their morale under physically demanding conditions. He scanned the environment constantly in his preparations. He tried to anticipate every contingency that could occur on the expedition and planned for his men's needs under those circumstances. Shackleton met his men's needs in thoughtful, selfless ways as well. Worsley (1931, p. 27) recounts an example: 'At dawn the next morning, Shackleton and Wild, like good Samaritans, made hot tea for all hands. This they took along to the inmates of the various tents.' He was known to provide his mittens to Frank Hurley when Hurley's were lost; he met the advance team who had been sent to survey the terrain with cups of hot milk; and he spent hours talking with the men, telling stories and at one point engaging the men in discussions about their next trip to Antarctica.

Shackleton was well known for exhibiting novel behaviors during the *Endurance* expedition. During Shackleton, Worsley and Crean's traverse of South Georgia Island to reach the whaling station the men found themselves at the top of a glacier with nightfall rapidly approaching. Shackleton knew the men could not survive a night on the glacier so he proposed that the three of them form a human sled and slide to the bottom of the glacier. 'Worsley and Crean were stunned – especially for such an insane solution to be coming from Shackleton' (Lansing, 1959, p. 266). Worsley (1931) estimated that they had traveled 3000 feet in under three minutes. This unexpected and novel behavior had saved the men from freezing to death on the glacier.

LEADERSHIP LESSONS

Several authors have written about the leadership lessons that can be learned from Shackleton and the *Endurance* expedition. 'He is a model of great leadership and, in particular, a master of guidance in crisis', Margot Morrell and Stephanie Capparell state in their book *Shackleton's Way: Leadership Lessons from the Great Antarctic Explorer* (2001, p. 1). Morrell and Capparell suggest that modern leaders should turn to Shackleton's example for guidance in creating a spirit of camaraderie, getting the best from each individual, and leading effectively in a crisis.

In *Leading at the Edge: Leadership Lessons from the Extraordinary Saga of Shackleton's Antarctic Expedition* Dennis Perkins and his co-authors (2000 [2012]) offer readers ten strategies for overcoming adversity. Perkins looks to leadership success among those groups that 'have been to the outer limits of human endurance' (Perkins et al. 2000 [2012], p. xxi). He calls this place The Edge and argues that 'by understanding the things that work when survival is at stake' (ibid.), one can learn to lead under other conditions. Perkins considers Shackleton's *Endurance* expedition an example of leading at The Edge and offers ten strategies that are necessary to successfully lead at The Edge. These strategies include instilling optimism and self-confidence, mastering conflict and never giving up.

In drawing our own conclusions about the leadership lessons that can be learned from Ernest Shackleton and the *Endurance* expedition we have chosen to focus on five lessons that may be of use to leaders who are confronted with today's versions of extreme situations. They are offered in the form of a packing list. We believe that these are the essential items that leaders should include when venturing into extreme situations.

Leadership Lesson 1: Pack Courage

The polar explorers were a courageous group. They faced extreme conditions that were far worse than those they had encountered in previous expeditions. This does not mean that they were not afraid. There were several times when Shackleton feared they would not survive another day. Yet they never lost their courage to forge ahead and meet the challenges that lay before them. Today's leaders are reminded to face the economic and environmental challenges confronting their organizations with courage and the confident belief that these conditions are surmountable.

Leadership Lesson 2: Pack Curiosity

Virtually every polar expedition was launched in part because of the curiosity of the expedition leader. The men who applied for positions on the *Endurance* expedition ventured into an unknown environment to find what had not yet been discovered. Virtually all of the polar expeditions that were launched during the Heroic Age of polar expeditions were scientific expeditions. Today's leaders are encouraged to tap into their own curiosity and lead their teams into unknown environments to explore new product lines, technologies and markets.

Leadership Lesson 3: Pack Nourishment

History illustrates that the need for proper food and nourishment could be the difference between life and death on a polar expedition. Shackleton turned back less than 97 miles from the South Pole because he knew there were not enough provisions to ensure the team's survival on the return journey. Additionally, Shackleton understood the importance of keeping his crew's minds and spirits nourished throughout the *Endurance* expedition. Not only was the *Endurance* well stocked with pemmican, wine and special treats to keep the men well nourished for the physical demands of their tasks, Shackleton also brought music and books on the expedition to maintain the men's spirits during the long, cold winter they spent on the ice. Frank Hurley, the official expedition photographer, took numerous photos of the men performing skits aboard ship, playing football on the ice, and competing in the dog sled races that Shackleton organized. Today's leaders are cautioned not to neglect the physical, psychological and spiritual needs of their employees. While the perquisites and lifestyle benefits offered by Google, Yahoo and other high-tech companies appear to consider the needs of their employees, organizations need to remember that nourishment means more than free cafeteria food.

Leadership Lesson 4: Pack Optimism

Years before psychologists began to study the effects of positivity (Seligman and Csikszentmihalyi, 2000); Shackleton knew the importance of remaining optimistic and fostering optimism in his crew. After the loss of the ship Shackleton made one of his most famous speeches, assuring the men 'that by hard effort, clean work, and loyal cooperation, they could make their way to land' (Worsley, 1931, p. 22). While Shackleton and a crew of six sailed to South Georgia to find help, Wild, second in command of the *Endurance* expedition, helped the men to remain optimistic with his daily reminder that the boss may return today. In an uncertain economy the importance of optimism cannot be stated enough. Leaders need to provide their followers with a realistic assessment of their current difficulties, as well as encourage them to remain optimistic and avoid falling victim to pessimism and doubt.

Leadership Lesson 5: Pack Your Compass

In the early 1900s Shackleton and the crew of the *Endurance* navigated using the stars, the horizon and a sextant. As they sailed across some of the world's most dangerous oceans and seas, they encountered storm conditions and ocean currents that pulled them off course and forced them to change direction several times. They were not always sure what their current location was, but Shackleton always knew where they wanted to end up. Today's leaders are encouraged to pack their own metaphorical compass and to have a clear vision of where they want to lead their companies. In today's fast-moving world leaders must recognize that the path to success might take longer than originally planned, may sometimes veer off course and is likely to involve extreme conditions. As Shackleton and the *Endurance* expedition illustrate, even if you do not always know where you are, never lose sight of where you want to end up.

CONCLUSION

The story of Sir Ernest Shackleton and the *Endurance* expedition has provided chief executive officers (CEOs), business students and management scholars with leadership lessons that are relevant a century after his expedition was mounted. The tale of the *Endurance* is an amazing story of courage, endurance and the human spirit. The extreme conditions experienced by Shackleton and his men during their three-year journey laid the foundation for Shackleton to demonstrate his charismatic leadership skills.

First-person accounts of the expedition can be found in *South*, Shackleton's (1919) personal description of the fate of his ship and its 27 crew members and *Endurance*, Sir Alfred Lansing's (1959) romantic retelling of the expedition based on interviews with surviving crew members and a content analysis of their personal diaries and expedition logs. The lessons to be learned from the *Endurance* expedition are not limited to leaders. The fortitude, optimism and trust exhibited by the crew of the *Endurance* also offer lessons for effective follower and team behavior. Shackleton's *Endurance* expedition provides management practitioners, scholars and educators with important lessons drawn from a most exciting time in history.

REFERENCES

Alexander, C. (1998). *The Endurance: Shackleton's Legendary Antarctic Expedition*, New York: Alfred A. Knopf.

Amundsen, R. (1912). *The South Pole, an Account of Norwegian Antarctic Expedition in the Fram, 1910–1912*. London: John Murray.

Amundsen, R. (1927 [2008]). *My Life as an Explorer* and Introduction by Campbell McCutcheon, 2008. Stroud: Amberley Publishing.

Bass, B.M. and R. Bass (2008). *The Bass Handbook of Leadership: Theory, Research, and Managerial Applications*, 4th edn. New York: Free Press.

Bullock, A.C. (2007). Charismatic leadership theory. In S.G. Rogelberg (ed.), *Encyclopedia of Industrial and Organizational Psychology*. London: Sage, pp. 71–2.

Conger, Jay A. and Rabindra N. Kanungo (1998). *Charismatic Leadership in Organizations*. Thousand Oaks, CA: Sage.

House, R.J. (1977). A 1976 theory of charismatic leadership. In J.G. Hunt and L.L. Larson (eds), *Leadership: The Cutting Edge*. Carbondale, IL: Southern Illinois University Press, pp. 189–207.

Huntford, R. (2010). *Race for the South Pole: The Expedition Diaries of Scott and Amundsen*. London: Continuum International Publishing Group.

Judge, T.A., E.F. Woolf, C. Hurst and B. Livingston (2006). Charismatic and transformational leadership: a review and agenda for future research. *Zeitschrift fu¨r Arbeits- und Organisationspsychologie*, 50 (4), 203–14.

Landis, M.J. (2001). *Antarctica: Exploring the Extreme 400 years of Adventure*. Chicago, IL: Chicago Review Press.

Lansing A. (1959). *Endurance: Shackleton's Incredible Voyage*. New York: Carroll and Graf.

Larson, E.J. (2011). *An Empire of Ice: Scott, Shackleton, and the Heroic Age of Antarctic Science*. New Haven, CT: Yale.

MacPhee, R.D.E. (2010). *Race to the End: Amundsen, Scott, and the Attainment of the South Pole*. New York: Sterling Innovation.

Morrell, M. and S. Capparell (2001). *Shackleton's Way: Leadership Lessons from the Great Antarctic Explorer*, New York: Penguin Books.

Mulvaney, K. (2003). Afterword. In Richard E. Byrd (ed.), *Alone*. Washington, DC: Island Press/Shearwater Books, pp. 297–313.

Perkins, D.N.T., M.P. Holtman, P.R. Kessler and C. McCarthy (2000 [2012]). *Leading at the Edge: Leadership Lessons from the Extraordinary Saga of Shackleton's Antarctic Expedition*. New York: AMACON – American Management Association.

Seligman, M.E.P. and M. Csikszentmihalyi (2000). Positive psychology: an introduction. *American Psychologist*, 55, 5–14.

Shackleton, E. (1919). *South: The Endurance Expedition*. New York: Signet.

Rogelberg, S.G. (2007). *Encyclopedia of Industrial and Organizational Psychology*. London: Sage.

Weber, Max (1947). *The Theory of Social and Economic Organization*, transl. A.M. Henderson and Talcott Parsons. Glencoe, IL: Free Press and Falcon's Bring Press.

Willis, C. (1999). *Ice: Stories of Survival from Polar Exploration*. New York: Thunder's Mouth Press/Balliett and Fitzgerald.

Worsley, F.A. (1931). *An Epic of Polar Adventure*. New York: W.W. Norton and Company.

2. Extreme leadership and decision-making: Scott and Amundsen and the race to the South Pole

Leon Mann

INTRODUCTION

The chapter examines the leadership and decision-making of Robert Falcon Scott and Roald Amundsen as their teams competed in 1911–1912 to be first to the South Pole, a return journey to base camp of approximately 1500 miles. Amundsen's Norwegian team succeeded and returned safely. Scott's British team reached the pole 33 days later than Amundsen's and perished on the return journey. A search party discovered their remains, journals and scientific materials eight months later.

The race to the South Pole in 1911–1912 is a rare historical episode. It involved two leaders, teams and expeditions with almost identical objectives competing in the same place and at the same time to become the first to conquer the South Pole. The two expeditions had two vastly different outcomes. The case captures the significance of leadership and decision-making in extreme situations. It demonstrates how seemingly minor choices can produce significant unforeseen outcomes, and how early and later decisions together produce a tipping point toward disaster. The chapter draws lessons about leadership and the importance of vigilant decision-making and learning from experience, for success and survival in extreme situations. I will examine a set of strategic, tactical and operational decisions made by the leaders in six key areas and how they might have affected the outcomes of the two expeditions. I draw on primary and secondary sources, such as Scott's and Amundsen's diaries and historical accounts, for the analysis and discussion.

THE RACE TO THE SOUTH POLE AS A CASE OF LEADERSHIP IN EXTREME SITUATIONS

The story of the race to the South Pole in 1911–1912 fits a category of leadership in extreme situations with the following features: a difficult, hazardous project involving a long journey across a remote and harsh environment to achieve a very challenging goal; the project requires good planning and preparation to succeed; the team is the first (or among the first) to attempt the project and will therefore be in unknown territory; much depends on the qualities and experience of the leader; excellent team coordination and performance is crucial for success; mishap and misfortune can spell disaster. Some, but not all, of these features relate to leadership in other extreme situations, for example leadership for survival and escape from prisoner of war (POW) camps, leadership of a group of survivors lost in the desert, or leadership following a shipwreck. But journeys of exploration in extremely harsh conditions are distinctive for the importance of preparation, planning and decision-making, both before and during the event, for determining outcomes.

TWO JOURNEYS TO THE POLE

Amundsen set out for the South Pole on 20 October 1911 from his base at Bay of Whales located 798 miles from the pole. He took an uncharted route and completed the return journey in just over three months (99 days from 20 October 1911 to 25 January 1912). Scott left his Cape Evans base, located 858 miles from the South Pole on 1 November 1911, 11 days later than Amundsen. Scott's journey from base followed a similar route to Ernest Shackleton's British Antarctic Expedition, the *Nimrod* expedition of 1907–1909, to the point where Shackleton turned back defeated at 88°23'S, approximately 113 miles from the pole. Scott then ventured into uncharted territory and reached the pole 33 days later than Amundsen. Scott's team was trapped in a severe blizzard on the return journey and perished from exhaustion, illness and starvation. Scott's unfinished journey took five months (150 days from 1 November 1911 to the estimated date of his death 29 March 1912).

The 'race' to the South Pole began long before the two teams set out from their separate bases on 20 October and 1 November 1911. The *Terra Nova* expedition (Scott's British Antarctic Expedition, 1910–1913) and the *Fram* expedition (Amundsen's Norwegian Antarctic Expedition, 1910–1912) had been years in the planning. Indeed in the Antarctic summer of 1910–1911, the two parties were already at their respective bases busy with preparations for the actual attempt to reach the pole that would begin at the earliest opportunity in the Antarctic summer of 1911–1912. Many decisions large and small were made in the two years leading up to and including the race to the pole. Thus a feature of this story is the way in which decisions taken (and not taken) across time and place played out in the different outcomes of the two expeditions.

The race to the South Pole in 1911–1912 has been analyzed by historians (for example, Roland Huntford, 1979; Stephanie Barczewski, 2007), scientists (Walter Sullivan, 1962; Susan Solomon, 2001) and management writers (for example, Jim Collins and Morten Hansen, 2011) for lessons about polar exploration and leadership. The tragic fate of Scott's team has become a matter of controversy. Some writers maintain the disaster was due primarily to extraordinarily severe weather conditions and misfortune (Fiennes, 2003; Preston, 1999; Solomon, 2001). Others argue the disaster was to a great extent due to Scott's leadership failings (for example, Huntford, 1979). They argue that Scott may have been overconfident and underestimated the challenges of the difficult journey, while in contrast Amundsen was very strategic and highly prepared, and benefited from good fortune. The achievements of both leaders were considerable. Amundsen's team conquered the pole and returned safely to base. Scott's polar team surpassed Shackleton's 'furthest south' mark of 1907–1909, was the first team to reach the pole on foot, and the team's collection of fossil-bearing minerals proved relevant to the theory of continental drift.

Much more has been written about Scott than about Amundsen. Several analyses compare the Scott and Amundsen expeditions on such factors as thoroughness of preparation, navigational skills, skiing proficiency, physical fitness, nutritional quality of the food, suitability of the protective clothing, and so on (see Fiennes, 2003; Huntford, 1979; Sullivan, 1962; Solomon, 2001). Comparisons have also been made of Scott and Amundsen's leadership styles and abilities (Collins and Hansen, 2011; Sengupta and Van der Heyden, 2011). A detailed comparison of the two leaders and their expeditions is beyond this chapter.

Mann (2006) identifies five major themes in leadership research and analysis: roles, character, relationships, decisions and journeys. In extreme situations, leadership relates to all five themes, but to decision-making in particular. Poor, ill-conceived decisions, in contrast to well-thought-out decisions, usually (but not always) spell the difference between survival and disaster.

The main aim is to examine leaders and their decision-making behavior in order to understand what factors may have affected their decisions and how they were made, as well as their effect on subsequent outcomes, in order to draw lessons about leadership in extreme situations. I propose that vigilant decision-making processes will be associated with positive outcomes, and inadequate decision-making processes, for example complacency and unnecessary risk taking, will be linked to poor outcomes (see Janis and Mann, 1977). Having a team perish, sick, starving and exhausted, on a journey of exploration is a disastrous outcome. The question is whether inadequate decision-making processes were linked to that outcome. I am mindful of the trap of hindsight bias, the tendency to overestimate the predictability and personal responsibility for events, accidents and outcomes beyond the individual's control (Fischhoff, 2007). There are traps also in interpreting and evaluating decision-making behavior from documents, some a century old, when the principals are not present to explain and respond. A final caveat: of necessity, the analysis will be incomplete, as it focuses only on individual choices and judgments, not on the myriad factors that invariably influence what happened in most historical events.

ORGANIZATIONAL FACTORS, LEADERSHIP AUTHORITY AND DECISION-MAKING

Hannah et al. (2009) propose a framework for studying leadership in extreme contexts that includes, *inter alia* the nature of the organizational context, the extremity of the situation, the stress level produced by extreme events and how it affects leader and follower responses (preparedness, vigilance) and, finally, leader responses at different phases as the situation unfolds (time dimension). Some elements of this framework are included in my analysis. Hannah et al.'s (2009) framework points to the role of organizational factors in determining leader selection, and degree of authority over strategic objectives and implementation of the project.

Scott and Amundsen were essentially powerful, 'heavyweight' leaders of major projects (see Clark and Wheelwright, 1992) with ultimate authority to champion, plan and conduct their expeditions. Scott, an officer in the British Navy, had led the British National Antarctic Expedition, the *Discovery* expedition, to Antarctica in 1901–1904, and with Edward Wilson and Ernest Shackleton was a member of the first British team to attempt to reach the South Pole. The three-man team got within 410 miles of the pole, setting a new 'furthest south' record for the time. The British Antarctic Expedition (the *Terra Nova* expedition) of 1910–1913 led by Scott was financed by the British Admiralty, the Royal Geographical Society, a government grant and public contributions. Scott was selected to lead the expedition and authorized to achieve two goals:

to reach the South Pole first for Britain and also conduct scientific work for the British Admiralty and Royal Geographical Society. The Norwegian Antarctic Expedition (Amundsen) was also funded by public subscription, supplemented by grants from Norwegian Royalty and Parliament. Amundsen was a self-selected rather than appointed leader. Amundsen, an accomplished sailor and cross-country skier, had led the Arctic sea expedition 1903–1906 that conquered the Northwest Passage, the Norwegian Northwest Passage Expedition, but had not been to Antarctica. Scott only learned in October 1910 while his ship *Terra Nova* was already well on the way to Antarctica that Amundsen, supposedly exploring in the Arctic, was also heading to Antarctica, signaling he would challenge for the pole. Amundsen had one paramount objective: to win the race to the South Pole for Norway.

Thus the race to the South Pole 1911–1912 involved two experienced explorers with considerable leadership experience in polar exploration, engaged in a race with a difference. Scott had returned to Antarctica to continue his quest to reach the pole, not to compete against another explorer for the honor. Amundsen had come to Antarctica to reach the pole before Scott.

LEADERSHIP AND VIGILANT DECISION-MAKING IN EXTREME SITUATIONS

Janis and Mann's (1977) decision conflict model provides a framework to describe the two leaders' decision-making processes, as inferred from published accounts. The conflict model identifies vigilance, complacency, defensive avoidance (procrastination, abandoning responsibility, distortion and rationalization) and hyper-vigilance (impulsiveness, panic) as common patterns used to deal with difficult decisions. The conflict model identifies psychological stress and arousal as an antecedent of the different patterns. The characteristics of vigilant decision processes are careful exploration of objectives and alternatives, careful evaluation of consequences, and thorough information search and implementation. I also refer to Janis's (1989) constraints model of decision-making, which describes the basic, occasionally naive, decision rules leaders sometimes use, even when dealing with serious, consequential issues. Examples of overly simple decision rules include 'follow tradition', 'do what we did last time' and 'do what's good enough'. The extent to which leaders exercise vigilance, do not rely on oversimple decision rules, are open to advice, and learn from their own and others' experience, improves the quality of their decisions and, in turn, the project outcomes.

STRATEGIC DECISIONS, TACTICAL DECISIONS AND OPERATIONAL DECISIONS

A key element of leadership and decision-making in extreme situations is the care taken with decisions at three levels: the major strategic decisions (setting fundamental objectives), the enabling tactical decisions (ways to achieve the objectives) and the operational decisions (routines for efficient use of time, resources and equipment).

Amundsen's objective was to conquer the South Pole. His strategy, knowing that Scott was heading for Antarctica with the same ambition, was to race to the pole as soon as possible. His tactics were to position his supply ship (*Fram*) and his base camp at a location as near as possible to the pole, and then in the summer of 1910–1911, establish a line of supply depots in easily identifiable locations using dog-hauled sledges for transport. He would begin the race to the pole at the first opportunity in summer 1911–1912, taking an eight-man team for the entire journey, using dog-hauled sledges to carry supplies and equipment. His operations at base camp focused on technical improvements to the sledges, skis, equipment, tents, clothing, and so on, to provide the most efficient passage over the Antarctic terrain. The three levels of decision-making – strategy, tactics and operations – were aligned in a very simple system.

Scott's objectives were to conquer the pole and conduct scientific work. He was unaware of Amundsen's challenge when he developed his strategy and tactics for the expedition. His strategy, having checked several sites, was to locate his base at the same place he used in the 1901–1904 polar expedition, and from there follow much the same route taken by Shackleton (on the 1907–1909 *Nimrod* expedition) to reach progressively closer to the pole. His tactics for the first season, the summer of 1910–1911, were to establish and supply a system of supply depots placed at regular intervals as far as possible along the route to the pole. His tactics for establishing the depots were to use a coordinated transport system of high-tech (motor-sledges) and low-tech methods (horses and dogs) to haul the supplies and equipment. Operations focused on procurement of motor-sledges, ponies and dogs, planning of depot locations, improving the equipment, precise estimations of food rations needed, and enhancing the men's knowledge of Antarctic weather, terrain and conditions. His tactics for the actual journey to the pole in summer 1911–1912 were first to deploy 16 men in four teams to establish additional depots closer to the pole, and then to hand over to a four-man team on skis for the final 150-mile trek to the pole, hauling a sledge with supplies and equipment, while the other teams returned to base.

Scott's strategy, tactics and operations were altogether more complex than Amundsen's. It is reasonable to ask whether that complexity contributed in some measure to the subsequent disaster.

SIX DECISION AREAS

In the two years of Scott's and Amundsen's polar expeditions, the leaders made hundreds of decisions. I focus on a subset that might have contributed to the outcomes of the two expeditions. The issues pertain to six decision areas: (1) expedition objectives; (2) places of departure; (3) when to begin the journey; (4) transport methods, and the decision to man-haul sledges; (5) location (and relocation) of supply depots; and (6) team selection, membership and fitness.

1.   Expedition Objectives (and the Decision to Collect Rock Samples)

Both expeditions had the same objective: to conquer the South Pole. Scott's expedition however, had a second objective, to collect scientific materials and make scientific measurements and observations.

Amundsen, with one objective – to get to the South Pole before Scott – focused his tactical and operational decisions almost entirely on the speed and efficiency required to get his team to the pole in the shortest time, and safely back to base. The urgency to move quickly (which nearly led to disaster when he set out prematurely on 8 September 1911), proved to be decisive in the success of his expedition, as his journey took a relatively short 99 days in the best part of spring and summer.

Scott's second objective – to gather scientific materials and information – had been determined by the *Terra Nova* expedition sponsors, the British Royal Geographical Society and the Admiralty. The two objectives do not appear to have added to the complexity of Scott's expedition, but while seemingly compatible, they sometimes conflicted. For Scott's team to reach the pole (and return safely) it was essential to keep moving and conserve energy, while to conduct scientific work it was necessary to carry instruments, stop to collect samples and make meteorological observations. This took time, and the longer the journey, the greater the risk of encountering blizzards and also suffering from injuries and illness. The two objectives clashed at a critical point in the harrowing return journey of Scott's team from the pole. On 7 February 1912 the team began its descent of the Beardmore Glacier. The weather was bad and the team had serious difficulty locating a depot. At this point in the return journey, Scott's team was struggling, suffering from frostbite, snow blindness and malnutrition, with only about five days of food left on the sledge, and the next depot about five days away. However, as the weather improved, Scott ordered a half-day's rest, allowing Wilson to 'geologise', and find 30 pounds of fossil-bearing samples to add to the sledge, which slowed progress to the next depot – and beyond – when the team resumed its journey.

Scott did not place scientific work above his men's safety; his weary team no doubt welcomed the rest. But it is a questionable judgment to haul an additional load of 30 pounds from depot to depot, rather than build and mark a pile of rocks for later collection, then move on. He might have underestimated the seriousness of the situation, or his judgment might have been influenced by a desire to maintain the scientific objective of the *Terra Nova* expedition and, despite the burden, proudly produce the scientific materials when the team returned to base. Scott's judgment might have also been affected by psychological stress due to setbacks and disappointment (see Janis and Mann, 1977). Weeks earlier, on 11 December 1911, Scott had referred in his diary to 'the stress of sighted failure of our whole plan'. Did the decision to stop to collect and add rock specimens to the sledge contribute to the eventual disaster? Possibly yes. Had Scott got his priorities wrong at that moment? Probably yes. While 'geologising' had provided a brief respite for the men, importantly, it added to the load the men were hauling across an icy plain – and added to their fatigue, further slowing the team's progress. When the fatal blizzard hit on 20 March 1912 and trapped Scott, Bowers and Wilson, they were only 11 miles short of One Ton Depot.

2.   Places of Departure: Base Camps

The overall strategic direction of an expedition dictates where the place of departure, base camp, is ideally located. Scott, having canvassed several options, decided to locate his base at Cape Evans, following the precedent of previous British polar expeditions. Cape Evans is located 858 miles from the South Pole. It was a vigilant decision, consistent with the two objectives of his expedition: to reach the pole and to conduct scientific work. From Cape Evans he could follow much the same route Shackleton had taken on his expedition, and the site was a suitable departure point for the extensive scientific work his party conducted during the *Terra Nova* expedition.

Amundsen located his base at the Bay of Whales, positioned 350 miles east of Cape Evans and 798 miles from the pole (therefore 60 miles closer to the South Pole than Scott's base). Amundsen studied the records of Scott's and Shackleton's previous polar expeditions as well as the journals of explorers who had visited the Bay of Whales since 1841. Amundsen's decision to locate his base at Bay of Whales seemed risky as it was located on an ice shelf, and therefore possibly unstable. However, Amundsen noted repeated mention in the journals of a fixed, dome-like structure at the Bay of Whales, and concluded that the ice shelf was stable. Amundsen was in a race and wanted to take the shortest possible journey to the pole. His decision, although unrelated to the outcome of the race, gave his team a shorter journey to and from the pole, approximately four days each way. Amundsen too had shown vigilance and while he took a calculated risk, it was based on convincing information.

3.   When to Begin: Timing

When a race begins usually determines when it will end, but in extreme situations, such as Antarctica, that principle can be illusory. Scott's bid to reach the pole began on 1 November 1911, when he set out from base at Cape Evans with three teams totaling 12 men, together with ponies and dogs. He allowed for a journey of 144 days to the pole and back. A four-man motor-sledge team had already set out with supplies to establish a depot located at lat. 80°35' south, where the entire 16-man party would rendezvous. The tactic was for the three support teams to establish and mark a chain of supply depots south of Camp 17 heading toward the pole and then return to base camp in succession, while Scott's selected 'polar' team would make the final push to the pole. However, the two motor-sledges broke down and the nine overworked ponies became ill. While the polar team eventually made up time, the entire complex arrangement was behind schedule. The failure of the transport support added to the strain of the polar team's subsequent journey. Scott's unfortunate decision to rely on motor-sledges and ponies for depot laying had affected when his polar team could take the final stage to the pole in 1911–1912, and now, unfortunately, the team was behind schedule.

An impatient Amundsen began his journey to the pole on 8 September 1911. Amundsen's plan was simple: a team of eight men on four sledges pulled by well-trained dogs would take the most direct route from base camp to the South Pole. But he set out much too early in the season and soon encountered dangerously cold temperatures of –40°C. Several men suffered frostbite and two dogs froze to death. On 16 September,

Amundsen recognized his huge mistake and ordered his team to return to base as quickly as possible. The men scrambled the 46 miles back to base in total disarray. Amundsen's decision to return to camp and wait for warmer temperature was pivotal for the outcome of his expedition. A near disaster had been averted, the men had time to recover from frostbite and further improve their clothing, boots and equipment, and Amundsen used the opportunity to reduce the team from eight to five men and in the process remove Hjalmar Johansen, an outspoken critic of the fiasco. On 20 October, in warmer weather, the smaller five-man team left camp with four sledges and 52 dogs. The journey went smoothly at first, but weather conditions soon deteriorated. Amundsen and Wisting's sledge nearly disappeared into a crevasse when a snow bridge collapsed below them. The remainder of the journey to the pole proceeded without mishap.

While the strategy to sprint to the pole ended in near disaster when Amundsen set out on 8 September, the emphasis on speed and efficiency served him well, to realize his objective to be first to the pole and achieve a quick return to base. By travelling quickly, he reduced the likelihood of exposure to extreme temperatures, severe blizzards and mishaps on the 1600-mile journey. Amundsen had made a highly risky decision on his first attempt, but was fortunate to be able to recover from his mistake and retain his leadership authority.

The decision of when to start – and how to maintain progress – was decisive for the two expeditions, significantly affecting the respective outcomes. Journeys to the pole are best taken in the summer months of December to February. The likelihood of encountering extreme weather, which can stall progress for days, must be factored into decisions about how far and fast a team can travel on a long arduous journey. To start early can bring disaster (Amundsen). To start late – and progress slowly – also courts disaster. When March arrives in Antarctica, the weather deteriorates. On 25 January 1912 Amundsen's team was safely back at camp. On 20 March 1912 the remainder of Scott's team were trapped in a blizzard 150 miles from camp.

4. Transport Methods, and the Decision to Man-Haul Sledges

Scott relied on a combination of transport methods – motorized sledges, ponies and dogs – to lay down depots and stock them with supplies in the first summer of the expedition, 1910–1911, and to extend the work in the second summer, 1911–1912. Scott's choice of transport methods for depot-laying was influenced, to a large extent, by Shackleton's 1907–1909 *Nimrod* expedition, which had used (with very limited success), pony transport and a motorcar adapted for the snow. The decision rules influencing his choice of methods might have been: 'multiple methods provide flexibility', 'do what's satisfactory' (satisficing), 'follow precedent' and 'try something new'.

None of the transport methods worked well in the southerly advance to the pole in the summer of 1911–1912. The two motor-sledges broke down, the dogs were unreliable and the ponies, which were not suited to tough work in extreme conditions, were mostly ill. Man-hauling of supply sledges became necessary. The inadequacy of the transport methods slowed the pace of depot laying and, in turn, delayed the departure of Scott's polar team for the long, grinding march to the pole.

Amundsen, invariably, used teams of well-trained and well-managed dogs to haul the sledges loaded with food and equipment to supply the depots dotted along the route south toward the Pole. This simple method worked well.

In the contest between a simple, but well executed, low-tech method (dogs and sledges) and a combination of high-tech and low-tech methods (motor-sledges, ponies with sledges, dogs with sledges) the simple method won. There are lessons for leaders in extreme situations. The technology and tools chosen for the project must be suited to the conditions. Expertise in the use of technology makes a great difference (the Norwegians used dogs and sledges competently; the British struggled). Finally, in extreme conditions, simplicity trumps complexity.

Transport to the Pole: Dog-Hauling Versus Man-Hauling

The crucial difference between the two expeditions was the means used to reach the pole. Amundsen, adopting the Inuit method, chose to travel the entire distance to the pole on four sledges hauled by teams of dogs. Scott chose to trek the final 150 miles to the pole with the team on skis hauling a single sledge. Thus Scott's team hauled a sledge loaded with a tent, sleeping bags, food and equipment up a glacier and across an ice plateau in freezing temperatures. The consequences of the decision were enormous. Well before Scott's team was trapped in a blizzard on 19 March 1912 the ill, hungry and exhausted men had hauled a heavy sledge for hundreds of miles across a vast icy plateau. The man-hauling decision, according to Sullivan (1962), was the decisive factor in the disaster.

It is important to provide some context to an apparently bizarre decision. Man-hauling was a strong tradition in nineteenth-century British polar exploration. Many British explorers, and Scott's mentor Sir Clements Markham, held the view that personal physical effort was noble and manly. Thus, while Scott believed that using dogs to haul supplies and equipment was acceptable, their use to haul men on a sledge was not.

Polar explorers often exchanged advice and information. The famous Norwegian explorer Fridtjof Nansen had advised Scott to 'take dogs, dogs and more dogs' for transporting men in the 1901–1904 *Discovery* expedition. Scott ignored the advice. Scott also assumed that Amundsen would be taking dogs to haul the sledges in his quest for the South Pole. Thus Scott's decision to man-haul a sledge to reach the pole was not capricious, but based on his basic values. It should be noted that Scott had found dogs difficult to work with on previous expeditions, and this might have been another reason for his decision. While Scott was seemingly confident about the chances of success, he must have harbored some doubts. On 3 January 1912 he wrote in his diary: 'Very anxious to see how we shall manage tomorrow. If we can march well with the full load we shall be practically safe, I take it'.

Amundsen had no qualms about using dog teams to haul sledges loaded with men and equipment all the way to the pole. He had experienced the effort of man-hauling while in the Arctic and was not impressed. He had two expert dog-handlers and over 50 well-trained dogs to haul the sledges. As Amundsen's team neared the pole and needed fewer dogs to pull the sledges, the weakest dogs were sacrificed to add vitamin-rich meat to the diet. Amundsen was pragmatic about animals and adopted the Inuit practise.

There are several decision-making lessons for leaders from this episode. Listen to advice from experts, note best practise (Inuit), note what potential (and actual) competitors are doing, check what colleagues think and prefer (Oates was critical of man-hauling), have a fallback position in case something goes wrong (Amundsen's team could have skied from depot to depot), learn how to use the best technology for the conditions (dogs), and most importantly, when survival is at stake do not allow outmoded sentimental values to dominate choices.

5. Location (and Relocation) of Supply Depots

The lifelines for each expedition were the supply depots established along a line from base camp extending south toward the pole. Ready access to depots located at manageable intervals along the route was important for obtaining food, cooking fuel, equipment and, ultimately, for survival.

Amundsen put great effort into the depots, and marked the route between them like a Norwegian ski course, using marker flags every eight miles, markers made out of food containers every mile, six-foot piles of rock every three miles, and a line of bamboo flags laid out transversely every half mile for five miles either side of each depot.

Scott laid down fewer depots than Amundsen, and they were less adequately marked and supplied. Scott's diaries describe his concerns with finding routes on the return journey, close calls in finding several depots, as well as discovering barely adequate food supplies, and leakage from the cooking fuel canisters. These problems suggest both a pattern of complacency, as well as the consequences of relying on inadequate transport methods to establish and supply the depots (see above). Did these problems contribute to the outcome? Possibly, yes. If the depots were hard to find, too far apart and inadequately stocked, there would have been a cost in valuable time and energy that made a difference at the edge of survival.

One Ton Depot
In January–February 1911, Scott's party laid out a chain of supply depots on the Great Ice Barrier down to approximately 80° south; the largest was to be One Ton Depot at 80° south. One Ton Depot would provide a large cache of supplies for the expedition on the march to and from the pole, to begin at the end of the year. In February 1911 sick ponies and poor weather conditions disrupted the depot-laying work. Scott decided to change the depot location plan and announced that One Ton Depot would now be established at 79°29' south (approximately 30 miles north of the planned location). His idea was to return the sick ponies to base to recover and be available to haul supplies at the end of the year. The decision to change the location of One Ton Depot was hotly contested. Captain Laurence Oates, in charge of ponies, was 'appalled' by the decision and urged Scott to push the ponies further to meet the original plan. Oates reportedly said to Scott, 'Sir, I'm afraid you'll come to regret not taking my advice.' Scott replied, 'Regret it or not, I have taken my decision as a Christian gentleman'.

The decision to relocate One Ton Depot had tragic consequences. A year later, on 20 March 1912, Scott's team on their return journey from the pole were trapped in a blizzard and perished about 11 miles short of One Ton Depot (but about 20 miles beyond where the depot had been originally planned).

6. Team Selection, Membership and Fitness

Leaders of challenging projects in extreme situations must ensure they select the very best team available. Team members must be capable and competent, have relevant experience, be physically fit and able to work well together. Character, hardiness, reliability, and even the need to ensure representation of different interest groups, are other considerations taken into account in team selection.

Amundsen chose an eight-man team for his first attempt on 8 September 1911 to race from base camp to the pole. Following the chaotic return to camp, he decided to trim his team from eight to five men. When he started out again on 20 October 1911, Amundsen led a highly capable team of Olav Bjaaland, a skilled carpenter and ski-maker; Hilmer Hanssen, a skillful dog driver; Sverre Hassel, an expert dog handler; and Oscar Wisting, a seaman and handyman. All team members were proficient navigators and skiers. By cutting to a smaller team, Amundsen was able to exclude Hjalmar Johansen, his fiercest critic. This meant a loss of valuable experience but a gain in team cohesion, essential for team performance in extreme situations.

Scott set out from base camp on 1 November with 16 men and only announced the members of his five-man polar team on 4 January 1912, when about 150 miles from the pole. The team, led by Scott, comprised Dr Edward Wilson (a scientist and medical doctor), Petty Officer Edgar Evans (Navy) in charge of sledging equipment, and Captain Laurence Oates (Army) in charge of pony transportation. The decision to select Oates is not obvious, as ponies were not part of this phase of the expedition and Scott and Oates often clashed. Oates's selection may have been to include an Army representative on a British polar team funded partially by the government. Lieutenant Henry Bowers (Navy), an experienced navigator, was an unexpected late addition to the team, as all the plans and preparations were for a four-man polar team.

It is noteworthy that Amundsen and Scott both changed their teams at the stage they were about to begin (or restart) the most critical part of the journey. Both teams probably benefited from the changes, Amundsen's especially. The new Amundsen team gained in efficiency and removed a potential irritant. The enlarged Scott team gained in navigational competence and manpower to help haul the sledge (Fiennes, 2003). Some analysts have criticized Scott's late decision to include Bowers, suggesting it added to the team's burden. Indeed, inclusion of Bowers created several logistical problems, for example greater load on the sledge, less room in the tent, altered food and cooking arrangements, and Bowers had to walk because his skis were already stored at another depot, many miles away. However, the inclusion of Bowers can be viewed as a fortunate (although ultimately futile) decision, as it provided three reasonably fit men (instead of two) when the health of Oates and Evans deteriorated sharply on the return from the pole in January–February 1912.

Leaders must be alert to the physical and mental fitness of team members. When the polar team was announced Oates had frostbitten feet, and Evans had a 'nasty cut on his hand. I hope it won't give him trouble', Scott noted in a diary entry three days into the trek. There were serious consequences from selecting team members who were carrying injuries. The team's progress slowed on the difficult return journey from the pole in February–March 1912 as the physical condition of Evans and Oates deteriorated rapidly. Evans died on 17 February and Oates walked to his death on 16 March. Scott, Wilson and Bowers struggled on until trapped in a severe blizzard. I speculate that if Scott's polar team had five fully fit men when it started the march to the pole, it could have moved faster and quite likely reached One Ton Depot, and from there, safety. From a modern-day perspective, Scott the team leader, and indeed Wilson the expedition doctor, appear complacent about the physical condition of men they selected for a highly demanding physical task. However, from the perspective of British values in the Victorian era of polar exploration, hardship and suffering were common, and Scott, as representative of a British Navy and Army tradition that valued highly bravery and stoicism in the face of adversity (Crane, 2005), might have been accepting of the men's condition.

What lessons can be learned about team selection? First, that selecting the right team for the task in extreme situations can be a matter of survival or disaster. Second, it is not simple to select the right team and adjustments may be necessary as the nature of tasks, and the suitability of the individuals needed to perform them, become apparent. Finally, out of loyalty for a friend or colleague, there may be a tendency to overlook or underestimate their physical and other problems, matters to be considered very seriously when selecting a team for a difficult project in an extreme situation.

REPRISE AND ASSESSMENT

My evaluation of the leaders' decision-making relates primarily to whether their decisions (or failure to decide) put at risk the men's lives and contributed to their hardship and suffering, not who won or lost the race to the pole. Scott made a number of mistakes that affected the condition of his men and in some cases cost precious time, which jeopardized their survival and his own. Some of the decisions contributing to the disaster were taken years earlier in planning the strategies and tactics for the expedition, their unforeseen consequences apparent only much later. The strategic objective to conduct scientific work as part of the expedition (a worthy objective) played out unfortunately when many months later Scott's team stopped to collect and add a load of rocks to the sledge. The decision to change the planned location of One Ton Depot in February 1911 played out disastrously one year later when the last members of the team perished just out of reach. Decisions in the final phase of the expedition, such as having two unfit men on the march to the pole, also contributed to the outcome. Errors and oversights made in the earlier phase of the expedition, for example the choice of inadequate transport methods, inadequate location and supply of depots, and neglect to address the well-known problem of faulty cooking fuel containers, combined later to steal precious time and add to the men's hardship and misery. In the post-mortem of why terrible disasters happen, multiple deficiencies in planning and preparation become apparent. Matters of little apparent importance at the time become, in retrospect, the defining factors that probably make the difference between survival and disaster.

I believe the two defining decisions that determined the disaster were relocation of One Ton Depot and choice of man-hauling, both putting the men at serious risk on the hard journey home. Relocation of One Ton Depot is the more obvious mistake, as it was a calculated risk taken despite strong opposition. The decision to man-haul the sledge, taken as an act of faith based on quaint outmoded values, ignored previous expert advice, contradicted good practice, was disapproved of by some of his team (for example, Oates), and was obviously risky. I emphasize these two decisions because they were contested at the time, and therefore it cannot be argued the consequences were unforeseen and unexpected. There were other decisions that contributed separately and together to the outcome, and they relate to unfortunate decisions about the overall transport methods and depot location and supplies for the entire expedition. While the expedition was certainly dogged by misfortune, decisions under the leader's control ultimately determined the fate of Scott's polar team, not bad luck.

The question arises for the study of leadership in extreme situations of what elements of Scott's leadership contributed to the outcome. Despite evidence of extensive planning and preparation, a distinct element of complacency and overconfidence is evident in how Scott led the *Terra Nova* expedition. He knew the seals of the cooking oil containers were unreliable, that the men's skiing skills needed improvement, the dogs were unreliable, but took little control of ensuring that the problems were fixed. He was unjustifiably optimistic about a variety of transport methods, which Shackleton on his 1907–1909 expedition had found were problematic. Scott understood the dangers of Antarctic exploration yet took unnecessary risks. Had he become overconfident from the experience of surviving many dangers over many expeditions? In his final diary entry, Scott wrote: 'We took risks, we knew we took them; things have come out against us, and therefore we have no cause for complaint, but bow to the will of Providence, determined still to do our best to the last'.

Amundsen the leader and decision-maker had a much simpler task. He was predominantly vigilant, highly ambitious and competitive, single-minded, highly planful, open to learning from his own and others' experience, impatient, a calculated risk-taker when he could see a clear advantage, made correctible mistakes, and was clearly very lucky. The overall picture is of a planful, highly determined, unsentimental and mostly vigilant leader of a smaller, simpler and more efficient operation than Scott's. Amundsen (1912) in his account attributed the success of his expedition to thorough preparation: 'I may say that this is the greatest factor – the way in which the expedition is equipped – the way in which every difficulty is foreseen, and precautions taken for meeting or avoiding it'.

THE CONNECTEDNESS OF DECISIONS

Disasters such as happened to Scott's polar team are frequently due to the result of a series of poor decisions, some made in preparation for the journey and some made during the journey. Weick (1990) in his analysis of the Tenerife air disaster of 1977, in which a KLM 747 and Pan Am 747 collided, suggests that catastrophes are rarely the result of one error or bad decision, but are mainly due to multiple small errors that become magnified into major problems. The more complex the system, the greater the likelihood of multiple errors and in turn the emergence of major problems. Amundsen's expedition was much simpler than Scott's, and there were fewer errors.

I accept that thoroughly considered plans might come unstuck when extreme weather sets in, and unforeseeable mishaps and accidents occur. However, I also maintain that the greater the practice of vigilant problem-solving in the fundamental decision areas identified in this analysis – the project objectives, places of location and timing of project commencement, the supporting infrastructure for the project (depots and methods of transport), and team quality and preparedness – the greater the likelihood of positive outcomes.

LEADERSHIP LESSONS

Several generalizations can be made from Scott and Amundsen in Antarctica about principles of leadership and decision-making in extreme situations:

1. Extreme situations place additional burden on the overall system and on the leader's decision-making capacity. In extreme situations leaders are operating within the bounds of unpredicted events, limited information, unknown risks and narrow options.
2. The leader's preferences and judgments tend to dominate in extreme situations. The extent to which leaders are well prepared, open-minded, learn from previous experience, learn from what others and competitors are doing, are open to advice from experts and colleagues, examine precedents but avoid preconceptions and bias, and avoid oversimple decision rules all determine the outcome of the project.
3. Decisions taken in extreme situations may be susceptible to error, the leader's judgment clouded by psychological stress engendered by danger, fatigue, loss and disappointment.
4. In extreme situations leaders must sort out and determine the very highest priorities. Previously compatible goals can become competing goals in an emergency and a recipe for disaster.
5. Strategic, tactical and operational decisions all count in extreme situations. Leaders must be vigilant at all three levels. Imprudent decisions even in apparently small matters can produce disastrous, irreversible outcomes.
6. Decisions made (and decisions not taken) in extreme situations are highly cumulative. Early mistakes and early neglect may combine with later errors to create a tipping point for disaster. Multiple small errors can produce a threshold for disaster.

Several research questions can be added about leaders in extreme situations. At what point do experienced leaders falter as they face new extreme situations? Are the best and worst qualities of leaders revealed and accentuated by the challenges of extreme situations? Do the same principles of leadership of complex projects in normal situations apply to leadership in extreme situations? (See Mann, 2005.)

The journeys of Scott and Amundsen to the South Pole provide an instructive account of how even highly experienced leaders are susceptible to error in extreme situations. One leader was able to recover from a major error and achieve his goal; the other, more error-prone, was able to achieve major goals, but ultimately met disaster.

ACKNOWLEDGMENTS

I am grateful to Professors Rex Brown and Joshua Klayman for their helpful and constructive comments and suggestions on the draft chapter.

REFERENCES

Amundsen, Roald (1912). *Sydpolen*. 2 vols, translated as *The South Pole: An Account of the Norwegian Antarctic Expedition in the 'Fram,' 1910–1912*. London: John Murray.

Barczewski, Stephanie (2007). *Antarctic Destinies, Scott, Shackleton and the Changing Face of Heroism*. London: Hambledon Continuum.

Clark, Kim and Steven C. Wheelwright (1992). Organizing and leading 'heavyweight' development teams. *California Management Review*, 34 (3), 9–28.

Collins, Jim and Morten Hansen (2011). *Great by Choice*. New York: Harper Collins.

Crane, David (2005). *Scott of the Antarctic*. London: Harper Collins.

Fiennes, Ranulph (2003). *Captain Scott*. London: Hodder and Stoughton.

Fischhoff, B. (2007). An early history of hindsight research. *Social Cognition*, 25, 10–13.

Hannah, Sean, Mary Uhl-Bien, Bruce Avolio and F. Cavaretta (2009). A framework for examining leadership in extreme contexts. *Leadership Quarterly*, 20, 897–919.

Huntford, Roland (1979). *Scott and Amundsen: Their Race to the South Pole*. London: Abacus.

Janis, Irving (1989). *Crucial Decisions: Leadership in Policymaking and Crisis Management*. New York: Free Press.

Janis, Irving and Leon Mann (1977). *Decision-making: A Psychological Analysis of Conflict, Choice and Commitment*. New York: Free Press.

Mann, Leon (2005). *Leadership, Management and Innovation in R&D Project Teams*. Westport, CT: Praeger.

Mann, Leon (2006). Investigating five leadership themes: roles, decisions, character, relationships, and journeys. In Qicheng Jing, Mark Rosenzweig, Gery d'Ydewalle, Houcan Zhang, Hsuan-Chih Chen and Kan Zhang (eds), *Progress in Psychological Science around the World*, Vol. 2. Hove: Psychology Press, pp. 125–43.

Preston, Diana (1999). *A First Rate Tragedy: Captain Scott's Antarctic Expeditions*. London: Constable.

Sengupta, Kishore and Ludo Van der Heyden (2011). The leadership lessons of the race to the South Pole. HBR Blog Network, December 13.

Solomon, Susan (2001). *The Coldest March. Scott's Fatal Antarctic Expedition*. New Haven, CT: Yale University Press.

Sullivan, Walter (1962). The South Pole fifty years later. *Arctic*, 15 (3), 175–78.

Weick, Karl E. (1990). The vulnerable system: an analysis of the Tenerife air disaster. *Journal of Management*, 16 (3), 571–93.

3. Leadership and organizational learning in extreme situations: lessons of a comparative study from two polar expeditions – one of the greatest disasters (Franklin, 1845) and one of the best achievements (Nansen, 1893)

Pascal Lièvre and Géraldine Rix-Lièvre

INTRODUCTION

The comparative study of two emblematic polar expeditions of the late nineteenth century, one of the greatest disasters (Captain Sir John Franklin's Royal Navy Northwest Passage Expedition, 1845–1848), and one of the greatest successes (Fridtjof Nansen's Norwegian North Polar Expedition, 1893–1896), directs the issue of leadership in extreme situations to manage collective action which takes the form of a process of organizational learning (Argyris and Schon, 1978, 1996) or a learning organization (Senge, 1994). This idea of understanding the development of a project under uncertainty as a process of organizational learning was developed for many years by Midler (1995). But there is no learning organization without individual learners, according to Argyris and Schon (1996). It is a necessary condition, but not sufficient. The history of these two expeditions shows that the first quality of a leader of the expedition is the ability to learn, with reference to the project he leads. Franklin did not learn throughout the project; this was the cause of its failure. Nansen learned throughout the expedition, and this was the cause of his achievement. In a first step, we propose some framework elements and definitions around extreme situations and polar expeditions. In a second step, we provide a comparative analysis of the Franklin expedition to conquer the Northwest Passage, and the Nansen expedition to the North Pole, in terms of organizational learning. In conclusion we identify some principles of the organizational learning process which are central to managing extreme situations.

FRAMEWORK AND DEFINITIONS

The Management of Extreme Situations as a Class of Situation

The management of extreme situations appears more and more as a class of situation away from traditional knowledge in the science of organizations, which we need to explore. As Hurley-Hanson and Giannantonio (2009) explain:

> There have been a number of crises that have affected organizations during this decade. The events of September 11th, 2001 and Hurricane Katrina in 2005 demonstrated that a majority of organizations' Crisis Response Plans (CRP) were not adequate to respond to either man made or natural disasters of this magnitude.

It becomes relevant to investigate extreme examples to understand what kind of management is required in this type of situation. What is an extreme situation? In agreement with Hurley-Hanson and Giannantonio (2011) 'An extreme situation is defined as one that falls outside the norm; that is, the situation falls outside the norm; that is, the situation falls outside the scope of daily experience'. Thus, we consider that an extreme situation management is a management of radical breaks with the past which requires organizational learning (Argyris and Schön, 1996; Senge, 1994). A traditional management situation can be defined as follows: 'when participants join together and have to accomplish in a determined period a collective action leading to a result which [is] going to be assessed by an external person' (Girin, 2011). A management situation is extreme when it presents three characteristics: time sensitivity, uncertainty and risk (Garel and Lièvre, 2010). Time sensitivity means that such a situation is disruptive. Uncertainty is a very well-known concept, but here we are facing radical uncertainty, because it is impossible to be ready for unforeseeable events. In this way, teams have to develop high resiliency capacities (Weick, 1993; Weick and Sutcliffe, 2007). The level of risks is high and their effects are often dramatic.

Polar or Mountaineering Expedition as Extreme Situation

For 15 years, researchers in management have taken expeditions in environment extremes as a field of research, such as polar expeditions and mountaineering expeditions. Expeditions offer good learning opportunities. First, they are in a confined environment in many aspects: geographical, social, economic, and so on. It is easier to concentrate on the evolution of this type of project from the very first idea up to complete closure. Second, risks are everywhere and not all of them can be managed, yet consequences can be dramatic, resulting in life-or-death situations. Expeditions are managed within a high level of uncertainty, which is often the case in management in 'normal' organizational life. They are prepared for with extreme rigor but their leaders must adapt continuously. Based on these two points, we believe that polar expeditions are ideal for research in management, representing an opportunity to learn about managing the unexpected (Aubry et al., 2010).

For example, Weick (1995) first opened the way by studying a Hungarian military expedition lost in the Alps. Perkins (2000) in his book *Leading at the Edge* was trying to draw lessons in leadership from Shackleton's expedition to the South Pole. Lievre since 2000 has investigated polar and mountaineering expeditions, as well as adopting the approach of a historian and anthropologist (Aubry and Lievre, 2010; Garel and Lievre, 2010; Recope et al., 2010; Lecoutre and Lievre, 2010). Hällgren (2007, 2011) is working on the management of deviations in a project on exemplary high-altitude expeditions. Savitt (2004) has investigated the conquering of the South Pole, from the archives of the Scott Polar Research Institute, to understand exploration management today. Recently, Musca et al. investigated a team of mountaineers whose goal was to explore an unknown land: the Cordillera Darwin in 2009 (Musca et al., 2009; Lievre, 2012).

What is a Polar Expedition?

A polar expedition is a temporary organization (Garel and Lièvre, 2010), which can be considered as a project. The project emerges around a relatively precise objective such as a crossing, reaching a summit, a particular point, having a scientific purpose, or as a leisure activity. We could say that the organization emerges from the moment the project is explicitly expressed. A certain number of actors will gather around the expedition's objective. Traditionally, the expedition leader, the hub of the organization, is the one who had the idea for the project. The leader is the one who will recruit the other members of the expedition. Recruiting is tricky because many criteria must be combined. The project can stop right there for lack of compatible 'comrades in arms', then pick up again two years later following certain encounters, or may never pick up. Depending on the level of difficulty of the expedition, preparation time can take from six months to ten years. During this time, the group will gather documents, meet with experts, assign tasks, plan the ideal course of the expedition, purchase the equipment and test it, provide individual and group training, and gather the administrative and financial documents to be able to leave on the start date. The expedition takes place in the field during a precise period of time, surrounded by the trip to and from home, except for any major incident that could force the expedition to be interrupted and to be brought back to civilization. The duration of the expedition can last from one month to three years. The project is finished not when the members of the expedition have returned to their respective homes, but when the books are closed and the commitments made to sponsors, scientific partners or organizations that may have subsidized the expedition have been fulfilled. Depending on the aforementioned operations, the organization may be prolonged for a few months or several years after the expedition proper. This type of project seems to have a few particularities. It is often the same team that follows the entire project. It appears that the implementation phase in the field always escapes complete planning and that the best attitude is not to want to apply the plan at all costs, but rather to place oneself in a permanent adaptation posture, with the plan having then to be considered as an overall resource for taking action in certain situations. At the same time, a lack of anticipation and preparation can have serious consequences further on in the course of the expedition. Acquired experience by members of the expedition throughout all of their various expeditions is a source of knowledge of unsurpassable value. Anything new must be tested before being implemented in the expedition.

CASE STUDIES: COMPARISON BETWEEN FRANKLIN EXPEDITION AND NANSEN EXPEDITION IN TERMS OF ORGANIZATIONAL LEARNING

In the framework of grounded theory (Glaser and Strauss, 1967), we purpose a historic comparative case study between two polar expeditions: the Franklin expedition to the North West Passage in 1845, and the Nansen expedition to the North Pole in 1893. We can learn from these two forms of organization of polar expedition with their different performance, and we can question the role of leadership. We analyze the life history of the expedition leader in order to determine the nature of commitment, expectations, skills vis-à-vis the shipping. We study all the organizational problems of the expedition and the organizational form, the social structure of the project team. These two expeditions are emblematic in the history of polar exploration. The first is the greatest disaster in Arctic exploration (Malaurie, 1990) with the total disappearance of two ships and 129 men. The Franklin expedition is also famous because many rescue expeditions (36 ships according to Ross, 2002) had been organized in order to search it. The work of Savours (1999), one of Britain's leading experts on polar expeditions, on the search for the Northwest Passage, is a history of the Franklin expedition.

The second expedition constitutes a landmark project in the history of polar expeditions. This expedition created the Norwegian polar expedition's school (Nansen, Sverdrup, Amundsen). This school is diametrically opposed to the English one (Franklin, Scott) based on the principles of maritime exploration developed by James Cook (1766–1779) and the Royal Navy. This Norwegian school claimed two world firsts: the first navigation of the Northwest Passage (1906) and reaching the South Pole (1911). The South Pole was the object of a confrontation between these two schools of exploration, with Amundsen on the one hand, and Scott on the other. Nansen's log of his expedition became a book (Nansen, 1897) which has been translated into many languages (including French) and has become a global benchmark for polar explorers. Explorers such as Victor (1958 [2004]) in the 1950s, Etienne of France (1996) and Ousland of Norway (2010), saw Nansen's account of his expedition as an essential reference.

We compare the two expeditions in terms of the issue of organizational learning. The expeditions were very difficult, very complex, because there were many unknowns and risks. The two expeditions were failures because they did not lead to their respective objectives. Franklin did not discover the Northwest Passage and Nansen did not reach the North Pole. But, the outcome of these two expeditions was very different. The Franklin expedition disappeared with no survivors. The Nansen expedition was very effective because it went geographically very near to the North Pole, and all the seamen returned safely to Norway. This comparative study is very interesting from the perspective of the learning organization. The Franklin expedition did not learn. The Nansen expedition learned. Why? In this chapter, we would like to suggest some avenues of research likely to describe Nansen's method regarding polar expedition, through a comparison with other expedition cases, and mostly through a close examination of what makes it different from the English

School's method. Sir John Franklin, its most famous representative, shared the idea that a polar expedition could only be considered as a sea military expedition, in accordance with James Cook's model. We will take Nansen's expedition as a starting point because it is virtuous.

A Project Consistent with Nansen's Ambitions

This expedition towards the North Pole was highly consistent with Nansen's aspirations, which are part of his life journey, and find their expression in the choices he made. For example, he chose to study biology instead of chemistry because it offered him opportunities of life and expeditions in the open air. Nansen was first of all a researcher, whose main objective was to discover as many things as possible in the unknown territories around the North Pole. At the same time this expedition was a total immersion in wilderness living, an experience which had always fascinated Nansen. He delighted in contemplating these landscapes but also in skiing across this polar desert, in hunting and fishing. This expedition fulfilled his quest for identity. He found real fulfilment through this expedition, which was not the case for some explorers belonging to the English school, for example Franklin or Scott coming from the Royal Navy. Franklin had never yearned to explore polar territories. He wanted to follow James Cook's path as a Royal Navy officer, but exploring meant cruising in the polar seas and discovering the lands beyond 70°N. Such exploration was very unlike Cook's, and Franklin never managed to understand that it was impossible to sail across polar seas, ice-bound for several months, as in free seas (Beettie and Geiger, 1987).

How Nansen's Successive and Progressive Learning since his Boyhood Seems to be Fundamental in the Organization of his North Pole Expedition

Three learning periods in Nansen's life can be identified, which allowed him to gain crucial skills in the design, preparation and implementation of an expedition to the North Pole. In his boyhood and throughout his teenage years, he had learned to live in a harsh natural environment, always choosing a self-sufficient way of life: bivouacking on the snow, skiing, hunting and fishing. These skills proved to be essential during the second part of the expedition to the North Pole. As a young adult, he took a five-month sea voyage in search of seals and whales between Greenland and Spitsbergen. The ship was trapped in the ice for almost one month near the Greenland coast. He then learned to ski on the ice floe and hit upon the idea of skiing across the Greenland. He also experienced life onboard an ice-bound ship, which proved useful in the first part of his voyage to the North Pole. Finally, a third period of apprenticeship was his expedition to Greenland (Nansen, 1890). He designed and led the expedition, during which he had his first real experience of decisive choices (including gear and companions). He gained two months' experience as a team leader, learned to ski on uneven surfaces, and used sledges pulled by dogs. He also learned to face bitter cold. All this new learning was fundamental for the second part of the expedition to the North Pole. The only gap in Nansen's know-how was seamanship. His meeting with Sverdrup was essential too. Sverdrup was one of Norway's foremost polar explorers; he played an important role in Nansen's successful Greenland crossing. All these successive elements were crucial in the organization of Nansen's expedition. Franklin, for his part, was invited by the British to command an expedition to chart and navigate a section of the Northwest Passage, without any experience of piloting a vessel beyond 70°N, as captain and sole master on board.

A Long and Methodical Preparation, where No Detail was Considered too Small, and where the Worst was Planned For

Nansen's expedition was prepared a long time in advance. From the project idea to the implementation, nine years were necessary. After several years of scientific study, he elaborated his strategy: let his boat be caught in the ice and drift to the Pole. He needed a boat able to drift without being crushed. He designed the boat with the best Norwegian naval architect, purpose-built for the specific conditions of the expedition. He nevertheless anticipated a possible sinking: lifeboats with supplies, all necessary material and vehicles enabling a party of several men to come back (dogs, sledges, clothing, tents), and food supplies depots in Siberia. Whereas many expeditions were prepared in a rush, Nansen took much time to choose his crew, equipment and food. Everything came under scrutiny. Nothing was to be overlooked in the preparation of the expedition. In contrast, the preparation of Franklin's expedition to the Northwest Passage only took six months, without any anticipation of a shipwreck and little thought given to an alternative plan.

An Ability to Adapt and to Move Away from the Original Plan

Whatever the level of preparation, of planning and anticipation, Nansen never considered his initial plan as the final one. The calculations made during the expedition showed that the ice floe drift was moving the boat more towards the south than planned. Nansen gradually convinced himself of the boat's inability to reach the North Pole. He then devised an alteration to his initial project, proposing that he and a companion would leave the *Fram* and travel on with sledges, dogs, skis and kayaks. He made sure that this second expedition would not endanger the first one (the *Fram*'s) and decided a party of two would be sufficient. Otto Sverdrup was given the command of the boat and was left in charge of it. This second expedition proved to require a succession of alterations that nobody could have forecast: first a ski trek with sledges and dogs, then without them, at last with sea kayaks. Franklin considered his plan to be the best, and that it must be followed carefully. He was certain of success; no alternative was envisaged.

The Different Modes of Acquiring Knowledge from Experience

Nansen had a thorough knowledge of all the polar expeditions of the time. He used to study the expedition leaders' logbooks in detail, which constituted for him the most precious pieces of knowledge. This was not the case for Franklin. Nansen used materials, clothing and techniques that he had already tested or tried out in real situations, such as his expedition to Greenland. During the second part of the expedition, when he left the *Fram*, even though he had already put this material to the test in real situations, he came back twice to the *Fram* to improve his equipment. They left for good at the third attempt. Franklin did not take into account feedback from recent expeditions undertaken in the Arctic which revealed that the passages were all blocked by ice. Furthermore, Franklin did not learn from his own previous land expeditions because as an officer of the Royal Navy, he thought of himself as a sailor not a land explorer. Thanks to Lieutenant Back, these previous expeditions did not become disasters (Franklin, 1827). As an officer of the Royal Navy, Franklin did not want to run in the woods! And he did not want to know anything to do.

The Use of Scientific Knowledge in the Organization of the Expedition

Reading a scientific article about polar ice drift after the wreck of the *Jeannette*, and the news of the discovery of bits of the ship's wreckage near the southern tip of Greenland, far from where it was known to have sunk, constituted for Nansen the cornerstone of his strategy to reach the North Pole. His project was explained in a scientific magazine article. He gave lectures on his future expedition to learned societies, for his project to be assessed. The food they would take with them was tested by chemists. He relied on medical knowledge about scurvy, and added lemon to the list of supplies. His choices did not correspond to Franklin's, who was neither a scientist nor an explorer willing to rely on science.

A Small Team Carefully Constituted with a Team Leader Close to his Team Mates

Nansen decided to select his team members for their technical abilities (experienced skiers or snow travellers, experienced seafarers) as well as for their commitment to the project and their team spirit. A party of 12 and the expedition leader boarded the *Fram*. Nansen was the kind of expedition leader who liked to live among his team mates. There was no hierarchical relationship, as there was in the Royal Navy expeditions. Franklin travelled with 120 men and used two military vessels (HMS *Erebus* at 370 long tons and HMS *Terror* at 340 long tons). For a similar project, to the Northwest Passage, Amundsen was successful with only six men.

CONCLUSION

These analyses lead us to draw comparisons between different ways of learning and different kinds of knowledge management between that of the 'English military school' born from the Royal Navy (Franklin) and that of Nansen. Nansen's successive and progressive learning throughout his life constituted the fundamental elements of his know-how, and was decisive throughout his project. Knowledge acquisition through other explorers' experience described in their logbooks, testing of materials and techniques used in real conditions seems to have been important. Scientific knowledge was used to solve problems related to the project. Knowledge learning was essential in Nansen's method in order to conduct his project, as well as the organizational flexibility: the ability to adapt to circumstances, and to manage alterations to the main project. It took Nansen several years of patient technical and scientific study to construct this project, despite the numerous objections he met. People expressed their strong doubts about the possibility of success. The expedition preparation included organizational aspects: no detail was considered too small, the worst scenarios were envisaged. A team is more ready to face hardships when these scenarios have been included in the preparation. We can see a logistic loop between strategy and implementation. Finally, we must ask ourselves if the deep coherence between Nansen's expedition project and his personal ambition was not the essential condition for his quick and efficient learning. A small group of men was carefully selected on technical and motivational attributes, but also on their capacity to integrate into a group whose leader shared their everyday life and played a central role in the project management.

This comparative study is very interesting from the perspective of the learning organization. The Franklin expedition did not learn. The Nansen expedition learned. Why? We can identify several human factors which represent some limits for organizational learning. We focus on the first stage of the organizational learning process, with the perception of gap by an actor or a group in situation. That is, the implementation of an organizational learning process depends on a first stage, which is the perception by at least one actor of a discrepancy in a given situation. In order to learn, someone has to be aware of a gap between intentions and achievements (Argyris, 1993) or between the capacities of an actor and those needed to cope with the situation (Senge, 1994). We were able to identify four factors which represent the limits for organizational learning (Gautier et al., 2008). The first factor concerns the differences between activity exercised by an actor and his own life project. That is to say, the reason why he is engaged in this activity, and the importance of the activity in the achievements of his life. The second factor concerns the differences between the style of actor and the style of project. The first two registers characterize the commitment and the sensitivity of the expedition leader with reference to the project. If the project is not meaningful for the expedition leader, no learning is possible. The project manager must be fully committed to the project. The third factor concerns the know-how necessary to act appropriately in the situation. It is about the difference between the know-how required to act in the situation, and the skills held by the actor at the time. If the difference is too great, the expedition leader sees nothing. First-year students of medicine cannot read X-rays to detect lung cancer. This will be easy for them after two years of study. The fourth factor concerns the structure of the organization, for example the type of leadership or the hierarchy of relationships between the actors. The question is whether and how the team mates of the expedition are able to express and to discuss the ways in which each of them makes sense of the events.

In all four factors, the two expeditions differed.[1] Franklin could not perceive his errors in situations, he could not adapt, contrary to Nansen. Also, the three main questions about leadership in extreme situations, to understand the potentiality of learning of the project leader, are: Does the project make sense for the leader? Does the leader have the minimum skills for the project's activity? Does the form of collective action make it possible to discuss the options to take in a situation, based on events? If the answer is no to all three questions, the possibility for the expedition leader to see discrepancies and errors in the course of the project are reduced, because the organizational learning process is blocked at source. This is a real obstacle to managing a project in extreme environments. These results are convergent with Weick's (1995) perspective on leadership: a leader has to be aware of the actors' sense-making.

NOTE

1.   The commitment of Franklin was to explore the world in the style of Cook: maritime exploration was important to him. But maritime expedition was not the style of expedition necessary to enable him to reach the Northwest Passage at the time. He did not understand that at this period, it was not possible to approach the exploration of the open seas and of ice and polar seas in the same way (Gautier et al. 2008). Thus, there was a gap between Franklin's style – maritime expedition – and the style of the project.

REFERENCES

Argyris, C. (1993). *Knowledge for Action: A Guide to Overcoming Barriers to Organizational Change*. San Francisco, CA: Jossey-Bass.

Argyris, C. and D. Schon (1978). *Organization Learning, a Theory of Action Perspective*. Reading, MA: Addison-Wesley.

Argyris, C. and D. Schon (1996). *Organization Learning II*. Reading, MA: Addison-Wesley

Aubry, M., B. Hobbs and P. Lièvre (2010). Project management and polar expeditions: more than a metaphor for project management. *Project Management Journal*, Special Issue, 41 (3), 2–3.

Aubry, M. and P. Lièvre (2010). Ambidexterity as a competence for project leaders: a case study from two polar expeditions. *Project Management Journal*, Special Issue, 41(3), 32–44.

Beettie, O. and J. Geiger (1987). *Frozen in Time: The Fate of Franklin Expedition*. Sakatoon: Western Producer Prairie Books.

Etienne, J.L. (1996). Préface. In F. Nansen, *Vers le pôle*. Paris: Edition Hoebeke, pp. 5–10.

Franklin, Sir J. (1998). *Journey to the Polar Sea*. Köln: Edition Konemann, Travel Classics.

Garel, G. and P. Lièvre (2010). Polar expedition project and project management. *Project Management Journal*, Special Issue, Project Management in Extreme Environment, 41(3), 21–31.

Gautier, A., P. Lièvre and G. Rix (2008). Les obstacles en matière d'apprentissage organisationnel au sein de l'organisation de la sécurité civile, une mise en perspective en termes de gestion des ressources humaines. *Revue Politique et Management Public*, 26 (2), 137–68.

Girin, J. (2011). Empirical analysis of management situations: elements of theory and method. *European Management Review*, 8 (4), 197–212.

Glaser, B.G. and A.A. Strauss (1967). *The Discovery of Grounded Theory: Strategies for Qualitative Research*. Piscataway, NJ: Transaction Publishers.

Hällgren, M. (2007). Beyond the point of no return: on the management of deviations. *International Journal of Project Management*, 25 (8), 773–80.

Hällgren, M. (2011). Mechanism in disaster: examining the structure of temporary organisation. In M. Aubry and P. Lievre, *Gestion de projet et expedition polaire: que pouvons-nous apprendre?* Montréal: Presses de l'Université du Québec, pp. 203–17.

Hurley-Hanson, A.E. and C.M. Giannantonio (2009). Crisis response plans post 9/11: Current status and future direction. *Academy of Strategic Management Journal*, 1 January, 23–35.

Hurley-Hanson, A.E. and C.M. Giannantonio (2012). Going to extremes: leadership lessons from outside the norm. Symposium, AOM, Boston, MA.

Lecoutre, M. and P. Lièvre (2010). Mobilizing social networks beyond project-team frontiers: the case of polar expeditions, *Project Management Journal*, Special Issue, 41(3), 74–85.

Lièvre, P. (2012). Du bon usage de la clique en situation extrême: l'expédition Darwin. 4th Conference on Management and Social Networks, HEC Geneve, 16–17 February.

Malaurie, J. (1990). *Ultima Thulé*. Paris: Edition Bordas.

Midler, C. (1995). Projectification of the firm, the Renault Case, *Scandinavian Journal of Management*, 11 (4), 363–75.

Musca, G., M. Perez, L. Rouleau and Y. Giordano (2009). A practice-based view of strategic leadership in a high-risk and ambiguous environment: the Darwin expedition in Patagonia. 25th Egos Colloquium, Barcelona, July.

Nansen, F. (1890). *The First Crossing of Greenland*. Transl. Hubert M. Gepp. London: Archibald Constable and Company.

Nansen, F. (1897). *Farthest North: Being the Record of a Voyage of Exploration of the Ship 'Fram', 1893-1896, and of a Fifteen Months' Sleigh Journey by Dr Nansen and Lt. Johansen*. 2 vols. New York: Harper.

Perkins, D.T. (2000). *Leading at the Edge*. New York: Amacom.

Recope, M., P. Lièvre and G. Rix-Lièvre (2010). The commitment of polar expedition members to a project: declared motivation or mobilization in situation? *Project Management Journal*, Special Issue, Project Management in Extreme Environment, 41 (3), 45–56.

Ross, W.G. (2002). The type and number of expeditions in the Franklin search, 1847–1859. *Arctic*, 55 (1), 55–69.

Savitt, R. (2004). Antarctic sledging preparations and tacit knowledge. *Polar Record*, 40 (213), 1–13.

Savours, A. (1999). *The Search for the North West Passage*, New York: St Martin's Press.

Senge, P. (1994). *The Fifth Discipline: Fieldbook Strategies and Tools for Building a Learning Organization.* New York: Doubleday.

Victor, P.E. (1958 [2004]). Les explorations polaires. In G. Stavridès and L.H. Parias (eds), *Les explorateurs, sous la dir.* Paris: Editions Robert Laffont, pp. 1022–1148.

Weick, K.E. (1995). *Sensemaking in Organizations.* London: Sage.

Weick K.E. and K.M. Sutcliffe (2007). *Managing the Unexpected.* San Francisco, CA: Jossey-Bass.

4. Leaders in Antarctica: characteristics of an Antarctic station manager

Ian Lovegrove

INTRODUCTION

This chapter focuses on leaders whose workplace is the world's coldest, windiest and driest continent: Antarctica. Sitting at the southern pole, this remote, hostile environment represents 10 percent of the world's land-mass, with its total summer surface area being approximately one and a half times the size of the US, twice the size of Australia and 50 times larger than the UK (Walker, 2012). The continent's highest point exceeds 16 000 feet (4892 meters) and temperatures fall to below −129 Fahrenheit (−89° Celsius). With wind speeds in excess of 200 miles (320 kilometers) per hour, snow is driven in blizzard conditions, while below 60 degrees latitude long months of complete darkness prevail.

Since the signing of the Antarctic Treaty in 1959, nations including the US, the UK, Australia and New Zealand have established a series of scientific stations. The British Antarctic Survey currently operates two permanent scientific stations in Antarctica, from which geologists, glaci-ologists, atmosphericists and biologists range to explore their disciplines. Technical personnel, such as electrical, heating and venting engineers, vehicle mechanics, radio and medical staff, support the central mission of scientific discovery and usually remain on station for two and a half years without a break. Most station personnel follow a 'normal' working day, with meals being taken communally, although at the day's close, 'home' is where they are. In this emptiest of the world's continents, devoid of indigenous people, around 1000 scientists and support person-nel overwinter on the various national stations. Station managers are appointed to lead each station and it is such leaders who form the basis of this chapter.

On British polar stations station managers are appointed by invitation and drawn from individuals who already have a proven record in Antarctica. Appointment confers a formal status on station managers, but within the predominately closed egalitarian society of a polar station, the differential between leader and follower is considerably less than expected for non-extreme environments. Station managers are ultimately responsible for their station and enjoy unfettered authority to take whatever decisions are required. Nonetheless, despite holding ultimate responsibility, station managers have limited formal sanctions available to them (Airey, 2001). During a crisis situation station managers are called on to make life-critical decisions independently, wherein error tolerance can be small and any mistake has the potential for fatal consequences (Hannah et al., 2009). Living in an isolated environment, work space is limited, facilities are functional and duties are both important and demanding, with the consequences of failure being extreme. Here, station managers carry out their duties in a 24-hour contact environment that is shared with followers and from which there is limited opportunity for parties to escape (Suedfeld, 2001).

In focusing on the British scientific stations in Antarctica, this chapter explores the leader characteristics needed to operate effectively in this extreme and isolated environment. The chapter predominately draws on empirical findings from a longitudinal study of 26 station managers and their followers, which embraced the psychometric measures of 16PF5 (the Sixteen Personality Factor Questionnaire) and emotional intelligence (Lovegrove, 2004). Data discussion is supported through participant observation and conclusions are derived on lessons learned which can be applied to less extreme work situations.

THE ANTARCTIC ENVIRONMENT: EXTREME ENVIRONMENT – PHYSICAL CHALLENGES AND SOCIAL CONSTRAINTS

Superlatives are often used to describe the polar environment, emphasizing the extreme physical aspects such as constant daylight or darkness, and the associated physical dangers of crevasses, blizzards and frozen seas, while on station there is an ever-present danger from fire. In many non-extreme environments temporary danger can manifest itself through accidents, disaster or human conflict (Yammarino et al., 2010). However, where exposure to danger is more continual, the term 'extreme and unusual environment' is applied. 'Extreme' refers to physical parameters that are substantially outside the optimum range of human survival, with 'unusual' referring to conditions that strongly deviate from the accustomed milieu (Suedfeld and Steel, 2000). The physical remoteness, or lack of access, is further identified in 'isolated' and 'confined' environments (Harrison, 1991). Antarctica comprises an extreme context, where the hostile and hazardous environment has the potential to harm an individual. With little external direction or support being available, the leader is often required to act independently.

An Antarctic station forms an extreme environment where confinement produces social restrictions on inhabitants. Polar residents need to contend with the social isolation of separation from significant others and being confined in a relatively inactive mode for many months. Indeed, social monotony, created through enforced togetherness with colleagues not of one's choosing and coupled with an absence of family and friends, has been identified as a major stressor for individuals in the confined environment of an Antarctic station (Steel and Suedfeld, 1992).

Within the restricted living space, followers and leaders experience the same 'closed' environment, which produces a status-leveling situation, wherein the leader is seen as a 'first among equals' (Stuster, 1996, p. 166). Here, with the leader and followers embedded in the same polar community, station managers have to rely on personal characteristics to encourage followers to 'go the extra mile' and to do things for them, as a person. In short, if followers are going to exceed expectations, station managers need to influence and lead.

Within the Antarctic context followers are often referred to as 'sojourners', which refers to those scientists and support personnel who are resident within the polar environment for the purpose of work, where their primary endeavor is the pursuance of professional goals (Steel et al., 1997). The leader is the station manager, the individual who holds overall responsibility for all aspects of their station, the resources, mission accomplishment and the welfare of their followers, the station personnel.

EXTREME LEADERSHIP

Leader Characteristics

Leadership studies often address aspects of the leader, rather than the nature of leadership (Barker, 2001), for it is the leader who mobilizes others to achieve goals. The phenomenon of leadership is ultimately an emotional bond between followers, leaders and their personal goals, with early studies identifying three pivotal components: leader, follower and situation (Pigors, 1935). The situational component tends to discard the earlier focus on nurture and the universal 'Great Man' theory of leader inheritance.

This chapter focuses on leader characteristics in the Antarctic, which combine within the situational-trait theory of leadership (Antonakis et al., 2012). This broad approach holds that leaders require specific characteristics for differing situations, wherein a concordant match is pursued between leader characteristics and a specific environment. Further, the personal characteristics associated with individual differences are most likely to produce follower commitment, hence the term 'leader influence' (Dinh and Lord, 2012). Within the influencing process, leader characteristics comprise important summary labels which assist followers in understanding and predicting leader outcomes (Shondrick et al., 2010). To be effective, leaders need to relate to the shared conceptions of followers, especially how closely they fit their schemata of a leader.

The remainder of this section explores the characteristics that station managers need to be successful in Antarctica, adopting both the leaders' and followers' perspective (Lovegrove, 2004). Characteristics are considered under three headings: relating to others, emotions and self-attitude, and style of thinking.

Relating to Others

Trust
Trust is a key leader characteristic in any workplace, although with the complexities and potential hazards apparent in isolated Antarctic living, it takes on greater importance. Thus, trust in extreme environments is not the same as 'office' trust, as the consequences of failure are infinitely greater. One key element that engenders trust is the personal characteristics concerning relationships and caring (Dirks and Ferrin, 2002). Station managers are significantly more trusting than leaders in non-extreme situations, with sojourners concurring that trust is a vitally important characteristic for an effective leader. Indeed, the station managers' natural propensity to be less vigilant and more accepting engenders trust in the sojourners they lead. Freewill influence is rarely possible unless followers trust their leader, with an increase in shared understanding being a positive outcome. In accepting trust as an important characteristic for influencing followers in extreme situations, effective communication can make an equally strong contribution (Sweeny et al., 2011).

Communication
One key leader characteristic of relationships and trust identified by sojourners refers to communication being open and honest, which is not unusual for extreme environments (Baran and Scott, 2010; Kolditz, 2007;

Taylor, 1987). One crucial element of communication in extreme situations relates to the process of reflection, especially the post hoc analysis of 'near misses'. Personal disclosure of errors is rarely comfortable, and before errors can be communicated openly, sojourners need supreme confidence and trust, in both the station manager and their companions. Inculcating a culture where openness is welcomed falls to the leader. Any subversion of failings is likely to expose others to similar risks, yet the station manager has to address the situation with caution. The person involved might be severely traumatized by the event and unable or unwilling to communicate openly. For example, on one such occasion a field leader experienced difficulty in communicating the circumstances of a 'near miss' and, having declined to undertake further field trips, was evacuated from the station. In this situation the accompanying sojourner was able to convey the details, although the thought processes behind the incident remained elusive.

Reserved warmth

Living in an extreme environment, in close proximity to their followers, it might be expected intuitively that station managers display a high degree of warmth in their relationships. Notably, sojourners seek a leader who is reasonably attentive, with an easy-going nature. In reality, station managers are significantly more reserved than leaders in non-extreme environments, which, given the conditions on an Antarctic station, produces advantages for mission accomplishment. Within the close confines of an isolated environment all parties inhabit the same living space, and following any chastisement by the station manager, or disagreement, a certain distancing is considered desirable (Leon et al., 2011). However, as with many extreme leader characteristics, a balance is required (Flin, 1996). Thus, while the station manager needs to demonstrate a high degree of empathy, which sojourners consider important, the warmth displayed is more moderated, with the process being aptly described as 'tough love' (Higgs and Dulewicz, 1999, p. 20).

Reduced sensitivity

Rather than being sentimental or tender-minded, station managers are significantly more objective and self-reliant than leaders who operate in less extreme environments, which finds agreement with sojourners. With no immediate escape from the confines of an Antarctic station, sojourners associate with individuals who would not normally constitute their preferred friendship choices. Indeed, a study of US wintering sojourners revealed that 60 percent of their waking time was spent alone (Carrere et al., 1991), which illustrates the nature of solitude on an Antarctic station.

Station managers need to recognize that a preference for solitude and privacy represent a personal choice characteristic, which is not necessarily symptomatic of unhappiness, or maladjustment (Larson and Lee, 1996; Wood et al., 2000). Indeed, privacy is an important factor in polar living, for which the leader characteristics of an objective, self-reliant station manager provide a strong environmental match.

Another example of an objective approach to relationships in Antarctica is acutely illustrated following a fatal accident. Although not commonplace, two sojourners were killed in a winter crevasse accident prior to my first Antarctic tour, and my first winter saw a further three British sojourners tragically lost on the sea ice. Such losses have a considerable emotional impact on the small close-knit community of sojourners who remain. Empty bed spaces and chairs stand as physical reminders of the loss, with psychological stresses being equally present in colleagues, who are themselves often wracked by guilt or survivor syndrome (Appelbaum et al., 1997). Sojourners may employ 'gallows humor' as a means of coping and the station manager needs to monitor the situation carefully, to reach an objective decision as to the best way forward. Thus, the leader characteristic for reduced sentimentality, or being more tough-minded or solution-orientated, assists the station manager in achieving optimal effectiveness. Given the environmental stressors present in an Antarctic station, characteristics that relate to a leader's emotional make-up are equally important.

Emotions and Self-Attitude

Self-awareness, stability and self-control

Leaders who are high in emotional awareness are able to monitor their own mood, along with that of their followers, and adapt accordingly. In understanding what drives and directs their behavior, they can engage in effective self-management strategies (Goleman et al., 2001). In relation to leaders in less extreme environments, station managers possess significantly higher levels of self-awareness, which results in greater awareness of their emotions and a powerful self-belief in their ability to manage these. In this respect, the station managers' emotional characteristics correspond with their more reserved and objective preferences, identified in their relationships with sojourners.

Given the solitude and limited external support that Antarctic station managers experience, there is a strong need for an emotionally stable and resilient leader, with a high level of hardiness. In numerous studies, involving sojourners from various nationalities, emotional stability has emerged as a key characteristic in both leader and follower success

(Palinkas and Suedfeld, 2008). British sojourners are equally convinced of emotional stableness as a characteristic of station manager success. Sir Vivian Fuchs (1964), leader of the first trans-Antarctic crossing, the Commonwealth Trans-Antarctic Expedition (1955–1958), identified the importance of emotional stability in a polar leader, with the characteristic being especially poignant when important, possibly life-critical decisions are being made. Station managers accrue further benefits from emotional stability in that it provides a platform from which status-leveling can be more easily tolerated, without the loss of personal respect.

The leader characteristic of self-control links with emotional stability, and station managers exhibit significantly higher levels than their non-extreme counterparts. This characteristic of conscientiousness, which is embraced by a self-disciplined, dutiful and ordered leader, is mirrored in other Antarctic nations (Sarris and Kirby, 2007). One possible negative impact of self-control, especially in relation to the station managers' ability to manage their emotions, is that sojourners can view the leader as lacking in passion. In short, leaders with high levels of emotional control can be perceived as being somewhat clinical and it may be this aspect that drives sojourners to seek warmer relationships with their station manager.

Low anxiety or neuroticism
In relation to emotional characteristics, sojourners are desirous of a station manager who is calm, relaxed, quietly confident and optimistic. With regards to temperament, successful station managers are extremely relaxed and significantly lower in neuroticism than non-extreme leaders. Sojourners similarly agree that station managers who have a greater tolerance for stress and adopt a positive attitude are more likely to succeed. Furthermore, not only do the low levels of neuroticism provide a stable platform from which to make decisions, but they also predispose the station manager to display a confident composure during crisis events, when timely decisions are often required.

The benefits of having a calm nature in Antarctica are not new. Early observations suggest a steadiness of mind being salient for a station manager, with Sir Vivian Fuchs arguing that this instills sojourner confidence in their leader (Fuchs, 1990). Similarly, Edward Wilson, the chief scientist on Scott's last expedition, valued a sojourner who saw what needed to be done, did it and said nothing about it (Cherry-Garrard, 1922 [1970]). Enthusiasm is an important leader characteristic, although in the Antarctic situation station managers represent a more subdued form of leader, exemplified in phrases such as 'calm judgment' and 'remaining cool under all circumstances', which have equally been identified in remote-duty leaders (Stuster, 1996, p. 105). Within the close confines of an Antarctic station, particularly during the dark winter months, the need for a calm, balanced leader precludes an extroverted or introverted personality, with neither providing an ideal situational match for the station manager (Palinkas et al., 2011), nor being supported by sojourner preference.

Optimism and humor

Sojourners champion leader optimism as a salient characteristic for station manager success. Optimism, which is related to being low for apprehension, is generally considered important to leader effectiveness in confined environments (Nicholas and Penwell, 1995; Sweeny et al., 2011). Optimism can equally combine with a sense of humor, with Sir Ernest Shackleton recognizing its value: 'the man with a cheerful disposition and ready laugh is a bright sun to his companions and a great help to the leader' (Shackleton, 1914, p. 142). Within extreme isolated environments, humor plays an important part in releasing tension; indeed studies in astronaut space-flight simulation value humor, although it needs to be in proportion (Sandal et al., 1995). Given the minimal opportunity for escape, the 'proportional' caveat is especially poignant on confined Antarctic stations, where the station manager needs to monitor this closely.

Integrity and leading by example

To operate effectively within the physical confines of a socially restricted Antarctic station, station managers' values have to be in accord with the situation. Sojourners are exceptionally clear that station managers have to be high in integrity, which is a distinct characteristic of an authentic leader (Avolio and Luthans, 2006).

In drawing a number of characteristics together, sojourners are desirous of a station manager who leads by example, which is a manifestation of leader integrity. Within the close social and physical confines of an Antarctic station there are, quite literally, few places for the station manager to hide. Sojourners look to the station manager as a role model, who leads from the front, which is also the case in other remote environments (Hannah and Avolio, 2012). Within this framework, sojourners particularly seek a leader who is fair and just in their dealings, with this characteristic equally finding favor in parallel situations (Kolditz, 2007; Sarris and Kirby, 2007). The process of social justice refers to the 'give and take' that Shackleton (1914) valued during his Antarctica endeavors. Sojourners currently see this important justice characteristic being manifested through the terms of tolerance and consideration; that is, tolerance of others' action and consideration in how one acts as an individual. Within the status-leveling environment of an Antarctic station, the characteristics of justice, fair play, tolerance and consideration equally apply to the station manager.

In leading, station managers encourage participative activity and recognize sojourners' needs, yet ultimate responsibility for decision-making remains theirs alone, with the notion of distributed leadership (Gronn, 2002) not being a consideration. In presenting an honest and transparent self, the station manager is endeavoring to build a high level of psychological well-being, which is akin to the conceptual framework of an authentic leader (Avolio and Gardner, 2005). In utilizing their ability for self-awareness, station managers draw on their true values, to function in an empathetic way that promotes trust and the well-being of sojourners. Humility and patience are practiced, with the bond being more of a relational (Avery, 2004) rather than transformational nature (Bass, 2008). Under the broader umbrella of integrity and the close proximity of Antarctic living, the station manager is constantly under scrutiny, wherein any display of non-authentic characteristics could lead to irrevocable damage of follower–leader trust. In addition to the emotional element, characteristics associated with a station manager's thought processes are equally important, to which the chapter's attention now turns.

Style of Thinking

Openness to change

With respect to their style of thinking, station managers are significantly more open to change than non-extreme leaders. Sojourners equally support the need for a high degree of flexibility within the dynamic Antarctic environment, particularly when responding to challenging situations. Indeed, a leader who is more experimenting and critical in their thinking supports earlier findings for openness in New Zealand station managers (Taylor, 1987). Besides the well-being of sojourners, station managers are equally responsible for ensuring that the station's scientific mission is accomplished. One aspect of the openness practiced by successful station managers relates to effective communication, which within the leader's style of relationships provides an authentic avenue with which to share information and build trust, particularly with regards to decision-making processes.

Grounded and consistent approach

While sojourners consider abstractedness to be a desirable leader characteristic, station managers are significantly more grounded and solution-orientated. Thus, although sojourners demonstrate a preference for an imaginative leader who is more absorbed in new ideas, in reality station managers are more inclined toward being practical. The characteristic is reflected in a station manager who is straightforward in their style of thinking, which can engender greater trust and integrity. It is equally important to sojourners that station managers are consistent in their performance, which relates to rule-consciousness and perfectionism, although in reality they are not significantly different to leaders in non-extreme environments.

It is important for station managers to be flexible in their outlook, particularly given the limited external support available. Thus, it would not be appropriate for station managers to overly ascribe to the dutiful and conforming characteristics associated with rule-consciousness, nor should they be overly expedient or prudent. Indeed, their central position for this characteristic, which shows shades of gray, supports a greater degree of flexibility. The station managers' flexible style of thinking is complemented by their neutral position for perfectionism. The poles of this characteristic are identified in a leader who is extremely organized, self-disciplined and precise, against an individual who tolerates disorder, is undisciplined and uncontrolled. Due to the high degree of planning required to cope with limited resource availability and pre-Antarctic organization, station managers might be expected to be higher in perfectionism. However, their flexible approach, evinced in the middle position for this characteristic, is particularly suited to reacting speedily to environmental stimuli or crisis and provides a strong match for station managers. Further, as station managers possess a high capacity for general intelligence, or reasoning, and are more open to change than non-extreme leaders, any rigid consistency effect is ameliorated.

LEADERSHIP LESSONS

Leadership is an emotion-laden social process of influencing and being influenced (Dinh and Lord, 2012), which relates to leader characteristics. In the absence of a universal theory, situational specificity provides the opportunity to match leader characteristics with the environment and, within the enforced confines of an Antarctic scientific station, it has been possible to identify characteristics that contribute toward leader success.

While the situational specificity of leader characteristics is apparent, less extreme environments can be identified. Here, the characteristics associated with successful station managers in Antarctica can be applied to offshore oil installations, disaster and relief workers, crisis and emergency services, and expatriate managers, who often operate in 'isolated' if not extreme environments. Lessons can also be drawn that are applicable to those who operate in the fast-moving corporate world, where economic challenges have sought to produce mental, if not physical isolation.

Environmental Fit

In the widest sense, leaders need to pay attention to their environmental fit. Individuals invariably self-select to enter extreme or challenging environments for which they consider themselves to be emotionally suited. Situational selection, be it individually or organizationally driven, is of importance in many work situations. While environments might not be as physically or mentally challenging as that experienced by station managers, leaders still need to be aware of their characteristic strengths and strive to match these with their target environment. In addition, once installed, there is a clear requirement for leaders to adapt their characteristics to meet unforeseen challenges associated with situational change.

Trust and Integrity

While trust is an important leader characteristic for extreme situations, it is of equal importance in work situations where the psychological and environmental stressors are not as severe. Several leader characteristics relate to trust, with integrity being of considerable importance. Indeed, in many work situations integrity provides the foundation for the symbiotic process of leader–follower trust. Thus, the trust and integrity associated with extreme situations can usefully be transposed to business in general, where leading by example has seen a decline in recent years. One particularly important element that all leaders need to understand is that personal competence is of paramount importance in engendering follower trust, as is the associated aspect of reaching just decisions.

Empathetic Communication

Sojourners are influenced by the stable characteristics of a leader who is calm and who communicates effectively, in an empathetic way. Dynamic and interactive communication is no less important in the wider work context. Indeed, despite advances in communication technology, workers can experience mental and physical isolation, particularly in the case of homeworkers. Regardless of the situational variables, leaders need to communicate hope and create a culture of openness, where trust is welcomed and individuals feel able to reflect on their actions and relate 'near misses', or failings, in an open and supportive environment.

Relating to others

Station managers are subject to the same environmental and psychological stressors as those they lead, which tends to favor a relational leader approach. In less intense environments a more flamboyant or extroverted leader can provide a successful fit, although the call for a 'quiet' and humble leader is spreading (Weis, 2007). In today's challenging work environment, good relations are needed for leaders to move from command-and-control to influence, which can be built though leader self-awareness and emotional stability.

Style of Thinking

While the innate characteristic of intelligence transcends many leader situations, an important factor is the leader's ability to use this astutely, particularly in listening, learning and empathizing with followers, which remain salient leader characteristics. A more open style of thinking is equally welcome in more routine situations, although a challenge for leaders in the current economic climate is to demonstrate consistency of core values while remaining flexible and responding to change.

Summary

While the consequences of leader failure in the corporate world may not be physically life-critical, a poor leader–environment match can be equally damaging to the mental well-being of followers. Extreme leaders also need to be true to themselves, and given the current uncertainty in business, an authentic approach to leader characteristics can bring wider benefits to the way non-extreme organizations function.

CONCLUSION

This chapter supports the integrationist contention which argues that specific environments attract a particular type of individual. Station managers are ultimately responsible for their actions and need to draw on their personal characteristics, often receiving little external support in a crisis situation. They need to trust those around them, in an open and honest way, and remain calm during challenging times. In functioning as a modest leader, station managers express gratitude for contributions followers make and, in dealing in optimism, present an image that goes beyond the extreme Antarctic environment. Above all, their hallmark of integrity identifies them as an authentic leader. Indeed, the characteristics of an authentic leader transcend the extreme Antarctic environment and need to be applied more widely if leader challenges within the current global crisis are to be addressed effectively.

REFERENCES

Airey, L. (2001). *On Antarctica*. San Ramon, CA: Luna Books.

Antonakis, J., D.V. Day and B. Schyns (2012). Leadership and individual differences: at the cusp of a renaissance. *Leadership Quarterly*, 23 (4), 643–50.

Appelbaum, S.H., C. Delage, N. Labib and G. Gault (1997). The survivor syndrome: aftermath of downsizing. *Career Development International*, 2 (6), 278–86.

Avery, G.C. (2004). *Understanding Leadership: Paradigms and Cases*. London: Sage Publications.

Avolio, B.J. and W.L. Gardner (2005). Authentic leadership development: getting to the positive forms of leadership. *Leadership Quarterly*, 16 (3), 315–38.

Avolio, B.J. and F. Luthans (2006). *The High-Impact Leader*, New York: McGraw-Hill.

Baran, B. and C. Scott (2010). Organizing ambiguity: a grounded theory of leadership and sense making within dangerous contexts. *Military Psychology*, 22 (Suppl.), S42–S69.

Barker, R. (2001). The nature of leadership. *Human Relations*, 54 (4), 469–94.

Bass, B.M. (2008). *Bass' Handbook of Leadership: Theory, Research and Managerial Implications*, 4th edn. New York: Free Press.

Carrere, S., G.W. Evans and D. Stokols (1991). Winter-over stress: physiological and psychological adaptation to an Antarctic isolated and confined environment. In A.A. Harrison, Y.A. Clearwater and C.P. McKay (eds), *From Antarctica to Outer Space: Life in Isolation and Confinement*. New York: Springer-Verlag, pp. 229–37.

Cherry-Garrard, A. (1922 [1970]). *The Worst Journey in the World: Antarctica 1910–1913*. Harmondsworth: Penguin.

Dinh, J.E. and R.G. Lord (2012). Implications of dispositional and process views of traits for individual difference research in leadership. *Leadership Quarterly*, 23 (4), 651–69.

Dirks, K. and D. Ferrin (2002). Trust in leadership: meta-analysis findings and implication for research and practice *Journal of Applied Psychology*, 87 (4), 611–28.

Flin, R. (1996). *Sitting in the Hot Seat: Leaders and Teams for Critical Incident Management*. Chichester: Wiley.

Fuchs, V. (1964). The qualities of an explorer. *Geographical Magazine*, 36 (4), 205–15.

Fuchs, V. (1990). *A Time to Speak*. Oswestry: Anthony Nelson.

Goleman, D., R.E. Boyatzis and A. McGee (2001). Primal leadership: the hidden driver of great performance. *Harvard Business Review*, 79 (11), 42–51.

Gronn, P. (2002). Distributed leadership as a unit of analysis. *Leadership Quarterly*, 13 (4), 423–51.

Hannah, S.T. and B.J. Avolio (2012). The locus of leader character. *Journal of Environmental Psychology*, 22 (5), 979–83.

Hannah, S.T., M. Uhl-Bien, B.J. Avolio and F.L. Cavarretta (2009). A framework for examining leadership in extreme contexts. *Leadership Quarterly*, 20 (6), 897–919.

Harrison, A.A. (1991). Antarctica: prototype for outer space. In A.J.W. Taylor (ed.), *Human Factors in Polar Psychology with some Implications for Space*. Presented at Polar Symposia 1, Cambridge, Scott Polar Research Institute. Cambridge: Cambridge University Press, pp. 43–9.

Higgs, M. and V. Dulewicz (1999). *Making Sense of Emotional Intelligence*. Windsor: NFER-NELSON.

Kolditz, T.A. (2007). *In Extremis Leadership*. San Francisco, CA: Jossey-Bass.

Larson, R.W. and M. Lee (1996). The capacity to be alone as a stress buffer. *Journal of Social Psychology*, 136 (1), 5–16.

Leon, G.R., G.M. Sandal and E. Larsen (2011). Human performance in polar environments. *Journal of Environmental Psychology*, 31 (4), 353–60.

Lovegrove, I.W. (2004). Leaders in extreme, isolated environments: a study of leader characteristics of managers of British Antarctic research stations. PhD Thesis, University of Manchester Institute of Science and Technology.

Nicholas, J.M. and L.W. Penwell (1995). A proposed profile of the effective leader in human spaceflight based on findings from analog environments. *Aviation, Space and Environmental Medicine*, 66 (1), 63–72.

Palinkas, L.A., K.E. Keeton, C. Shea and L.B. Leveton (2011). *Psychosocial Characteristics of Optimum Performance in Isolated and Confined Environments*. NASA Report TM-2011-216149. Hanover, MD: NASA.

Palinkas, L.A. and P. Suedfeld (2008). Psychological effects of polar expeditions. *Lancet*, 371 (9607), 153–63.

Pigors, P. (1935). *Leadership or Domination?* London: Harrap.

Sandal, G.M., R.J. Værnes and H. Ursin (1995). Interpersonal relations during simulated space missions. *Aviation, Space and Environmental Medicine*, 66 (7), 617–24.

Sarris, A. and N. Kirby (2007). Behavioral norms and expectations on Antarctic stations. *Environment and Behavior*, 39 (5), 706–3.

Shackleton, E.H. (1914). The making of an explorer. *Pearson's Magazine*, 38 (224), 138–42.

Shondrick, S.J., J.E. Dinh and R.G. Lord (2010). Developments in implicit leadership theory and cognitive science: applications to improving measurement and understanding alternatives to hierarchical leadership. *Leadership Quarterly*, 21 (6), 959–78.

Steel, G.D. and P. Suedfeld (1992). Temporal patterns of affect in an isolated group. *Environment and Behavior*, 23 (6), 749–65.

Steel, G.D., P. Suedfeld, A. Peri and L.A. Palinkas (1997). People in high latitudes: the 'Big Five' personality characteristics of the circumpolar sojourner. *Environment and Behavior*, 29 (3), 324–47.

Stuster, J. (1996). *Bold Endeavors: Lessons from Space and Polar Exploration.* Annapolis, MD: Naval Institute Press.

Suedfeld, P. (2001). Groups in special environments. In N. Smelser and P. Baltes (eds), *International Encyclopedia of the Social and Behavioral Sciences.* Oxford: Elsevier, pp. 6430–34.

Suedfeld, P. and G.D. Steel (2000). The environmental psychology of capsule habitats. *Annual Review of Psychology*, 51, 227–53.

Sweeny, P.J., M.D. Matthews and P.B. Lester (eds) (2011). *Leadership in Dangerous Situations: A Handbook for the Armed Forces, Emergency Services, and First Responders.* Annapolis, MD: Naval Institute Press.

Taylor, A.J.W. (1987). *Antarctic Psychology.* Wellington, NZ: DSIR Science Information Publishing Centre.

Walker, G. (2012). *Antarctica: An Intimate Portrait of the World's most Mysterious Continent.* London: Bloomsbury Publishing.

Weis, E.J. (2007). Quiet leadership. In D. Crandall (ed.), *Leadership Lessons from West Point.* San Francisco, CA: Jossey-Bass, pp. 206–17.

Wood, J., S.J. Hysong, D.J. Lugg and D.L. Harm (2000). Is it really so bad? A comparison of positive and negative experiences in Antarctic winter stations. *Environment and Behavior*, 32 (1), 84–110.

Yammarino, F., M. Mumford, M. Connerly and S. Dionne (2010). Leadership and team dynamics for dangerous military contexts. *Military Psychology*, 22 (Suppl.), S15–S41.

5. The Darwin mountaineering expedition in Patagonia: a case of successful leadership failure

Linda Rouleau, Geneviève Musca, Marie Perez and Yvonne Giordano

INTRODUCTION

Why do some leaders succeed while others fail? The literature on leadership provides many different answers to this fundamental question (Avolio et al., 2009; Burke et al., 2011). Successful leadership is generally attributed to the leaders themselves, to the heroic qualities possessed and to the capacity to influence followers in order to achieve organizational goals (Hambrick, 2007; Carpenter et al., 2004). In contrast, leadership that does not provide positive outcomes tends to be attributed to political factors or to the lack of supportive conditions for the leader's action (Smith et al., 2006). These answers largely come from leadership studies undertaken in traditional settings and which predominately explore leadership through quantitative data, gathered retrospectively (Boal and Hooijberg, 2000). In extreme conditions (Hannah et al., 2009), leadership that fails to achieve goals might also be perceived as being successful, as great leadership might still end up with poor results.

In this chapter we propose an alternative view of leadership success and failure founded on the basic premise that success may translate into failure and vice versa. Under unusual circumstances this simple maxim needs to be applied more seriously in order to better understand the meaning of leadership in situations that lie outside the scope of daily experiences. In fast-paced, unexpected and uncertain environments, the failure of reliable leadership may be a prerequisite to coping successfully with leadership challenges (Weick and Sutcliffe, 2007).

In order to better understand leadership success under extreme conditions, we draw on the Darwin mountaineering expedition, Project Darwin (www.projet-darwin.com). After explaining the expedition we briefly describe three discursive micro-practices – storytelling, world-bridging and justification work – through which the expedition leader succeeded in keeping the team together, even though the climbers did not achieve their primary goal. We then discuss how the notion of 'successful leadership failure' advances the emerging leadership-as-practice field (Carroll et al., 2008; Crevani et al., 2010; Denis et al., 2010; Raelin, 2011; Simon, 2006).

THE DARWIN EXPEDITION

The primary goal of this exploratory expedition by French climbers was to traverse the Cordillera Darwin in Tierra del Fuego (Chilean Patagonia). The mountain range is in one of the world's least explored regions, which is located close to the tip of South America and is only accessible from the sea. No detailed maps or GPS data are available. The inherent difficulties associated with the expedition's goal were virtually unknown to the team of ten climbers (including eight professional mountain guides), yet these were to be ultimately exacerbated by extremely hostile climatic conditions. Subsidiary endeavors were to produce a film record of the expedition and gather data on relationships within the team.

The Darwin expedition comprised three phases: preparatory (autumn 2008 to summer 2009), the actual expedition (autumn 2009) and post-expedition (autumn 2009, extending into 2010). Four researchers, working in pairs, were given the opportunity to join the expedition, allowing them to directly observe numerous situations and conversations during all three phases. In addition, they engaged in face-to-face interactions and conducted interviews with expedition team members. The ethnographic study allowed the researchers to take part in certain selected team activities.

The actual expedition deviated substantially from the original plan. First, it took nearly two weeks, instead of the three days projected, to reach the cordillera by boat, with this being partly due to poor weather conditions and unsuccessful meteorological forecasting. Second, the team landed at a site on the east side of the mountains, instead of the west as was initially planned. Third, two teams were formed to traverse different routes, yet each team found itself facing impenetrable mountainous terrain, whereupon the expedition leader instructed both teams to make their way back down the mountain. As the climbers were unable to advance, once again plans had to be changed, with an alternative strategy being devised. This recast the expedition around the more modest goals of 'ascending a series of peaks in a star-shaped pattern' and undertaking

a number of first assents. Fourth, the boat required repairs, by which time
four of the six weeks allotted to the expedition had elapsed. To salvage
the film project, the expedition leader decided to separate the team, with
one group aiming to accomplish a series of mountain climbs, while a
second group traveled to Cape Horn to record images of Patagonia and
its inhabitants. The climbers who remained in the mountains succeeded
in conquering two lower summits in the range, both of which were first
assents. The team then set their sights on Mount Shipton, a well-known
peak in the cordillera, but again, weather conditions prevented the
summit being reached.

   During this expedition the expedition leader and members faced a
succession of unexpected and uncertain situations, including injury,
inclement weather and shipboard mechanical problems, all of which
prevented them from achieving their primary objective of traversing the
Darwin Cordillera. A first-level analysis of the expedition's events
quickly reveals that the expedition leader did not spend sufficient time
preparing the expedition for the physical and cultural conditions that they
might have been expected to deal with. Moreover, during the expedition,
the leader mainly practiced top-down leadership, whereby the lines of
communication between expedition leader and climbers remained somewhat directive and unambiguous. Yet the existing literature on unusual
and uncertain situations suggests that, under such conditions, an effective
leader should adopt a more collaborative approach, in order to create a
climate for a shared experience; thus effective communication is seen as
central to successful extreme leadership (Kayes, 2004; Klein et al., 2006;
Tempest et al., 2007). This might be another reason why the expedition
failed to achieve its primary goal.

LEADERSHIP-AS-PRACTICE IN EXTREME SITUATIONS

However, a more refined analysis of the leader's in situ deliberations and
actions yields a nuanced interpretation of what constitutes leadership in
extreme situations. In reality, behind the 'official' objective of traversing
the Darwin Cordillera, other 'unofficial' goals were present, such as team
morale. These need to be taken into account to gain a better understanding of leadership in extreme situations. A second-level analysis of the
data suggests that the expedition leader was mainly preoccupied with the
need to develop and preserve good relationships between team members,
so as to help ensure their safety in this dangerous environment. Indeed, in
expeditions of this type, when events are not going according to plan, as

was the case with the Darwin venture, team members may engage in dangerous behaviors: pursuit of the goal at any cost, competition, breakdown of group cohesiveness and so on (Kayes, 2006). In contrast, a positive social and emotional climate can make a significant difference to the overall well-being of the group (Bigley and Roberts, 2001; Kayes, 2004; Lièvre and Rix, 2008; Roberto, 2002). The social climate was particularly important during the Darwin expedition, as the team members, although well versed in climbing expeditions in the Alps, Himalayas, China, Alaska and the Andes, lacked the maritime experience needed for the range. In particular, they failed to appreciate that the ship-borne approach to the mountains and the unexplored mountain setting, unlike any other on Earth, were capable of denying them their success. In regard to social climate and maintenance of group cohesiveness, the expedition leader appears to have provided effective, possibly even successful leadership during the three phases of the expedition.

Following Raelin (2011) who suggests that a leadership-as-practice view focuses on the activity and everyday practice of leadership, we have identified three micro-practices through which the expedition leader successfully asserted leadership during the expedition, despite the failure to achieve the expedition's primary goal of traversing the cordillera.

First, leadership in extreme situations as storytelling. During the expedition, stories relating to previous mountaineering and epic expeditions played a crucial role in maintaining the climbers' morale. As the situation deteriorated, the leader recounted previous expeditions in which he 'heroized' either himself or specific team members, depending on the contextual situation. For example, when the climbers were forced to return to the boat-camp, after failing to climb an impassable col, they felt dejected, as though they had lost the first battle with the mountain. At the end of the meal that followed their return, the expedition leader, who was struggling with a knee injury, eloquently recounted how once, when preparing to join a group of climbers, he had been forced to descend the mountain alone with the body of a man that he had found dead on the trail. While this story served to enhance the leader's image among the climbers, it also conveyed that he understood perfectly that it is not always possible to follow a plan, especially when an inescapable contingency intervenes. Moreover, this story had a specific emotional tone that was not as incidental as one might expect. By recounting a story involving a dead man, the leader was metaphorically introducing a fundamental taboo for climbers, in that they tend not to talk about mortality, even though it is part of the climbing 'game'. In so doing, he was using his story to re-emphasize that safety should be prioritized above all else.

Second, leadership in extreme situations as a means of world-bridging. During the Darwin expedition two competing rationalities were present, the 'performance' and the 'adventure' rationalities. While the former is centered on technical mountaineering skill and non-commercial activities, the latter has to do with leading commercial expeditions with clients (Mitchell, 1983). As experienced mountaineers the Darwin project climbers take part in 'amateur' high-level mountaineering expeditions, while as professional mountain guides they lead commercial expeditions designed for enjoyment and adventure. Using his discursive abilities, the expedition leader was able to balance, or bridge, these two competing rationalities which were constantly in play. As an alpinist with numerous years' experience in guiding climbing expeditions, he was able to draw on his previous mountain experiences. Thus, in an effort to balance the two contrasting rationalities, he constantly reminded the climbers of the importance of seeking enjoyment in the expedition, even though events were continually going awry. During an interview conducted at the expedition's conclusion, the leader stated:

> We were constantly having problems, all the time, and nothing was really working ... but fortunately the guys were there to support the adventure ... I've been doing expeditions for 30 years ... we can say that an expedition is successful when we set out as friends and we come home as friends, whether the goal has been achieved or not ... These mountains, they are not on a human scale, I had to work hard to make sure everyone was enjoying the trip despite everything and got along with one another.

Third, leadership in extreme situations as justification work. A filmmaker specializing in mountain settings formed part of the expedition and the film they sought to produce represented a major financial stake for the Darwin venture, as well as for the expedition's sponsors. The expedition leader frequently had to comment on the current situation in front of the camera, and here he proved capable of adapting his discourse for the audience by offering coherent justification for his decisions, even when they appeared contradictory. For example, at the beginning of the expedition, in an endeavor to produce an original mountain exploration film, his discourse centered on the importance of following the initial plan, regardless of what might happen. However, later, when he had to justify sending a group of climbers to Cape Horn, he varied his approach and extolled the team's ability to take advantage of unexpected opportunities. In this way, he adapted the tenet of his discourse in relation to the circumstances. On completion of the expedition, the leader stated:

We had to find something to make the film work. We had to find something else. The film might have worked if we had succeeded in crossing the Darwin, but as it was, we sent an expedition party to Cape Horn, so we are going to refocus the film on Patagonia, the Land of Fire. I hope we will have a very good film, a film of discoveries, a film that will interest people through the pictures and the story we will tell.

These three leaderful micro practices in extreme situations did not assist the expedition leader in crossing the Darwin Cordillera. However, while failing as a leader with respect to not achieving the expedition's formal objective, he did succeed in creating a positive community and holding the expedition members together, despite the tumult of unexpected events that constantly endangered their lives. This bonding is particularly important, because the community of French mountaineers is extremely small. Thus, the climbers have an interest in maintaining a strong positive relationship with one another, so as to protect their future in the climbing community. In addition, the team members might have to work together in future expeditions. Indeed, in a post-expedition interview, the leader reflected: 'The expedition continues, life continues and our experience continues, our adventure continues in another form, but it continues.' Since then, most of the Darwin alpinists have worked together on diverse guided expeditions, with a number teaming up as climbing partners in their free time.

SUCCESSFUL LEADERSHIP FAILURE IN EXTREME SITUATIONS

Until now, a number of studies have attributed leadership to managers and colleagues who are able to influence others or develop their adaptive capacities in order to drive their organization toward success (Burke et al., 2011; Hambrick, 2007; Uhl-Bien et al., 2007). The Project Darwin expedition, on the other hand, constitutes a case of what we label 'successful leadership failure'. This concept takes into account the unofficial or hidden dimensions that are intrinsic to the team dynamic. In extreme situations, the social dynamic created between group members is often a matter of survival and can make a significant difference when confronting danger. In these situations, effective leadership constitutes being attentive to the social norms that are temporarily established between team members.

The concept of successful leadership failure is based on the notion that success and failure relate to the expectations of various stakeholders

(Vaara, 2002). Success and failure are often viewed as totally separate entities. Yet while success and failure can appear to be opposites, the boundaries are less clear than is often thought, particularly in extreme situations. In other words, success and failure are like two sides of the same coin – one is related to the other and cannot exist without it. Leaders are not perfect human beings who are incapable of doing anything wrong. Their success and failure implies an underlying question that needs to be brought to the fore, that is: to what extent does leadership success relate solely or primarily to goal achievement, or are the people involved in the process more salient than the goal? This question equally works in reverse, with regards to leadership failure. The Darwin expedition can be viewed as a failure in terms of the initial objective to cross the cordillera. But from the sponsors' perspective, as well as that of the climbers and the multiple TV broadcasts and conferences audiences, the venture is, in many ways, viewed as having a successful outcome.

The concept of successful leadership failure allows us to take into account both the objective and the relational aspects of leadership and is consistent with a practice perspective of leadership (Carroll et al., 2008; Crevani et al., 2010; Denis et al., 2010; Raelin, 2011). This perspective is concerned with understanding the 'doing' of leadership and the associated situational and contextualized nature. By suggesting that leadership is predominately accomplished through daily activities, which require experience, social awareness and relational capability, a leadership-as-practice perspective pays greater attention to the hidden activities and discourses. Within this focus on practice, the Darwin expedition offers the potential to revisit the black box of leadership processes and practices so as to close some of the existing gaps in leadership literature (Boal and Hooijberg, 2000; Carpenter et al., 2004; Hambrick, 2007; Smith et al., 2006).

LEADERSHIP LESSONS

The literature on leadership recognizes that mountain climbing is not unlike running a business. More specifically, a climbing expedition can be viewed as a temporary organization that has all the multifaceted characteristics of project-based organizations (Hällgren, 2010). Therefore, lessons can be drawn from the Darwin expedition that are applicable to those practitioners who lead complex initiatives and make critical decisions in any type of environment.

First, leaders need to pay attention to what they say and do in their daily activities (Raelin, 2011). Being skillful in interacting with others and particularly in the art of conversation can assist leaders in patiently and persistently moving events in a direction they seek to promote informally, despite the occurrence of unexpected events and ambiguity. Such skillfulness draws on the leader's discursive abilities that are embedded contextually. The stories used in the Darwin case were particularly appropriate, in that when climbers are resting in shelters, they invariably sing, or recount and discuss past and present adventures. Therefore, by using relevant stories related to their specific context, leaders have a greater chance of getting their message across.

Second, the ability to deal with the tensions that are created by divergent goals or fast-changing circumstances is central for being leaderful. In order to invoke this ability, leaders need to transpose their knowledge into action and function as socially competent performers. In practice, leadership needs to be enacted by the leader demonstrating a strong affiliation with the core values that are central to the specific organizational context. Thus, in many organizational circumstances, leaders should be able to demonstrate their virtuosity in those social competencies and behaviors that are viewed as appropriate, particularly with respect to different competing rationalities. Successful leaders are invariably people who are able to navigate, with credibility, between different rationalities to inculcate different rationalities, thereby bridging the differences at the personal level.

Third, leaders need to be able to change the way events are interpreted and transform perceptions on how they reinforce or disentangle the pattern of multiple stakeholder interactions. In holding a broader vision of how various elements are working, leaders need to constantly pattern and repattern their discourse with respect to valid stakeholders, which can be achieved through the use of subtle dialogues and meaningful micro-acts that relate to changes in the environment. Leaders equally need to use words that are appropriate to any changes that arise, so as to co-construct meaningful explanations of those changes.

To sum up, leaders in extreme situations need to pay particular attention to what they do and say in their daily activities. Being skillful in employing stories, bridging divergent goals and justifying their decisions can assist them in influencing, despite any unexpected events that may arise. From a leadership-as-practice perspective, achieving effective leadership is much less about playing a role than it is about the ability to enact skillful knowledge through everyday discursive activities.

CONCLUSION

This chapter has developed the concept of successful leadership failure by drawing on the Darwin expedition to Patagonia. In extreme situations, it is difficult to identify exact conditions for successful or unsuccessful leadership. While the Darwin expedition failed in its objective to cross the cordillera, from the sponsors' perspective, as well as in terms of team cohesion and safeguarding the climbers' future, a feeling of success was evident. Storytelling, world-bridging and justification work emerged as three discursive micro-practices through which the expedition leader succeeded in binding the team together, even though the climbers did not achieve their primary goal.

This mountain-climbing expedition has parallels with organizational projects or project-based organizations (Turner and Müller, 2003), in that not all are perceived as being successful. Indeed, many fail without the exact reason being known. Thus, the concept of successful leadership failure needs to be further developed in order to advance our knowledge of project manager leadership, which presents a number of similarities to mountaineering expedition leadership.

REFERENCES

Avolio, B.J., F.O. Walumbwa and T.J. Weber (2009). Leadership: current theories, research, and future directions. *Annual Review of Psychology*, 60, 421–49.

Bigley, G. and K. Roberts (2001). The incident command system: high reliability organizing for complex and volatile task environments. *Academy of Management Journal*, 44 (6), 1281–99.

Boal, K.B. and R. Hooijberg (2000). Strategic leadership research: moving on. *Leadership Quarterly*, 11 (4), 515–49.

Burke, C.S., D. Diaz-Granados and E. Salas (2011). Team leadership: a review and look ahead. In A. Bryman, D. Collinson, B. Jackson, M. Uhl-Bien and K. Grint (eds), *The Sage Handbook of Leadership*. London: Sage, pp. 338–51.

Carpenter, M.A., M.A. Geletkanycz and W.G. Sanders (2004). Upper echelons research revisited: antecedents, elements, and consequences of top management team composition. *Journal of Management*, 30 (6), 749–78.

Carroll, B., L. Levy and D. Richmond (2008). Leadership as practice: challenging the competency paradigm. *Leadership*, 4 (4), 363–79.

Crevani, L., M. Lindgren and J. Packendorff (2010). Leadership, not leaders: on the study of leadership as practices and interactions. *Scandinavian Journal of Management*, 26 (1), 77–86.

Denis, J.-L., A. Langley and L. Rouleau (2010). The practice of leadership in the messy world of organizations. *Leadership*, 6 (1), 67–88.

Hällgren, M. (2010). Groupthink in temporary organizations. *International Journal of Managing Projects in Business*, 3 (1), 94–110.

Hannah, S.T., M. Uhl-Bien, B.J. Avolio and F. Cavarretta (2009). A framework for examining leadership in extreme contexts. *Leadership Quarterly*, 20, 897–919.

Hambrick, D.C. (2007). Upper echelons theory: an update. *Academy of Management Review*, 32 (2), 334–43.

Kayes, D.C. (2004). The 1996 Mount Everest climbing disaster: the breakdown of learning in teams. *Human Relations*, 57 (10), 1263–84.

Kayes, D.C. (2006). *Destructive Goal Pursuit: The Mt Everest Disaster*. New York: Palgrave Macmillan.

Klein, K.J., J.C. Ziegert, A.P. Knight and Y. Xiao (2006). Dynamic delegation: shared, hierarchical and deindividualized leadership in extreme action teams. *Administrative Science Quarterly*, 51 (4), 590–621.

Lièvre, P. and G. Rix (2008). Vers un observatoire de l'organisant: le cas des expéditions Polaires. Association International de Management Stratégique (AIMS-International Association of Strategic Management), Qualitative Analysis Workshop, May, IAE de Lille.

Mitchell, R. (1983). *Mountain Experience. The Psychology and Sociology of Adventure*. Chicago, IL: Chicago University Press.

Raelin, J. (2011). From leadership-as-practice to leaderful practice. *Leadership*, 7 (2), 195–211.

Roberto, M. (2002). Lessons from Everest: the interaction of cognitive bias, psychological safety and system complexity. *California Management Review*, 45 (1), 136–58.

Simon, L. (2006). Managing creative projects: an empirical synthesis of activities. *International Journal of Project Management*, 24, 116–26.

Smith, A., S.M. Houghton, J.N. Hood and J.A. Ryman (2006). Power relationships among top managers: Does top management team power distribution matter for organizational performance? *Journal of Business Research*, 59 (5), 622–9.

Tempest, S., K. Starkey and C. Ennew (2007). In the death zone: a study of limits in the 1996 Mount Everest disaster. *Human Relations*, 60 (7), 1039–64.

Turner, R.J. and R. Müller (2003). On the nature of projects as a temporary organization. *International Journal of Project Management*, 21 (1), 1–8.

Uhl-Bien, M., R. Marion and B. McKelvey (2007). Complexity leadership theory: shifting leadership from the industrial age to the knowledge era. *Leadership Quarterly*, 18 (4), 298–318.

Vaara, E. (2002). On the discursive construction of success/failure in narratives of post-merger integration. *Organization Studies*, 23 (2), 211–48.

Weick K.E. and K.M. Sutcliffe (2007). *Managing the Unexpected: Resilient Performance in an Age of Uncertainty*, 2nd edn. San Francisco, CA: Jossey Bass.

6.   Leadership at the edge of the summit
Betty S. Coffey and Stella E. Anderson

INTRODUCTION

In 2006 a four-person team attempting to summit Mount Everest encountered another climber in need of rescue. The story of this Mount Everest climb-turned-rescue garnered international attention that focused on the team's decision to abandon their summit attempt in order to help the stranded climber. This particular case provides a powerful example of leadership and team dynamics in extreme conditions. In this chapter, we explore the context of the mission to summit-turned-rescue utilizing a framework for examining leadership in extreme situations (Hannah et al., 2009). The situation is extreme in every sense of the word. Climbing teams on Mount Everest face a harsh environment where physical and psychological challenges are exacerbated in the life-threatening conditions. This specific climbing team made decisions of extreme consequence in that helping the stranded climber meant abandoning the mission to the summit despite significant personal commitment and investment.

THE CLIMB

High-altitude mountaineering is a risky undertaking even under the best conditions. Mount Everest, part of the Himalayan mountain range, is the world's highest peak with an elevation of 29 029 feet. Mountaineers often refer to high altitudes above 26 246 feet (8000 meters) as the 'Death Zone', aptly named because the human body will begin to significantly deteriorate with prolonged exposure at this high altitude (Tempest et al., 2007). The extreme cold, strong winds and icy conditions often create life-threatening conditions for climbers. Climbers undertake the endeavor knowing that humans can survive only for a short period of time at the extreme high altitudes. When asked about the passion to summit Mount

Everest, climbers describe the unique challenge and adventure of climbing the highest peak in the world. High-altitude mountaineers often have different motives, but generally share the ultimate purpose of reaching the top. As Useem (1998) described, 'To the uninitiated, such a purpose can appear irrational, even absurd. But to the expeditionary climber, to place a foot on the top of the world and see it dropping off in all directions is the driving ambition' (p. 95).

Given the unpredictable life-threatening conditions on Mount Everest, climbers always face a very narrow window of time to summit and descend safely. Climbers seeking to reach the summit and descend safely usually plan and anticipate their climb for years, knowing they may have one chance to reach the summit. High-altitude climbers make a substantial personal investment of time, money and energy. Many climbers join an expedition organized and led by experienced professional climbing team leaders accompanied by climbing staff and sherpas. A typical expedition to Mount Everest may involve at least two months or more, including several weeks of training, preparation and acclimatization.

Such was the situation of the climbers who joined the 2006 expedition to attempt the summit and descent of Mount Everest during the April to May climbing season. The expedition leader Dan Mazur was an experienced high-altitude mountaineer guide, having led several expeditions climbing the world's highest peaks including Mount Everest (Brash, 2006; Free, 2006). Mazur's 2006 Mount Everest expedition team included 13 paying clients and several climbing staff and sherpas (SummitClimb.com, 2006). Several weeks were spent in preparation, training and acclimatization. As events unfolded during the course of the expedition, many factors, including the weather, route conditions, and the physical and mental preparedness of individual climbers, led to four climbers attempting to summit together on 26 May 2006.

As it turned out, on this particular day, Mazur was teamed with Andrew Brash, Myles Osborne and Jangbu Sherpa in the attempt to summit. Brash, one of the clients and an experienced climber himself, had previously climbed with Mazur and has said, 'I felt I knew Dan very well, and trusted him like I do few others' (Brash, 2006, p. 47). The other client, Osborne, was an experienced climber who knew Mazur and had spent three years training and saving for the climb (Robinson, 2007). Jangbu Sherpa was a highly experienced Mount Everest guide and had climbed with Mazur on other expeditions (Mazur, 2012).

The weather conditions on the morning of 26 May 2006 were near perfect as the climbing team ascended deliberately along the north ridge toward the summit of Mount Everest. Already eight hours into the climb, the four climbers were optimistic about reaching the summit on the morning of their attempt. They estimated that in about two hours they should be standing on the top of the world. Shortly after sunrise, with the rugged peak in sight, Mazur was stunned to realize that the speck of bright yellow fabric moving in the wind was actually an incoherent climber sitting precariously on the dangerous ridge line (Broom, 2006; Free, 2006; Mazur, 2012). The team could not believe it when Lincoln Hall asked, 'I imagine you are surprised to see me here' (Hall, 2007, p. 195). Little did the four team members know that the fateful encounter was about to change their mission from summit to rescue.

Shortly after 7 a.m. on the morning of the summit attempt, the climbing team had reached about 28 200 feet when they encountered Hall. At the time of the encounter, it was unclear to Mazur's team how the individual was there alive and alone. It later became known that Hall had collapsed the day before on his descent from the mountain after having reached the summit. Other members of Hall's expedition had apparently concluded that Hall was unresponsive and could not be revived, so he was left behind. In essence, Hall's expedition did not realize that he was, in fact, still alive (Hall, 2007).

Mazur's team, realizing that Hall was alive and without essential equipment for survival, stopped to pull him away from the extremely dangerous ledge where he was found. They shared their vital oxygen, water and food supplies and replaced his hat, gloves and jacket. Mazur radioed the base camp to alert Hall's expedition that he was alive. It took precious time to convince Hall's expedition that he was in fact still alive. Meanwhile, Mazur, Brash, Osborne and Sherpa gave their immediate attention to caring for Hall. As time passed, they made the decision to stay with him until rescuers from Hall's expedition could arrive.

It took approximately four hours for Hall's rescue party to finally arrive. As Mazur's team waited with Hall, they became mindful that their narrow window of opportunity to summit and descend safely was slipping away. They had lost precious time and critical supplies helping Hall, making it highly improbable that they could make the summit and safely descend in daylight. They had expended considerable energy as they cared for Hall, making them potentially vulnerable to effects of high-altitude sickness, hypothermia and oxygen deprivation that could impair judgment. In addition, as usual on Everest, weather conditions were expected to worsen by late afternoon. The team would risk having insufficient oxygen, supplies and daylight hours to support a summit attempt and safe descent.

Despite the incredible sense of disappointment, there was a realization among the four climbers that if they went for the summit they might not make it back themselves. As described by Osborne at the time:

But as we turned our attention back to our original morning's objective of Everest's top, we realized that time had been slipping away; we were still perhaps 3 hours from the summit, and although we were strong and eager to go on, the early afternoon storms were not far away. They could trap us high on the mountain at 2 or 3 p.m., probably culminating in a greater tragedy. So after years of fundraising, and months of training and climbing, we made the tough call to turn around. And as it turned out, the storms did indeed blow in that afternoon. (Dispatch, 28 May 2006)

Instead of summiting the mountain, the four climbers had to begin their long journey back down the mountain. As Osborne recalled (Robinson, 2007):

An incredible sense of disappointment came over me. But if we'd gone for it, we wouldn't have made it back. I took one last look at the summit, standing between a 10 000-foot drop to my left and a 7000-foot drop to my right. And then we started down as quickly as we could.

Undoubtedly, there was significant disappointment from sacrificing their personal quest for the summit. As stated at the time, 'Coming back down the ridge, to be honest feelings were of nothing but disappointment at not making the summit' (Dispatch, 28 May 2006). From Mazur's perspective it was disappointment that Brash and Osborne would not have the opportunity to attempt the summit, given that his job is getting people up to the summit of Everest and getting them down safely (Broom, 2006). Mazur respected that Brash and Osborne, who had paid to climb Everest, and Sherpa, who would be paid in part by reaching the summit, never hesitated to abandon their summit attempt to help. From the individual accounts at the time, the team members believed they made the right decision to help the stranded climber and they would not have acted differently. Mazur has often stated that saving a life is more important than reaching the peak. 'We just all felt like we knew that's what we had to do', and, 'the summit is still there and we can go back. Lincoln only has one life' (Broom, 2006). Likewise Osborne commented that they could not leave the stranded climber, 'Mount Everest is just a big hill, there's nothing more to it than that' (Gray, 2006). Brash stated, 'The day we climbed, we saw Lincoln and there wasn't a choice; it was instinct to stop and help' (Cook, 2006), and, 'I've had time to reflect on what happened up there, and I feel we reached the best conclusion' (Everest News.com, 2006).

When the team initially encountered Hall and realized he was in trouble, Mazur immediately began the process of assessing Hall's condition and the situation facing the team. Mazur comprehensively assessed the situation, guided by his prior experiences at high altitudes attempting to rescue others. The team provided oxygen, food and water, contacted Hall's expedition, finally convincing them that Hall was alive so that they would come to help in the rescue. In stopping to help and staying with Hall until his other rescuers arrived, approximately four hours passed and oxygen supplies were being depleted.

Mazur's recollection was that by 11 a.m. or so, while it was still a beautiful day, it was getting too late to attempt the summit. There had to be a realistic assessment of the time and conditions that would be needed not only to summit, but also to safely descend in daylight before weather worsened. This involved a comprehensive assessment of the weather conditions that were worsening, time remaining to climb and descend safely in daylight, availability of required oxygen and the climbers' energy that had been expended having spent several hours already at these high altitudes. Helping rescue Hall became the priority. From Mazur's perspective, with the passage of time, a shared realization and understanding developed among the team members: it was too late in the day and summiting was no longer a realistic option. This realization was based on an assessment of the calculated risks for their own survival and safe return (Bell, 2006; Mazur, 2012).

When asked to reflect on how the experience that day changed him, Mazur explained that the experience reaffirmed the goodness in people and that many individuals inspired by the team's efforts have reached out to express their positive sentiments (Mazur, 2012). The experience has helped strengthen skills for subsequent climbs through learning from the rescue and sharpening instincts. The realization of making the decision to help another person was a simple but powerful choice: the team could stop to help, or walk away to pursue the summit (Mazur, 2012). As Mazur has said, 'We didn't discuss the decision to help. We all know what we had to do' (Bartley, 2006).

The team members had an opportunity to meet Hall shortly after the rescue while he was recovering in Nepal. Since the event occurred, most have stayed in touch. In an epilogue to this story, Hall passed away on 20 March 2012 (Nelson, 2012). Mazur was deeply moved and inspired by Hall's courage and ability to survive the experience on Mount Everest beyond what others thought was a hopeless situation. Mazur conveyed that he would be thinking of Hall whenever climbing Everest in the future, and especially near Mushroom Rock where the team first encountered Hall in 2006 (Mazur, 2012).

EXTREME LEADERSHIP

This case provides a powerful example of leadership and team dynamics under extreme conditions. In analyzing the situation, we utilized the framework provided by Hannah et al. (2009). They define an extreme context as 'an environment where one or more extreme events are occurring or are likely to occur that may exceed the organization's capacity to prevent and result in an extensive and intolerable magnitude of physical, psychological, or material consequences to – or in close physical or psycho-social proximity to – organization members' (p. 898). This framework identifies several dimensions of extreme contexts that create specific leadership requirements and challenges. Effective leadership varies over the stages of preparation, response and recovery from extreme events. In addition, the leadership challenge involves managing the transitions that dynamically occur as extreme events transpire. This framework calls for an examination of the degree of extremity of any given context and how that context influences the leader and followers' response to leaders.

In terms of the 2006 expedition and rescue, Mazur and his team had painstakingly planned, trained and prepared for the opportunity to summit Mount Everest. A critical part of this process required that Mazur prepare the team members to realize and understand the potential threats as well as the vigilance and preparedness required for this endeavor. As team leader, Mazur's challenge on the front end was to emphasize safety, develop the capacity of the climbing team to make realistic risk assessments, plan for contingencies and adapt in the face of changing circumstances. In fact, as the climbing team ascended Mount Everest they encountered a most unexpected circumstance when they came upon the climber in need. This altered situation required a reassessment of circumstances, realistic options and mission. The magnitude of the team's decision in this context was extreme in that it required them to abandon a goal despite significant personal commitment and investment.

The decisions made by Mazur's team stand in contrast to the breakdown in decision processes that presumably led to disasters in other extreme events (for example, Burnette et al., 2011; Kayes, 2004; Roberto, 2002; Tempest et al., 2007). In realistically assessing the considerable risks, Mazur's team members became keenly aware of very real limits on their ability to summit and safely descend. This keen awareness of the limits successfully tempered their drive to push on to summit. Moreover, there was a narrow window of time in which the team could assess the changing circumstances and determine how best to respond. Thus, the reassessment and awareness of their limits materialized in relatively short order as the situation unfolded.

According to Hannah et al. (2009), the preparation, in-situation and post-event actions and decisions should be analyzed to better understand the leadership implications. A leader in this extreme context likely will be challenged to manage the transitions from stable to extreme, and back to relatively stable. Rebalancing the team with respect to emotional, cognitive and physical perspectives is central to this challenge. Mazur and the climbing team invested heavily in planning, training and otherwise preparing to reach the summit. When the team approached the final ascent to the summit and encountered Hall, this encounter likely created a significant 'cognitive shift', thereby making it critical for Mazur to help team members rapidly make sense of the altered situation (Foldy et al., 2008). One major responsibility of the team leader is to help team members gain an accurate, shared understanding of their environment and how they need to respond as a team (Zaccaro et al., 2001).

The team faced an unanticipated event when they came upon Hall that altered their situation and ability to achieve their ultimate goal to summit. They had a very narrow window of time in which to act and the team members had to coalesce around a fundamentally different goal. Their mission essentially changed from summiting to rescuing. In terms of leadership, the case illustrates the importance of a leader fostering among team members a shared understanding and sense of responsibility for the consequences of the team's decisions (Day et al., 2006; Kayes, 2004; Zaccaro et al., 2001). The team members worked together and devoted their efforts and resources to rescue the stranded climber.

Perceived expertise, competence and confidence in a leader (Yukl, 2010) and trust (Burke et al., 2007) become critical in extreme situations for sustaining the focus and effort of team members. Trust generally must have formed with team members prior to encountering extreme events. Mazur's influence with team members appears to have resulted from perceived expertise, competence, confidence and trust. Mazur had prior experience with rescuing other stranded climbers and knew what to look for in terms of 'rescuability'. He drew upon what he described as a 'backlog of experience' from other climbs, witnessing frightening traumatic situations and trying to rescue others. Instinctively Mazur knew what he must do with regard to getting necessary oxygen for Hall and locating Hall's climbing expedition.

Also, team members relied on Mazur for his experience, judgment and expertise in safely and successfully leading Mount Everest expeditions. While research indicates that team members in crisis situations are more likely to follow a directive of a leader perceived as competent, confident and focused (for example, Yukl, 2010), in the case of Mazur's team, he did not need to issue a directive or make any apparent attempt to get team members to forgo summiting. There was no debate or dissent about the decision to devote time and resources to rescuing Hall, even when it became apparent that in doing so they would be abandoning their summit attempt. One account (Burman, 2006) reported that 'Mazur said later none of the team questioned stopping to rescue Hall. The weather was good, they were close to their goal, but no one mentioned going on.' By consensus the team reached a decision agreeing that this was the right and only choice. As a leader, Mazur emphasized being receptive to input from team members, explaining needed actions and communicating openly. In these actions, Mazur may well have been demonstrating what others (Peterson et al., 2012) have indicated is the most effective approach for leading a team in an extreme context.

As precious time passed, the team came to the realization that they were forgoing their attempt to reach the summit. In reaching this decision they seemed keenly aware that there would be no opportunity for them to reach the summit and safely descend. Mazur's team appeared to be highly cognizant of the fact that, beyond a point in time, the chances of safely descending from the summit were drastically reduced. Basically, the team understood that reaching the summit of Everest is less than half the task as the descent is the most difficult and dangerous part of the journey. This mindfulness or realistic appraisal of the risks associated with descent late in the day stands in stark contrast to the decision processes evident in one of the deadliest Mount Everest expeditions that occurred in 1996 (Tempest et al., 2007). The 1996 expedition teams appeared to be unrealistic about the very real limits and restrictions faced in their situation, such that in forging to the summit they sacrificed their ability to descend in the safety of daylight. Mazur's team recognized that the passage of time represented a very real limit that would restrict their ability to safely descend. Thus, they abandoned their summit attempt.

LEADERSHIP LESSONS

By implication this case illustrates several key leadership lessons. One lesson is that leaders and team members need to have the ability to reassess in rapidly changing circumstances when the nature of the mission and the commitment to preconceived goals is challenged. This is extremely difficult when the individuals are substantially invested psychologically and materially in a goal that is virtually within reach. To shift focus and resources requires a significant transition in both leadership and team processing and decision-making. Furthermore, teams and leaders often need to be prepared to make these transitions under severe time constraints. The ability to reassess circumstances and to shift focus and resources as situations emerge over time is critical for leaders and teams operating in most contemporary organizations.

Another lesson relates to the need for leaders to foster a shared sense of responsibility for a team's actions and decisions. Leaders often recognize that their leadership can only be as good as the team and they must work to make the team as a whole stronger. When circumstances require collective decision-making and performance, there may be no clear leader–team member distinction. By fostering a shared sense of responsibility for decisions and outcomes, leaders and team members can better respond to a rapidly changing situation. This is a timely relevant lesson for many organizational settings today, as illustrated in research (Klein et al., 2006) on highly skilled specialist teams (for example, medical trauma teams) that require rapid assessment and the ability to collectively improvise with changing circumstances.

The case also illustrates the significance of a leader's and team's ability to realistically and accurately assess risk and limits. In the case of Mazur's team this pragmatic assessment of several factors, including the loss of precious time and diminished resources, led them to accept that summiting was no longer a realistic option. Risk assessment is vital for organizations of any size. Teams, such as top management teams, product development teams or cross-functional teams, need the capability for each team member to accurately assess changing circumstances and factors that may well limit the team's ability to achieve their goals. Leaders generally play a pivotal role in getting team members to assess limits in order to make a realistic assessment of alternatives and choices.

A final lesson is that individuals, teams and leaders can benefit from reflecting on their reactions and decisions in an extreme situation (Hannah et al., 2009). Reflection may be necessary to fully make sense of decisions made in complex and uncertain conditions. In doing so, the individual and the team build an expanded experience base of additional knowledge, skills and judgment that can be incorporated into subsequent experiences and decisions. Following an extreme situation or event, it is critical that leaders and team members assess the impact of the event and the implications for individuals and teams. It is not uncommon in today's environment that many organizations face challenges and hardships as well as successes. Leaders likely play a central role in providing the opportunity and the time for teams and individuals to engage in post-event reflection and ensuring a supportive environment for learning to occur. In the absence of post-event processing and reflection, organizations likely fail to capture lessons learned in order to build the capacity of individuals and teams to meet future challenges.

CONCLUSION

The team's efforts to summit Mount Everest and their decision to rescue Hall illustrate positive lessons for leadership and team behavior in an extreme situation. The team's decision to help the climber and stay with him came at an inconvenient time, with unexpected circumstances. The four climbers coalesced on their new goal to help the stranded climber and made the decision to wait with him, despite knowing that they were very close to accomplishing their personal goal to summit. The team also made the difficult decision to abandon the summit despite having invested significant time, energy and training. The case contributes to our understanding of the leadership required to get a team to realistically appraise limits and risks and then coalesce around a decision that represents a significant change in a goal or mission.

REFERENCES

Bartley, N. (2006). Risking it all. *Pacific Northwest Magazine. The Seattle Times*, 19 November. Available at http://community.seattletimes.nwsource.com/archive/?date=20061119&slug=pacificpclimb191 (accessed 26 June 2012).

Bell, T. (2006). Saving a stranger left for dead. *People*, 65 (24). Available at http://www.people.com/people/archive/article/0,,20061208,00.html (accessed 26 June 2012).

Brash, A. (2006). Rescue from the Death Zone. *Explore*, September–October, 44–9.

Broom, J. (2006). Olympia guide helped save life of Everest climber left for dead. *Seattle Times*, May 30. Available at http://seattletimes.nwsource.com/html/localnews/2003027261_climber30m.html (accessed 26 June 2012).

Burke, C.S., D.E. Sims, E.H. Lazzara and E. Salas (2007). Trust in leadership: a multi-level review and integration. *Leadership Quarterly*, 18 (6), 606–32.

Burman, J. (2006). Ancaster man would make Sir Edmund proud. *The Spectator*, June 2. Available at http://www.thespec.com/news/world/article/691407–ancaster-man-would-make-sir-edmund-proud (accessed 26 June 2012).

Burnette, J.L., J.M. Pollack and D.R. Forsyth (2011). Leadership in extreme contexts: a groupthink analysis of the May 1996 Mount Everest disaster. *Journal of Leadership Studies*, 4 (4), 29–40.

Cook, M. (2006). On top of the world. *U Magazine*, Fall. Available at http://www.ucalgary.ca/news/uofcpublications/umagazine/fall2006/brash (accessed 26 June 2012).

Day, D.V., P. Gronn and E. Salas (2006). Leadership in team-based organizations: on the threshold of a new era. *Leadership Quarterly*, 17 (3), 211–16.

Dispatch, May 28 (2006). SummitClimb.com. Available at http://summitclimb.com/new/default.asp?linktype=r&mtype=smenu&vid=18&nid=41 (accessed 26 June 2012).

EverestNews.com (2006). Mt. Everest 2006: sometimes, who lives and who dies depends on who cares. Available at http://www.everestnews.com/2006expeditions/everest006252006.htm (accessed 26 June 2012).

Foldy, E. G., L. Goldman and S. Ospina (2008). Sensegiving and the role of cognitive shifts in the work of leadership. *Leadership Quarterly*, 19 (5), 514–29.

Free, C. (2006). Hiker left for dead on Mount Everest. *Reader's Digest*, December. Available at http://www.rd.com/true-stories/survival/hiker-left-for-dead-on-mount-everest (accessed 26 June 2012).

Gray, K.M. (2006). Cabot tutor saves man on Everest. *Harvard Crimson*, June 5. Available at http://www.thecrimson.com/article/2006/6/5/cabot-tutor-saves-man-on-everst (accessed 26 June 2012).

Hall, L. (2007). *Dead Lucky: Life after Death on Mount Everest*. London: Penguin Books.

Hannah, S.T., M. Uhl-Bien, B.J. Avolio and F.L. Cavarretta (2009). A framework for examining leadership in extreme contexts. *Leadership Quarterly*, 20 (6), 897–919.

Kayes, D.C. (2004). The 1996 Mount Everest climbing disaster: the breakdown of learning in teams. *Human Relations*, 57 (10), 1263–84.

Klein, K.J., J.C. Ziegert, A.P. Knight and Y. Xiao (2006). Dynamic delegation: shared, hierarchical, and deindividualized leadership in extreme action teams. *Administrative Science Quarterly*, 51 (4), 590–621.

Mazur, D. (2012). Personal interview, 4 April.

Nelson, V.J. (2012). Lincoln Hall dies at 56; climber survived Mt Everest ordeal. *Los Angeles Times*, March 25. Available at http://articles.latimes.com/2012/mar/25/local/la-me-lincoln-hall-20120325 (accessed 26 June 2012).

Peterson, S.J., F.O. Walumbwa, B.J. Avolio and S.T. Hannah (2012). The relationship between authentic leadership and follower job performance: the mediating role of follower positivity in extreme contexts. *Leadership Quarterly*, 23 (3), 502–16.

Roberto, M.A. (2002). Lessons from Everest: the interaction of cognitive bias, psychological safety, and system complexity. *California Management Review*, 45 (1), 136–58.

Robinson, J. (2007). Rescue on top of the world. *Columbia College Today*, January–February. Available at http://www.college.columbia.edu/cct_archive/jan_feb07/features1.php (accessed 26 June 2012).

SummitClimb.com (2006). Available at http://summitclimb.com/new/default.asp?linktype=r&mtype=smenu&vid=18&nid=41 (accessed 26 June 2012).

Tempest, S., K. Starkey and C. Ennew (2007). In the Death Zone: a study of limits in the 1996 Mount Everest disaster. *Human Relations*, 60 (7), 1039–64.

Useem, M. (1998). *The Leadership Moment: Nine True Stories of Triumph and Disaster and their Lessons for Us All*. New York: Three Rivers Press.

Yukl, G. (2010). *Leadership in Organizations*, 7th edn. Upper Saddle River, NJ: Prentice Hall.

Zaccaro, S.J., A.L. Rittman and M.A. Marks (2001). Team leadership. *Leadership Quarterly*, 12 (4), 451–83.

7. The ghosts of shared leadership: on decision-making and subconscious followership in the 'death zone' of K2

Markus Hällgren, Marcus Lindahl and Alf Rehn

INTRODUCTION

Extreme environments are characterized in part by the romance and mystique ascribed to them, something that goes for leadership as well. Whereas the mystique of the former is connected to the perception of danger and risk, both have connections to transcending the mundane, heroism and the challenge and character of the self. Extreme environments would thus be highly likely to bring out extreme perceptions of leadership as well, including but not limited to attempted heroics and confusing risk-taking with leadership. In addition to this, the romantic notion of extreme environments would seem to dictate the necessity of a leader, and be influenced by the notion that leadership should emerge in such circumstances. Arguably, this would make people in extreme environments more likely to look for a leader to follow, or even – as we will argue herein – follow a leader that is simply not there.

This chapter focuses on high-altitude mountaineering and the manner in which leadership patterns and roles emerge in the same. More precisely, we are inquiring into notions of leadership in the 'death zone', defined as the area above 8000 meters on a mountain where the human body quickly deteriorates due to the lack of oxygen. This is an environment that is both unambiguous and hellishly difficult, and where decisions have clear-cut and potentially fatal consequences. In 1996, eight climbers were killed on Mount Everest in what has become known as 'the most widely publicized mountain-climbing disaster in history' (Kayes, 2004, p. 1267). Many researchers have analyzed the events on that particular mountain and attributed the events to failures at a cognitive, group and industry level. Flaws in leadership have for example been argued to contribute to the disaster, together with considerations of a commercial nature (Burnette et al., 2011; Hällgren, 2010; Tempest et al., 2007; Useem, 2001).

Less well known, although more recent and with more fatalities, are the events on K2 in 2008, events that led to the death of 11 climbers. In contrast to Everest, K2 attracts far more experienced climbers who do not climb with the aid of guides. The climbers are supposed to make most decisions by themselves, and only on some occasions together with others. In other words, in comparison to Everest, climbing K2 is to a larger extent to take part in a process of shared leadership, where each climber is supposed to be capable of making their own decision on when it is time to turn around. Drawing upon accounts in biographies and books, 30 hours of raw film material, and extensive and repeated interviews with six of the survivors, we analyze the K2 case and find that up until the final summit push the climbers followed an intentional shared leadership approach (Pearce and Conger, 2003).

This, however, is not our main concern. More interesting, we believe, is the manner in which this shared leadership broke down, and how during the summit push something we have taken to calling a 'spectral leader' emerged (cf. O'Connor and Quinn, 2004). We will argue that this idea of a leader, or notion that there existed someone who had a more complete plan, contributed to the disaster by giving climbers a false sense of control. Thus, we focus on the emergence of this kind of specter, and how shared leadership in extreme environments can be derailed.

K2: THE HOLY GRAIL OF MOUNTAINEERING

Located in the Karakoram mountain range on the border of Pakistan and China, 8611-meter-high K2 is the second-highest summit in the world and more technically challenging than Mount Everest. For comparison, up until 2012 Everest had been summited about 5600 times and K2 about 300 times. Because of the technical demands bearing on the climbers, the relative inaccessibility of the mountain (it takes at least ten days of hiking to get to base camp) and its unpredictable and harsh weather conditions (wind gusts up to 75 mph and temperatures below 40 celsius are not rare), K2 has a very high status and symbolic value in the mountaineering community, and has attracted far more experienced climbers than Everest. Because of the height of the mountain, mountaineers have to establish at least four camps to be able to make the last push for the summit. These camps are established with great effort since they have to be carefully stocked with supplies that can only be transported in the climbers' backpacks. Literally, to stock a camp means going up with a full backpack of supplies, down with an empty one, and then doing this camp by camp while battling high winds and snow conditions. Because of the scarcity of the supplies this is a delicate process where the logistical challenge is immense, since a climber stuck in a camp for too long would use precious supplies. K2 is usually climbed in June to August and most time is spent getting struck back by the conditions of the mountain. After months of tedious work and preparations the climbers hope for a short weather window that some years never emerges, and they scramble up the mountain to be in position for the last summit push where all their hard work comes together in one attempt of reaching the summit. The last push is however the hardest part of the mountain. It requires the climbers to negotiate a passage through the infamous Bottleneck and Traverse. The Bottleneck is a narrow and steep gully that ends beneath the huge end of the summit glacier under which the climbers have to make a traverse to the summit shoulder. Because of the daunting task of traversing the rockfall and icefall exposed, the Traverse has also been nicknamed 'The Motivator' by Ed Viesturs, one of a few expert mountaineers to have climbed all the world's summits over 8000 meters without supplemental oxygen.

In the following, we will detail how one attempt to conquer the mountain was organized, and how the shared leadership established in this attempt fell apart – with lethal consequences.

PHASE 1: SHARED LEADERSHIP AND PREPARING FOR THE PUSH

K2 was first conquered in 1954, but 2008 will remain in its annals as a particularly bad year, as 11 people were killed between 1 and 3 August 2008 during a final push for the summit. In 2008 there were 15 expeditions on the mountain, of which eight (with a total of 29 climbers) were directly involved in the tragedy. These expeditions were trying to summit K2 simultaneously, all by different routes but merging for the final push. The total group of climbers was heterogeneous ability-wise, which created situations of distrust between individuals. Still, due to the inherent difficulty of climbing K2, the climbers had to partially depend on each other as collaboration was crucial for the climb. Therefore there were voluntarily and detailed coordination meetings for the effort in the base camp before the summit push. The meetings at base camp served the purpose of collectively deciding and agreeing beforehand on how everyone should act – preferably in a predefined manner. This was essential on all levels, as on-the-fly decision-making in the death zone is exceptionally hard and dangerous. Climbers therefore claim that there was a feeling of being well prepared for the final push, and that there was some safety provided by the number of climbers.

During these meetings, which most climbers attended, many aspects of the push were negotiated between expeditions. It was decided what each expedition should bring and do, such as who was responsible for bringing the ropes, who should affix them and at what time. Moreover it was decided in what order the expeditions were to go. In this, every expedition was expected to contribute with resources and/or tasks. After the meeting the climbers knew what they and others had to do in order to be able to summit, while the execution of this was mainly up to them as individuals and their own discretion. There was thus no formal leader assigned to the task of coordinating the different activities, besides a leader for the first summit team that was supposed to affix the ropes – but who later became sick.

Some individuals with previous experience from the mountain, such as the Dutch climber and expedition leader Wilco Van Rooijen, had a more pronounced role within the group of climbers. Still, neither he nor anyone else had any explicit formal or even informal leader role. The meetings were open discussions where the climbers agreed upon the rules together, following a pattern of shared leadership. This was however not without its problems.

PHASE 2: THE EMERGENCE OF A SPECTRAL LEADER

Despite the best of efforts, things started to go wrong during the final summit push, that is, the last, very hard climb of approximately 15 hours between the uppermost camp and the summit. During the push, safety measures such as ropes were misplaced or not fixed at all, and poles and strings to mark the way back were not put out. Moreover, the climbers came to a late start that increased the exposure through the treacherous Bottleneck, followed by the Traverse under a ice-cliff famous for rock falls. Because of the late start and subsequent slow progress, a few climbers turned around early, even as the majority continued. Soon, the first fatality occurred in the Bottleneck, when one of the climbers disengaged from the fixed rope and fell to his death. In the attempt to recover his body another climber died, and others had a close call.

Among the 23 who continued, no single individual had a distinct role as a overall leader. There were some administrative rather than formal leaders, for example Van Rooijen for the Norit K2 expedition and Cecile Skog for the Norwegian K2 expedition, but most climbers were essentially free agents expected to make decisions related to execution at their own discretion. For example, Christopher Klinke, an American climber whose climbing partners had turned around, made the decision to turn around in the Bottleneck due to the exposure to altitude and slow progress (interview with Klinke, 16 December 2011). Progress was slowed by being forced to climb sequentially with no possibility of overtaking slower (and sometimes inexperienced) climbers. The slow progress was generally recognized and created worries and some possibilities for climbers to discuss concerns about the progress and the conditions that bore witness of possible future icefalls. These were however quickly suppressed by several highly experienced and recognized climbers with reference to the exceptional weather and snow conditions and earlier successful summits of the same mountain (interview with Van Rooijen, 23 November 2011, making his third attempt on K2). Earlier disastrous summit attempts were not mentioned, nor statistics bearing witness to the significantly increased risks of summiting past 4 p.m. Although the emergence had started earlier when no formal leaders were nominated in base camp nor in camp 4, this is the first step toward the 'spectral leader' since the discussions referred to a external process that legitimized and normalized the present conditions. These brief discussions were moreover of limited scope and impact, as the 23 climbers were geographically dispersed, lacked communication devices and did not share a common language. Instead the discussions were isolated to the climbers that happened to be next to each other in the line and happened to share a language and/or climbing philosophy. It was widely recognized that turning around would effectively cancel any later summit attempts due to logistics for example, as well as energy and resource levels among the climbers.

As the remaining climbers approached the summit they had had significant exposure to both altitude and cold. Moreover the climbers were down to their last available bottles of supplemental oxygen, but instead of turning they continued since no one and nothing told them to. In addition, many were exhausted, with several of the climbers approaching the summit on their knees. The first climber summited at about 3 p.m. but the majority of the climbers reached the summit between 5.30 p.m. and 8 p.m. The first climber to summit soon started the descent and saw the long line of climbers still ascending. This caused some concern, but rather than expressing this he kept quiet and/or answered questions on estimations of how long it was to go to the summit (about two hours). He did that since he found that it was not his task to tell them, and it was in a sense 'him against them'. With the last climber summiting as late as 8 p.m., this meant a night-time descent for him and for many other climbers. A night-time descent of K2 is not impossible, but increases risks due to the required technical skill, the darkness, the cold and the long exposure to altitude.

Soon after the first climbers to descend had passed the Traverse, there was a collapse of ice and rocks in the Traverse that tore the fixed ropes and killed a Norwegian climber. Without a fixed rope the climbers above the Traverse were effectively stranded unless they had the skill and/or strength to descend without ropes. Some of the climbers made it back, some fell, and yet others bivouacked and waited for the next day. There was, however, little coordination between the stranded climbers, and climbers were left to survive on their own or together with two or three climbers who happened to be at the same place. The perfect conditions that were referenced to earlier however worked in their favor and contributed to keeping the deaths relatively low, thanks to somewhat mild weather during the night. One of the most remarkable events was that a Nepalese climber more or less carried another climber down the Traverse, at significant risk to his own life. In either case, survival was in many cases more of a fluke than a result of deliberate choice because of the cold and the effects of hypoxia. After daybreak on 3 August, as the last survivor was located, the total death-count was confirmed at 11.

THE SPECTER OF LEADERSHIP

Leadership theories tend to assume that leadership is an intentional act in which a leader influences others to act through varied means (Avolio et al., 2009). There has, however, been a move away from so-called 'heroic' theories of leadership, where the leader is perceived as a solitary agent with specific qualities. This trait-based conception has gradually been questioned and replaced by more complex theories focusing on the interrelationship between leaders and followers (Howell and Shamir, 2005; Uhl-Bien, 2006; Uhl-Bien et al., 2007) and the so-called cultural turn in leadership theories where formal leaders may even be obsolete as subjects in a strong, coherent culture could lead themselves (Manz and Sims, 1987) through shared, collective or distributed leadership (Gronn, 2002). This particular type of leadership involves intentionally con-structed peer and lateral influence where the result of the whole is larger than what the individual members and leaders would have accomplished by themselves (O'Connor and Quinn, 2004; Pearce and Conger, 2003). Pearce and Conger (2003, p. 1) defined shared or distributed leadership as 'a dynamic, interactive influence process among individuals in groups for which the objective is to lead one another to the achievement of group or organizational goals or both. This influence process often involves peer, or lateral, influence and at other times involves upward or downward hierarchical influence.'

Despite the substantial increase of self-managed teams in post-bureaucratic industrial settings (for example, Whittington et al., 1999) as well as the increase of knowledge workers in late modernity (Kärreman and Alvesson, 2004), relatively little research has been carried out on the consequences of this new way of organizing or its further implications (Carson et al., 2007), particularly in extreme environments (Hannah et al., 2009). As Avioli et al. (2009) points out, there is a need to investigate boundary conditions, mediators and moderating mechanisms for shared leadership, and not least the local environment's impact. Extreme environments, being in and of themselves boundary conditions, would seem well suited to acknowledge this call of Avioli et al. (2009).

Theories of shared leadership have tended to emphasize situations where this works well, or at least in a satisfactory manner. In the case of K2, we propose that we can see a case of how shared leadership falls apart and how during the summit push something we have taken to calling a 'spectral leader' emerged. This idea of a leader, or notion that there existed someone who had a more complete plan, contributed to the disaster by giving climbers a false sense of control through the normalization of the conditions (for example the reference to previous attempts and the good weather) by experienced climbers. This leadership configuration is somewhat different than shared leadership, and the issue of leadership is more a property of the whole system rather than of its members. The quality of leadership then is the resulting 'vector' of the interacting parts (O'Connor and Quinn, 2004). These interacting parts refer to the non-existence of either a formal leader or a shared leadership, the weather, previous summit attempts, the geographical dispersion of the climbers and the difficult communication situation. Drawing upon O'Connor and Quinn we will use the term 'spectral leader' or 'specter' to refer not to an existing leader or leadership process, but rather to the belief in that there – despite everything – would be someone who is leading an endeavor. In extreme environments, where pressures are high and decisions have life-or-death consequences, such a belief may be both irrational and psychologically quite understandable.

The manner in which we approach this is by highlighting how people, despite having partaken in shared planning, can still act as if there is a leader present, and how this belief in a leader can cause a breakdown in the shared leadership model (Weick, 1993). In a manner of speaking, the community had established a specter of leadership through their planning processes and through the hierarchy that still existed among the climbers. Although people such as Van Rooijen were explicitly not the leaders of the summit push, the existence of a hierarchy created a situation where it was assumed that there existed a control of the process, established by the existence of more experienced members of the party.

However, as this belief in experience and shared leadership was not directed toward anyone in particular, and not directly voiced, the 'spectral leader' existed mainly as an idea that was further exacerbated as numerous choices were made by the separate individuals. As leadership was shared and everyone still afforded a great deal of individual freedom, the process through which leadership was assumed cannot be looked for in any specific choice made on the mountain, but rather in the manner in which actors assumed that something still controlled the process. This 'something' refers to the experience of others, the sense of safety provided by the numbers, the reference to earlier successful expeditions and the pre-staged process of climbing. Despite recognizing the slow progress, the climbers were literally left with three choices: (1) remain quiet and continue; (2) voice their concerns; or (3) turn around. Once they turned around they knew that was it. Any attempt to turn around typically included at least a short discussion with a fellow climber before turning around, and by selection among the remaining climbers any growing unease was therefore quickly rejected. The remaining group thus consisted of climbers who had bought into the perfect conditions, and safety in the preparations paradigm despite objective evidence of the opposite (several safety measures were never implemented, and the statistics are clear that climbers who turn around normally never get a second chance during that season). At K2 the expeditions shared the physical setting but the climbers were not part of one team. The climb was thus rather a collaboration of subjects who made decisions at their own discretion. The individuals collaborated on a voluntary basis but without any democratic foundations or shared, agreed-upon culture beside a common, but not necessarily shared, idea of mountaineering. If someone did not like what was happening, that individual was free to descend. During the final push for the summit the climbers thus shared a physical and mental context of time and space that exercised control over their actions, and subsequently had them take risks that they might have not taken otherwise. Instead of following one distinct leader the group acted as if the process as a whole was coordinated by an immaterial force, a spectral leader.

Gronn (2002, pp. 429–31) attributes three forms of concertive action to distributed leadership: a collaborative mode of engagement that arises spontaneously; an intuitive understanding that emerges from working relations among individuals; and structural relations and institutionalized processes may or may not regularize distributed action. Through these forms a sense of conjoint agency may emerge where individuals 'synchronize their actions by having regard to their own plans, those of their peers, and their sense of unit membership' (Gronn, 2002, p. 431) and where synergies such as cross-hierarchy, trusteeship, parity of relations, separation of powers and friendship may emerge (Gronn, 2002, p. 437). Although the leadership that emerged among the climbers arose spontaneously (no formal leader), a somewhat intuitive understanding emerged (outstanding conditions) and there were institutionalized processes (a climber summits mountains), the leadership was not distributed per se since the mutual influence of the individuals was very limited on a formal basis and hardly recognized by anyone in the interaction among the individuals (cf. Carson et al., 2007, p. 1218).

We might say that the climbers followed an unintended, spectral leader rather than a true shared leadership model, and that this emerged out of the vectors of influence that the extremity of the environment established. The notion of a spectral leader gave a sense of direction and exercised a concertive control of the subjects and the whole (Barker, 1993). Concertive control here means that each member of a group functioned as a peer but also, more importantly, as a control point of what appropriate behavior is. This, in combination with the individual acknowledgment of sunk costs and what were conceived as favorable conditions by most climbers, all contributed to the disaster. In combination, the conditions and the sense of direction made it difficult for the subjects to turn around, particularly as the process was continuously nudged by the notion that there was some form of specific leadership, transcending the individual, guiding the effort. There was thus no leader to object and/or question without openly disagreeing with everyone else, an act that has been found to be socially difficult (Janis, 1972).

At K2 this concertive control was implicit rather than explicit as in the shared culture of Barker. It is implicit in that no one openly expressed any concerns about the others so that they heard, neither were there any serious coordination efforts beyond a few formal activities of fixing ropes, bringing poles and strings to attach to the poles. Comments instead remained between friends and those who were considered as peers.

This understanding of leadership – which would emphasize people's assumption of what guides an effort, an assumption which can be irrational – is different from the heroic strong type of leadership often attributed to leadership in extreme environments, for example in military settings (Hannah et al., 2009; Kolditz, 2007). In extreme environments the existence of a strong leader and a shared culture is often assumed, thus creating a potential problem when attempting to follow a shared leadership model. By what we have here called a spectral leader this chapter thus tries to contribute to the cultural turn within leadership studies. Since this chapter relies on a single case study it is hard to make generalizations. Future research therefore could deepen and widen the research effort by inquiring in more depth as to how assumptions of leadership can derail shared leadership engagements.

LEADERSHIP LESSONS

Despite the inherent shortcomings in using a single case study, some reflections on the leadership lessons seem in order. There are three lessons we would like to particularly emphasize, lessons that follow from our case:

1. Leadership does not require a body.
2. A spectral leader is hard to question.
3. Leadership in extreme environments is different from leadership in extreme events.

Leadership Does Not Require a Body

The contemporary understanding of leadership is created around the notion of body and intention, regardless of whether it is individual-, or group-based. The findings in our case and in the wider work on leadership building on 'the cultural turn' questions these assumptions. Applicable to any setting, mountaineering or engineering alike, rather than being tied to an individual, leadership can be seen as a product of tacitly shaped group dynamics that limits the individual's ability or wish to voice particular concerns. From a leadership perspective a neither a formal or informal leader is necessary for leadership to affect a process. The leader may in fact be found as a spectral presence in other dynamics and interrelationships. Naturally, any individual, leader or member of an organization have to recognize the potential of an existing spectral leader.

A Spectral Leader is Hard to Question

With the emergence of a spectral leader – a leadership constituted as a shared if flawed understanding in a group – there is no body or intention to object against. The leadership characteristics are therefore systemic rather than individualistic, whereby the solution to the problem cannot be found within an individual but rather within the system (or culture) itself. The tacitness makes the leadership that an individual might want to exercise to prevent similar future disasters difficult, as there is no formal power to relate to. Moreover, there is no formal authority to act beyond what is given by a group of highly competitive individuals. Instead of convincing an individual or a group, a person who wants to voice concerns or lead a group in conditions where there is no formal authority needs to consider the group dynamics in play. These conditions are most likely found in settings where teams exercise concertive control and shared leadership. Still, this is inherently difficult since he or she must first be recognized as someone with the right to make such claims, which is particularly difficult in isolated, dispersed teams.

Leadership in Extreme Environments is Different from Leadership in Extreme Events

Had it not been for the torn ropes at the Traverse, most of the fatalities would probably not have happened, as this was the last difficult point before safe arrival at the highest camp, and the emergence of the spectral leader would have been relatively uneventful. However, instead of coming together as a group when the ropes were torn, the torn ropes disintegrated the group even further since there was no one in charge over the situation and event. Here the role of a strong formal leader would have been beneficial, as no one made sense of the situation or coordinated a joint effort to reach safe ground. This leads us to argue that one of the leadership lessons that can be drawn is that the belief in a spectral leader can hinder the establishment of a formal leader, and that the effect of the emergence of a spectral leader when things are progressing according to plan is different than when unexpected events occur. That is, the demands for leadership are different during a uneventful process and an unexpected event, and by focusing on the latter we can understand the shortcomings of the former. For the practicing manager this suggests that one has to pay close attention to the process, since a spectral leader lowers the margins to be able to recuperate from failure.

CONCLUSION

The purpose of this chapter has been to investigate how shared leadership can fall apart in an extreme environment, and to note the specter of leadership that emerged in this. What we call a 'spectral leader' can emerge in any kind of setting where all and no one is the leader, and where leadership therefore may become assumed yet cannot be questioned. This has implications for settings beyond extreme environments, since self-managed teams are getting increasingly popular. Through this rather extreme example we argue that shared leadership, at least where collectiveness is implicit and not distinctly pronounced as a joint effort towards a joint goal, can fall apart in environments with a high level of flux and change. The sharedness of meaning and the calibration of action and perception are relative processes, and can constitute unintended consequences. Moreover the chapter has significant implications for operations in extreme environments with competitive actors, as spectral leaders are more likely to emerge in situations where self-coercion, a strong focus on goals and an unwillingness to show weakness is accentuated.

REFERENCES

Avolio, B.J., F.O. Walumbwa and T.J. Weber (2009). Leadership: current theories, research, and future directions. *Annual Review of Psychology*, 60, 421–49.
Barker, J.R. (1993). Tightening the iron cage: concertive control in self-managing teams. *Administrative Science Quarterly*, 38 (3), 408–37.
Burnette, J.L., J.M. Pollack and D.R. Forsyth (2011). Leadership in extreme contexts: a groupthink analysis of the May 1996 Mount Everest disaster. *Journal of Leadership Studies*, 4 (4), 29–40.
Carson, J.B., P.E. Tesluk and J.A. Marrone (2007). Shared leadership in teams: an investigation of antecedent conditions and performance. *Academy of Management Journal*, 50 (5), 1217–34.
Gronn, P. (2002). Distributed leadership as a unit of analysis. *Leadership Quarterly*, 13 (4), 423–51.
Hällgren, M. (2010). Groupthink in temporary organizations. *International Journal of Project Management in Business*, 3 (1), 94–110.
Hannah, S.T., M. Uhl-Bien, B.J. Avolio and F.L. Cavarretta (2009). A framework for examining leadership in extreme contexts. *Leadership Quarterly*, 20 (6), 897–919. DOI: 10.1016/j.leaqua.2009.09.006.
Howell, J.M. and B. Shamir (2005). The role of followers in the charismatic leadership process: Relationships and their consequences. *Academy of Management Review*, 30 (1), 96–112.
Janis, I.L. (1972), *Victims of Groupthink: A Psychological Study of Foreign-Policy Decisions and Fiascoes*, Boston MA: Houghton Mifflin.

Kayes, C.D. (2004). The 1996 Mount Everest climbing disaster: the breakdown of learning in teams. *Human Relations*, 57 (10), 1263–84.

Kärreman, D. and M. Alvesson (2004). Cages in tandem: management control, social identity, and identification in a knowledge-intensive firm. *Organization*, 11 (1), 149–75.

Kolditz, T.A. (2007), *In Extremis Leadership: Leading as if Your Life Depended on It*. San Francisco, CA: Jossey-Bass.

Manz, C.C. and H.P. Sims Jr (1987). Leading workers to lead themselves: the external leadership of self-managing work teams. *Administrative Science Quarterly*, 32 (1), 106–29.

O'Connor, P. and L. Quinn (2004). Organizational capacity for leadership. In C.D. McCauley and E. Van Velsor (eds), *The Center for Creative Leadership: Handbook of Leadership Development*. San Francisco, CA: Jossey-Bass, pp. 417–37.

Pearce, C.L. and J.A. Conger (eds) (2003). *Shared Leadership: Reframing the Hows and Whys of Leadership*. Thousand Oaks, CA: Sage Publications.

Tempest, S., K. Starkey and C. Ennew (2007). In the Death Zone: a study of limits in the 1996 Mount Everest disaster. *Human Relations*, 60 (7), 1039–64.

Uhl-Bien, M. (2006). Relational leadership theory: exploring the social processes of leadership and organizing. *Leadership Quarterly*, 17 (6), 654–76.

Uhl-Bien, M., R. Marion and B. McKelvey (2007). Complexity leadership theory: Shifting leadership from the industrial age to the knowledge era. *Leadership Quarterly*, 18 (4), 298–318

Useem, M. (2001). The leadership lessons of Mount Everest. *Harvard Business Review*, October, 51–8.

Weick, K.E. (1993). The collapse of sensemaking in organizations: the Mann Gulch disaster. *Administrative Science Quarterly*, 38 (4), 628–52.

Whittington, R., A. Pettigrew, S. Peck, E. Fenton and M. Conyon (1999). Change and complementarities in the new competitive landscape: a European panel study, 1992–1996. *Organization Science*, 10 (5), 583–600.

8. Greenland: creating world-class teams

James G. Clawson

INTRODUCTION

In the summer of 1991, four young, unknown Norwegian men set out in an attempt to break the world record for crossing Greenland unsupported. The existing record was 26 days and the average crossing time was 42 days. 'Unsupported' means no outside assistance, just human power; no snowmobiles, no airdrops, just man and sled. Greenland is the world's largest island, a large bowl of ice with mountains on the east and west coasts and as such is a severe place. Temperatures frequently drop to the minus 60°C range, blinding furious blizzards regularly sweep across the ice cap, and there is nothing but ice – no grass, no shrubs, no rocks, no huts, no relief – just ice and more ice for 400 miles. More people have summited Mount Everest than have crossed Greenland unsupported. The Darden School case study (Clawson, 2004; Clawson and Lie, 2008) chronicles this remarkable expedition in some detail.

The story is powerful for many reasons, not least of which is that these young men were not just giving lip service to the phrase 'world class', they were attempting to prove that they could indeed be the best in the world at something. Many corporations, and teams within them, claim to offer 'world-class goods and services that delight our customers beyond their expectations' while in reality their efforts fall far short of that lofty objective. True, there is no harm in striving – unless your results are consistently sub-par and your customers are repeatedly disappointed. In that case, corporate and team credibility is eroded. What does it take to create a real world-class team? The Greenland expedition provides more than 20 answers.

THE CHALLENGE

The typical Greenland crossing route begins on the east coast in an area with the worldwide highest number of polar bear attacks on humans. The route crosses the eastern mountain range and begins a long ascent to the mid-point of the island about 7500 feet above sea level. The altitude change on the route including the rises for the mountains on both coasts is shown in Figure 8.1.

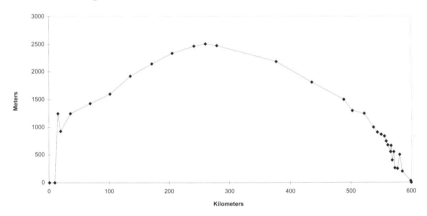

Figure 8.1   Greenland expedition altitude

The route then continues downhill, across a vast ice field riddled with crevasses that sink several hundred feet down. Then up over the western range and steeply down to the sea. This is a daunting challenge just to complete, much less to become the fastest ever.

Suppose you wanted to be world-class at something. Suppose you have already declared to the world that your team, your company, is a 'world-class' provider but you have yet to prove that. How would you go about building a team of people who could set a world record – at anything? Perhaps the first question is, 'Who would want to do this?' The second might be, 'Why?' Let me introduce you to the team, and let us see if these are the people you are expecting:

- 'Odd' Harald Hauge, 35, Chief Financial Editor of Norway's largest newspaper, *Aftenposten*. Hauge finished gymnasium[1] top of class. He served his mandatory military service in the Coastal Artillery, top of class. He earned an MBA from one of Norway's best business schools, Norges Handelshøyskole, in 1980. Hauge has

been married twice to the same woman (divorced while in Greenland in 1991). He has one child.

- Ivar Erik Tollefsen, 30, entrepreneur. Tollefsen found school to be
  boring and too slow for him. After he started his own public
  company in 1980, he did not have time to finish gymnasium and
  dropped out when he had three months left. At 24, he sold his
  company for $3 million. He went bankrupt when he was 27, with
  $1 million in debt. In 1986, one of his British suppliers got
  involved in organized crime in Britain, and Tollefsen was kid-
  napped and held for ransom. Tollefsen is divorced with two
  children from that marriage and has another child from a second,
  broken relationship.
- Bård Stokkan, 31, IBM operator and customer support representative. After the compulsory nine years of school, Stokkan mustered
  on the Norwegian full-rigged school ship *Christian Radich*. After
  serving six months on the ship, he got a 'temporary' job at IBM
  that lasted 17 years. Stokkan is unmarried with no children.
- Morten Lie, 28, a Lieutenant Commander in the Royal Norwegian
  Navy. His father died when Lie was 14 years old. He was an
  exchange student in Sacramento, CA, from 1978 to 1979. After
  graduating from gymnasium in 1982 at the top of his class, he was
  accepted into the Royal Norwegian Naval Academy. After graduating from the academy in 1986 (third in his class) with a major in
  economics, he served as supply officer and substituting executive
  officer on fast patrol boats for two years, as a financial officer in
  NATO for 18 months, and at Norwegian Defense Headquarters for
  12 months. He is unmarried with no children.

LEADERSHIP LESSONS

- Recruitment and selection. The group began with eight individuals
  who were interested in pursuing this venture. By the time the
  expedition began, the number had been winnowed in half. What
  kind of skill, determination and stamina does it take to perform at
  the world-class level?
- Instruction. The group found a climbing instructor and went
  through a crash course in technical climbing. This was not an
  experienced group of climbers.
- Preparation. The group began going on training trips on weekends
  in the far north of Norway. Many of these training trips were, they
  said, more severe than the actual expedition. They pursued this

training for a year before venturing to Greenland. So, the preparation-to-execution ratio was about 26:1. Sometimes executives declare that they do not have time for 26:1 preparation ratios. Then someone else will say something like, 'Well, I spent six months working my boss's 45-minute PowerPoint presentation for the annual meeting', or, 'Well, I hope the guys building the 787 get it right the first time!' The severity of the training trips was what trimmed the final group down to four.

- Trust. What kind of trust would develop between four people who were climbing in life-threatening conditions week after week after week? One would learn soon who one could count on, and who one could not. One would learn the other team members' stamina, mental condition, physical condition and dependability.

- Personnel types. Brousseau et al. (1996) identified four common career concepts in society: Linears (managers), Experts (independent contributors), Spirals (learners) and Transitories (focused on something other than work), a group that most Linears detest. These four young men were Transitories, their work was intermittent, their home lives were somewhat of a mess. It is not always, in fact perhaps not usually, the traditional career types who make the big breakthroughs.

- Rotating leadership. Leadership in the emerging team rotated. First, the lead position in skiing is the most difficult because one must break trail. Second, assignments for cooking, melting ice for water, and so on rotated so that no one could complain they had the crummy job. This often leads to a discussion of the weight of leadership. Having been the CEO of a 3000-person non-profit organization, I can attest to this mantle of responsibility and the density of its mass. Sharing the load is very helpful.

- Inflexible strategy. They had a simple but powerful and almost inviolate core strategy. Their formula was $L = F = S$: light is fast and fast is safe. This strategy fit both their objective and their concerns for safety. The longer one is on the ice pack, the more dangerous it becomes.

- Flexible tactics. That said, the team demonstrated remarkable flexibility and ingenuity in the application of their strategy, their tactics. When the tent pole broke, they devised a way to solve the problem. When the fuel leaked into the food, they dealt with it.

- Strategic planning. If 'light' is a core strategic principle, then one must re-engineer one's equipment to be as light as it can be. They stripped the edges off their skis, saving a few grams here and there. They repackaged their food to lighten the load. In the end, the sleds still weighed 250 pounds each. Because of the weight issue, they decided not to carry a rifle – in a dangerous region. They carried minimal redundancies in all areas of their equipment.

- Equipment. They searched for the latest in mountaineering equipment and frequently re-engineered that equipment to suit their own purposes. They did not just take what was on the shelf. Their harnesses for pulling the sleds was of their own design and creation.
- Technology. The team used the latest technology they could find, in this case global positioning systems (GPS) which was not yet commercially available, by negotiating with the military. This technology solved a critical problem: location. Without knowing their location they would be at a major disadvantage.
- Benchmarking. The team visited a number of 'experts' who had made the crossing before, and pumped them for data and information. In the end, they discarded much of what they heard. That seems arrogant and brash. On the other hand, there is a way in which benchmarking, a common business practice, prepares you for someone else's yesterday, not your own tomorrow. If they had followed the benchmarking advice, they would have crossed in 26 days.
- Common goal. They all had a single, focused common goal: to set a world record. This is a very high standard. What does it take to become the best at something among 7 billion people? Most people do not even think about striving for that level of achievement. In Collins' terms, this was a big, hairy, audacious goal (BHAG).
- Metrics. They were measuring some very important variables. By knowing their location they could measure distance. By knowing time, they could measure speed. But they also measured fuel, or in this case, calories. There were two stores of fuel/calories: on the sleds and on their bodies. They were calculating body fat along with the infant formula and energy bars they were carrying.
- Calculated risk taking. With good measurements of key conditions such as location, speed, weight, body mass index (BMI) and calorie consumption, they could make some risky decisions with greater confidence. They crossed the polar bear region without incident. About two-thirds of the way across they calculated that they were carrying too much food, so in the middle of nowhere, they discarded a significant portion of their stores. They calculated and retained a two-day buffer of food in case someone fell into a crevasse on the western slope and it took them two days to make the rescue or recover the body.

- Luck. They did not encounter any polar bears. When the tent pole broke during a white-out blizzard and they were all in danger of suffocation, the man nearest the tent door awoke in time to dig their way out. Otherwise, they would all still be out there.
- Competition. The team knew that the Norwegian Olympic gold medalist in cross-country skiing was behind them. This gave them extra energy as they wanted to show that they could beat his time.
- Short-term goals. The plane from Oslo to Greenland arrived once a week. If they got to the west coast too late, they would miss the plane and have to wait another week for the ride home.
- Persistence. The team concluded that the longer they were on the ice field, the more dangerous it was. They also concluded that if they were sick or the weather was bad, they could be miserable in the tent or miserable walking, so they decided on the walking alternative. That fit their strategy anyway and aligned with their ultimate goal.
- Social support. Because of improper stowing, the kerosene fuel leaked into their food supply and they all got sick. Soon they were out of toilet paper. One fellow was particularly hard hit. So, to encourage him, one teammate walked along beside him. Wait a minute: that meant breaking two trails and using twice as much energy. This was a net energy loss for the team. Why would they do this? This leads to a fascinating discussion about the 'social construction of energy'. The teammate was not giving food or drink, just encouragement, so where was the energy transfer here? Some kind of Frankensteinian wireless energy field? Do you believe in the social construction of energy? Where does that come from? We talk about how encouragement can unlock the linkages between a depressed brain and underutilized muscles.
- Caring. From the above, it is clear that these men cared about each other. We could fold this one in with trust and social support but it deserves separate mention.
- Failure is not an option. Cortez burned his men's ships. Here, the four young Norwegians knew that if they sat down, they died. The threat of danger and even death (or figuratively, the health of a company) is a big motivator – for some.
- Social conflict management. The team planned in advance, probably from their experience on the training hikes, for managing conflict. In extreme conditions (weather, deadlines, difficult technical problems, and so on), people will tend to get testy and usually critical. They decided a priori that when any conflicts arose they would not play the 'blame game', but focus all their precious

energy on solutions. So when the fuel leaked and the tent pole broke, they were all primed to avoid blaming and focus on problem-solving. Many corporations expend enormous amounts of energy in finding scapegoats and hanging them.

- Breaking assumptions. The team decided two-thirds of the way through that they could relax what is probably the most pervasive assumption in the world: the number of hours in a day. They calculated their condition, body fat, sled calories, location, and so on, and decided to work 30-hour days. They changed their view of time.

- Boredom. The daily grind of this expedition was pretty overwhelming. Put one foot in front of the other, pull your 250-pound sled, over and over again. There is little that was exciting about this, yet they were able to maintain high energy levels and performance.

- Passion. Many will note that no one could do what these young men did if they did not love what they were doing. Passion is an important element here.

- Discipline. Many participants will mention discipline as a key component. The stamina of this team was remarkable, built no doubt in large part by the intensity of their self-imposed training period. 'You play like you practice.'

- Humility. Some participants will mention humility: the willingness to listen, to not blame, to keep an open mind (flexibility) and support others even when it costs you something.

- Celebrating. This is akin to the social support lesson. They, contradicting their prime strategy, brought along a bottle of cognac with which to celebrate Norwegian Independence Day. Survival experts loudly proclaim that in conditions of hypothermia you should never drink alcohol. Further, the liquid is heavy. They calculated that the energy release (internally) would be greater than the energy cost of bringing along the bottle. This is similar to the social support hypothesis that social support will create more energy in total than the extra spent by breaking two trails.

- Breaking up. Near the end of their journey as they neared the west coast, the team 'broke up'. That is, they began skiing as fast as they could. Later, they regretted this. Yet, we might predict that no world-class team can persist indefinitely; the energy required to perform at that level is just too much. Despite that, there were no individual medals or awards. In fact, there were no awards at all. Just the team's satisfaction that they had done this thing that no one else had. In the end they not only broke the world record, they smashed it, crossing in 13 days and several days ahead of the Olympic gold medalist. And they made the plane to Oslo.

There is one more big lesson here, though. Why do people do things like this? Money? Fame? Uniqueness? Power? I am voting for 'flow', or what my co-author Doug Newburg (Clawson and Newburg, 2008) would call 'resonance' or what ball players call the 'zone'. After completing the Greenland expedition, Odd Harald immediately began planning his next expedition: twice as long, in more severe conditions, 800 miles to the South Pole with two other men, one injured in an electrical accident with only one arm and no hands. 'World's best' is a fleeting thing; the power, the energy, lies in the chase. If one can figure out, before one dies, what one's flow or resonance is, and how to recreate it, and how to feed it, and how to share it with others, then, and perhaps only then, can one hope to perform at the world-class level.

So my personal, published, definition of leadership is an unusual one. It is not the common 'the ability to organize a group of people around a common goal'. Rather, I say, leadership is the ability to manage energy, first in yourself and then in those around you. Too many executives focus on motivating others, when the first lens should probably be trained on themselves. If you have the passion, and the strategy – well, all of the items listed above – then you could probably hope to perform truly, not just in lip service, at the world-class level. It is an extreme target.

NOTE

1. Gymnasium: a secondary school that prepares students for university. Gymnasium is a three-year education after the compulsory nine years of school.

REFERENCES

Brousseau, Kenneth R., Michael J. Driver, Kristina Eneroth and Rikard Larson (1996). Career pandemonium: realigning organizations and individuals. *Academy of Management Perspective*, 10 (4), 52–66.

Clawson, J.G. (2004). Greenland teaching note. *Darden Case No. UVA-OB-0581TN*.

Clawson, J.G. and M. Lie (2008). Greenland. *Darden Case No. UVA-OB-0581*.

Clawson, James and Doug Newburg (2008). *Powered by Feel: How Individuals, Teams and Companies Excel*. Singapore: World Scientific.

PART II

Extreme work teams

9. Dr Lehman: extreme healthcare leadership along the shores of Lake Tanganyika

Robert O. Harris

There are leaders who are innately driven to serve people and provide hope in extremely remote areas on earth. One such area exists where tour buses refuse to travel and cannot reach due to road conditions or where only charter flights land with little or no radar. The indigenous people travel primarily by boat or walk hours for healthcare. This story is about a team of intrepid doctors and healthcare workers willing to work along the Lake Tanganyika region in Tanzania, East Africa inhabited by over 3 million people. Most of all this is a short story about a medical doctor with an infectious laugh, walk-on-hot coals attitude and the professional capability to save thousands of lives, named Amy Lehman, MBA, MD.

Today the African continent stands on the edge of extraordinary growth and development overshadowed by healthcare demands connected to escalating disease and healthcare worker shortages. It is a major dilemma for most developing countries caught in a race for economic growth. Historically, rural healthcare services in developing countries lags behind urban, 'big city' healthcare and economic resources. Consequently, in developing countries most of the population lives in rural to extremely remote towns or villages, especially in sub-Saharan Africa (SSA). The rural population is loosely organized and often isolated, beyond the reach of social safety nets or infrastructure: high-capacity roads, 24-hour electricity and safe, clean drinking water.

According to the World Health Organization's *World Health Report 2006*, 1 billion people or 11 percent of the world's population lives in SSA (WHO, 2006). Historically, SSA has experienced a critical shortage of trained healthcare workers. In 2004, Lesotho had only 89 doctors for a population of 1.8 million. Malawi had some 265 clinicians for 13 million people in 2008. In comparison, the Americas represent approximately 14 percent of the world's population, less than half of the burden of disease, and almost 50 percent of the world's healthcare workers. This is a sobering comparison to SSA, which has only 3 percent of the world's healthcare workers. The World Health Organization (WHO) recommends a minimum of one physician for a population of 10 000. In SSA only 17 countries reached this standard; the other 37 are below (Conway et al., 2007; Kumar, 2007).

The exodus of trained doctors and nurses or so-called 'brain drain' of local talent is a brutal consequence left over from past decades of war, corruption, inadequate healthcare and low wages. Moreover, the lure of Western society urban big cities in Europe, Australia and the United States is especially attractive for many African healthcare professionals (Hagopian et al., 2004; Kalipeni et al., 2012). According to the *British Medical Journal*, nine sub-Saharan African countries lost the equivalent of $2 billion as doctors left the African continent to work overseas (Mills et al., 2011). The World Health Organization (WHO) and United Nations proclaim the SSA shortage of trained healthcare workers as a fundamental barrier to achieving the Millennium Development Goals (Kinfu et al., 2009; Ogilvie et al., 2007).

The Tanzania Ministry of Health and Social Welfare (MoHSW) estimated that as of 2006, the healthcare system was operating with a 65 percent shortage of the required skilled workforce. In addition, the MoHSW has launched a ten-year program to ensure that all Tanzanians have access to healthcare services. This program, called the Primary Health Services Development Program (PHSDP), is intended to expand and improve the provision of health services to every village (Nartker et al., 2010).

In 2007 McKinsey and Company conducted a healthcare study which revealed that 820 000 additional doctors and nurses are needed to provide basic care in SSA (Conway et al., 2007). Reducing child mortality, maternal mortality and tackling diseases such as HIV/AIDS, malaria and tuberculosis (TB) requires more trained healthcare personnel each year (Nyoni et al., 2006). Without a sustained increase in trained healthcare workers, no amount of aid, medical technology or infrastructure can save lives. Skilled human resources are the backbone of any performing healthcare system (Skeldon, 2008).

Like many other developing countries in SSA, Tanzania faces a crisis in human resources for healthcare. Tanzania has one of the most severe health worker challenges, with only 1200 doctors estimated to be in the country of 40 million people (Madulu, 2005). Based on the WHO minimum standard of 23 health workers per 10 000 people, Tanzania is approximately 84 000 health workers short of meeting the most basic health needs. Over the next ten years, if left unchecked, this gap is expected to grow to 104 000 (Bryan et al., 2010 ; Conway et al., 2007). This is the core challenge for Dr Amy Lehman's organization and philosophy to fill in the medical gap along the shores of Lake Tanganyika.

CREATING A SUSTAINING VISION AND LEADERSHIP: LAKE TANGANYIKA FLOATING HEALTH CLINIC

In 2011 during a University of Chicago Africa Conference, Lehman was one of the program speakers on innovation and social entrepreneurship. During her introduction, I noticed that she had the 'it factor': a smart, young and attractive person who smiled very easily, yet there was this sense of toughness and blunt honesty. Lehman was one of the most memorable and emotionally descriptive regarding critical healthcare conditions along the shores of Lake Tanganyika that day. Perhaps it was my misperception of a soon-to-be-rich white female surgeon leaving fortune and fame for the war-torn areas of the Democratic Republic of the Congo (DRC), but I wondered why she would leave the First World comfort of Chicago for Third World TB, malaria and AIDS-infested Tanzania, Burundi and Zambia. What was the motivation? I concluded later that it was not for money or notoriety. In addition to disease burdens in rural areas, healthcare workers are overwhelmed by the magnitude of the medical needs and unsustainable medical resources. Moreover, healthcare workers suffer from isolation from their peers, low income and government assistance irregularities which are all factors contributing to higher attrition rates. Many native doctors lose their lives medically treating patients in that part of the world.

After 15 minutes into her presentation, punctuated by an infectious laugh, unbridled courage and compassion, I looked around the room to notice that Lehman had hypnotized everyone. Oh my God, even the waiters in the room slowed down to listen. Beyond the stories of triumph, trials and terror, Lehman showed a remarkable commitment to that part of the world by displaying a huge map of Lake Tanganyika tattooed on her back.

As a child, Lehman struggled with an autoimmune disease, spending many years at home in a wheelchair. As a result, she struggled with severe nerve damage in her right arm that would later threaten her medical career. This is a sobering character-developmental phase. Collins (2005) provides a unique explanation regarding skills development called Level 5 leadership: leadership capacity builds through a paradoxical combination of personal humility plus professional will (Collins, 2005).

The Level 5 leader sits on top of a hierarchy of capabilities that are necessary requirements for transforming an organization from good to great.

Lehman trained as a cardio-thoracic surgeon at the University of Chicago Medical Center for over ten years, while balancing medical team duties and responsibilities as a single mother. Perhaps the personal isolation as a child in a wheelchair, training as a thoracic surgeon and performing life-altering operations on the heart, lungs and other chest organs shaped her values and propelled her ambitions into a life devoted to healthcare services. Altruism is fundamental to the identity of doctors, nurses and non-governmental organization (NGO) leaders who face extraordinary health challenges (Lee, 2010; Ancona et al., 2007).

Beginning in 2009, Lehman established an NGO to serve 3 million people: Lake Tanganyika Floating Health Clinic (LTFHC). The organization's mission is to provide mobile hospital care to the hard-to-reach population along the Lake Tanganyika shores that border the DRC, Burundi, Tanzania and Zambia. This is an ultra-remote area where cellphone coverage, roads, clean water, electricity and medical care are scarce to non-existent. Due to unreliable road conditions, especially during the rainy season, a fully functional ship is the most efficient platform to deliver state-of-the-art healthcare to those port locations.

CONSTRUCTING THE FUTURE VISION WITH INNOVATION

Project HOPE and Mercy Ships have made remarkable achievements in providing mobile healthcare to communities on hard-to-reach shores such as West Africa, the Amazon, India, Cambodia, Haiti and Honduras. In 2013, the award-winning CBS TV show *60 Minutes* featured the MV *Africa Mercy* providing healthcare along the coast of West Africa. This proves the viability and overwhelming response to mobile healthcare.

Lehman's goal is to use the region's major lifeline, Lake Tanganyika, to bring a hospital ship to villagers rather than villagers traveling to a remote location. A hospital ship provides a controlled, safe and clean medical environment ideally suited for serving patients. For the local community living along the lake, such a journey is unrealistic in an area where roads, electricity, running water and access to governmental health facilities are scarce or understaffed.

To safely and efficiently provide the highest level of care, the ship's design requirements include two onboard operating rooms, intensive care facilities and a small inpatient ward, ship-to-shore loading equipment for the establishment of temporary land-based patient registration and treatment areas where the majority of services would be performed, and an outboard motorboat to serve as a water-based ambulance.

LTFHC staff will provide ongoing training for local healthcare workers in SSA and around the world by way of medical student exchange programs. The opportunity to rotate on the ship fulfills a growing demand voiced by Western medical schools and students to include rotations in global healthcare as part of their curriculum. Moreover, the ship provides a platform for an invaluable cross-cultural and medical exchange of ideas, experience and knowledge (Schein, 2010).

DEVELOPING SUPPORT AND BUILDING COMMUNITY RELATIONS

Wireless cellphone coverage and wired communications options in the Lake Tanganyika basin are extremely limited due to the remoteness of healthcare centers, the terrain and distances between locations. To address this critical infrastructure issue, Lehman's LTFHC established a partnership with Hewlett-Packard (HP) in March 2012 to install high-frequency radios at eight health centers in Moba, DRC. This new system has enabled the health centers to communicate with the Moba Regional Hospital and submit reports as required, and provide monitoring and surveillance for DRC Ministry of Health activities. 'Technology can play an enabling and transformational role, improving the quality of life', says Paul Ellingstad, Global Health Director, HP Sustainability and Social Innovation. Prior to this network, nurses had to walk miles on foot just to submit reports to the central office. This is a major breakthrough and an invaluable contribution toward improving the quality of life for the area. Transformational leaders challenge the process, inspire new vision and demonstrate highly effective behavior.

Collaboration and support is an operational mandate of LTFHC. To insure sustained success, Lehman had to meet with, and win over, officials from all four nations bordering the lake and has had to familiarize herself with the various cultures. Moreover, Lehman established relationships with local business people, NGOs, multilateral organizations and, most importantly, lakeside communities. As a result, LTFHC has developed a truly unique perspective respected by the local communities. Few organizations can claim the on-the-ground knowledge and community relationship equity LTFHC has attained (Van de Ven and

Poole, 1995). As a medical organization, LTFHC has vigorously managed shipping, customs and immigration nightmares and has been steadily building community partners.

MANAGING WHERE EXTREME LEADERSHIP IS NEEDED

As a transformative leader working in extreme situations, Lehman is opening a window to capacity building and mobile healthcare access in one of the most remote regions in sub-Saharan Africa. According to Bernard Bass, leadership expert, four unique factors define transformational leadership: charisma, inspiration, intellectual stimulation and individual consideration. Transformational leaders challenge the process, inspire new vision, demonstrate highly effective behavior and encourage independent thought process (Bass, 1990). They are change agents.

In addition to being a change agent and transformational, it is paramount for the LTFHC leadership efforts to address organization culture adaptation. Organizational theorist Edgar Schein suggests that groups and organizations face two archetypical problems: (1) survival in and adaptation to the external environment; and (2) integration of the internal process to ensure the capacity to continue to survive and adapt (Schein, 2010).

Despite occasional uncertainty, risk, volatile political and economic circumstances, the team shares the leadership vision set by Lehman to serve the communities along the lake (Hailey, 2009). Academic research proclaims that leaders should possess four essential skills. First is the ability to engage others in shared meaning. Second is a distinctive and compelling voice. Third is a sense of integrity. The most critical skill of the four is called adaptive capacity (Bennis and Thomas, 2002).

FIGHTING MALARIA IN MOBA TERRITORY, DEMOCRATIC REPUBLIC OF THE CONGO, 2010

Malaria is the leading cause of morbidity and mortality in the DRC; 97 percent of the population lives in areas where disease is endemic and transmitted throughout the year. About 200 000 people die every year from this disease, many of whom are children under five years of age. Recognizing that malaria has and continues to ravage its population, the DRC is taking steps to eradicate this preventable disease. However, approximately 90 percent of the population does not have or use the recommended mosquito nets.

Long-lasting insecticide treated bed nets (LLINs) are vital tools used to decrease morbidity and mortality from malaria. The LLINS are highly cost-effective, easy to use and a major component of the WHO's anti-malaria program. In 2009, there was an 11 million net gap in the DRC, preventing the country from reaching one of the Millennium Development Goals of achieving universal bed net coverage. The Great Lakes Region Katanga Province has the single largest component of this gap, requiring some 5.5 million nets.

In 2010, Lehman and the LTFHC team developed an outreach educational project to increase awareness of malaria prevention using the LLIN insecticide nets. The outreach project is named Katanga Kicks Malaria 2010 (KKM). LTFHC launched the program to engage youth and community leaders in a sport-based malaria education project in the Katanga region of the DRC. The LTFHC team collaborated with local and national DRC government, healthcare professionals, NGOs, Congolese football players, United Nations officials and the United Nations Children's Fund (UNICEF).

WOMEN'S REPRODUCTIVE HEALTH OUTREACH PROJECT FOR FISTULA, FALL 2011

The location is Rukwa Region, Tanzania and Moba Territory, DRC, where childbearing often begins during the teen years, extreme poverty is the norm, and the population has an extremely low socio-economic status. Most births take place in ultra-rural areas along the lakeshore, with traditional birth attendants present, if anyone is present at all. This is a major contributor to the 20–25 percent childhood death rate. Women injured during childbirth can develop fistula while simultaneously experiencing the death of their child from obstructed labor.

Due to cultural norms, a women's life may change for the worse with this injury, even if she lives. Women with this condition are segregated from normal life and social interaction. Additionally, the spouse often abandons her. Furthermore, most fistula injuries can be treated successfully through appropriate surgery, if women have access to 'VVF' repair procedures. The LTFHC spearheaded a VVF repair outreach along Lake Tanganyika, on the Tanzanian side of the lake in the remote southern region of Rukwa. To carry out this outreach, the LTFHC upgraded the Kirando Health Center. The Kirando Health Center is the area's central care provider designed to serve 250 000 persons. Until the LTFHC performed the upgrade, the Kirando Health Centre functioned without running water and electricity.

Lehman shipped to Kirando from Yonkers, New York, a 40-foot container full of medical supplies and equipment needed to help refurbish the clinic and conduct planned outreach activities. Additional infrastructural work was performed to repair plumbing, sink access points and install electrical wiring. The center is currently operating at United Nations standards.

During the outreach, the Lehman's LTFHC team based in Kipili and Kirando, Tanzania, treated 44 women. LTFHC registered women identified as having fistula and who agreed to the procedure. Furthermore, during the registration period, several patients were identified and placed into LTFHC files for future treatment.

Transformational leaders challenge the process, inspire new vision and demonstrate highly effective behavior. They find projects that strategically fit their skill set or philosophy and challenge the community's status quo.

CONCLUSION

Leadership is not a position, it is a process. As a transformative leader working in extreme situations, Lehman and the LTFHC team are opening windows to capacity building and mobile healthcare access in one of the most remote regions in sub-Saharan Africa. Lehman's leadership and vision regarding the LTFHC is an example of the new generation of policy-makers and organizational leaders. Some may call their skills or traits charismatic, transformative, humility, sustaining, or just-in-time healthcare management.

Reality reveals a chilling fact that these communities do not have the required capacity to train new healthcare workers and meet the expected demand. More training and infrastructure development is clearly important but this is a long-term solution projected to take at least a decade. At the same time, there is a variety of complementary, shorter-term responses strategies to consider. For instance, the World Health Organization suggests that shifting some tasks from people requiring longer-term training to those requiring less intensive training will enable more services to be made available in a shorter time (Kinfu et al., 2009).

WHAT IS THE IMPACT OF DR LEHMAN'S LEADERSHIP?

According to Lehman:

> we've touched around 300 000 people so far. One good example is all our malaria work, including the supply of bed nets and training community health workers. We installed radios in eight health centers, which are in communications black spots. We've made a huge difference for such a tiny organization with very little funding.

Hope springs eternal.

REFERENCES

Ancona, D., T.W. Malone, W.J. Orlikowski and P.M. Senge (2007). In praise of the incomplete leader. *Harvard Business Review*, 85 (2), 92–100.

Bass, B.M. (1990). *Handbook of Leadership*. New York: Simon and Schuster.

Bennis, W.G. and R.J. Thomas (2002). Crucibles of leadership. *Harvard Business Review*, 80 (9), 39–45.

Bryan, L., M. Conway, T. Keesmaat, S. McKenna and B. Richardson (2010). Strengthening sub-Saharan Africa's health systems: a practical approach. *McKinsey Quarterly*. Retrieved from http://www.mckinsey.com/insights/health_systems_and_services/strengthening_sub-saharan_africas_health_systems_a_practical_approach.

Collins, J. (2005). Level 5 leadership: the triumph of humility and fierce resolve. *Harvard Business Review*, 83 (7–8), 136–46.

Conway, M.D., S. Gupta and K. Khajavi (2007). Addressing Africa's health workforce crisis. *McKinsey Quarterly*. Retrieved from http://www.mckinsey.it/storage/first/uploadfile/attach/139896/file/adaf07.pdf.

Hagopian, A., M.J. Thompson, M. Fordyce, K.E. Johnson and L.G. Hart (2004). The migration of physicians from sub-Saharan Africa to the United States of America: measures of the African brain drain. *Human Resources for Health*, 2 (1), 17.

Hailey, J. (2009). NGO leadership development: a review of the literature. International NGO Training and Research Centre (INTRAC).

Kalipeni, E., L.L. Semu and M.A. Mbilizi (2012). The brain drain of health care professionals from sub-Saharan Africa: a geographic perspective. *Progress in Development Studies*, 12 (2–3), 153–71. DOI: 10.1177/146499341101200305.

Kinfu, Y., M.R. Dal Poz, H. Mercer and D.B. Evans (2009). The health worker shortage in Africa: are enough physicians and nurses being trained? *Bulletin of the World Health Organization*, 87 (3), 225–30.

Kumar, P. (2007). Providing the providers – remedying Africa's shortage of health care workers. *New England Journal of Medicine*, 356 (25), 2564–7.

Lee, T.H. (2010). Turning doctors into leaders. *Harvard Business Review*, 88 (4), 50–58.

Madulu, N.F. (2005). Population distribution and density in Tanzania: experiences from 2002 population and housing census. *African Journal of Environmental Assessment and Management*, 10, 26–49.

Mills, E.J., S. Kanters and A. Hagopian (2011). The financial cost of doctors emigrating from sub-Saharan Africa: human capital analysis. *British Medical Journal*, 243, 13.

Nartker, A.J., L. Stevens, A. Shumays, M. Kalowela, D. Kisimbo and K. Potter (2010). Increasing health worker capacity through distance learning: a comprehensive review of programmes in Tanzania. *Human Resources for Health*, 10. DOI: 10.1186/1478-4491-8-30.

Nyoni, J., A. Gbary, M. Awases, P. Ndecki and R. Chatora (2006). *Policies and Plans for Human Resources for Health. Guidelines for Countries in the WHO African Region*. Brazzaville: WHO Regional Office for Africa.

Ogilvie, L., J.E. Mill, B. Astle, A. Fanning and M. Opare (2007). The exodus of health professionals from sub-Saharan Africa: balancing human rights and societal needs in the twenty-first century. *Nursing Inquiry*, 14 (2), 114–24.

Schein, E.H. (2010). *Organizational Culture and Leadership*, 4th edn. San Francisco, CA: Jossey-Bass.

Skeldon, R. (2008). International migration as a tool in development policy: a passing phase? *Population and Development Review*, 34 (1), 1–18.

Van de Ven, A.H. and M.S. Poole (1995). Explaining development and change in organizations. *Academy of Management Review*, 20 (3), 510–40.

WHO (2006). *Working Together for Health: The World Health Report 2006*. Geneva: World Health Organization.

10. Bringing up the Thirty-Three: emergent principles in multi-tiered leadership

Michael Useem, Rodrigo Jordán and Matko Koljatic*

> You need to collect all the information and then decide on a plan and then get the whole country behind the plan. Accelerate the speed of the process; set goals and don't waste time. Ask for help. Show that you are in charge. Act specifically. Spread out the responsibility.
>
> Sebastián Piñera, President of the Republic of Chile

Disaster struck on 5 August 2010. A massive cave-in entombed 33 miners drilling 700 meters below the surface. They had been working in a medium-sized copper and gold mine beneath the moon-like wilderness of the Atacama Desert near the city of Copiapó, Republic of Chile, 800 kilometers north of Chile's capital, Santiago.

Chilean mining minister Laurence Golborne arrived that evening in Quito, Ecuador on a state visit with the Chilean president, Sebastián Piñera. At 11 p.m., Golborne's smartphone came to life with a message whose starkness spoke its urgency: 'Mine cave-in, Copiapó; 33 victims.'

Golborne, an engineer, entrepreneur and manager, had served as chief executive of Cencosud S.A., a large retail firm, and under his eight-year direction, the company had expanded annual sales tenfold. He had been called by President Piñera to join the government less than five months before. With plenty of management experience but no background in mining and just months in office, he knew he would have to act. How to do so and with whom was less obvious.

TIERS OF LEADERSHIP

If Golborne were to engage in or even lead the miners' recovery, it would have to be in tandem with a leader among the stranded miners themselves, most probably shift supervisor Luis Urzúa. Unknown to those above, the group of 33 would hunker down as the dust settled in a small cavity. The miners quickly concluded that the odds of a rescue were small but not zero. Organizing themselves to survive with water but virtually no food until a rescue became Urzúa's calling.

Two separate leadership efforts at the stricken mine – one already underway below, one getting underway above – would have to be combined for either to succeed, just as they were in 1970 when NASA, the National Aeronautics and Space Administration, successfully returned the damaged spacecraft, *Apollo 13*, to Earth after the near fatal explosion of an oxygen tank.

Three astronauts aboard *Apollo 13*, led by flight commander James Lovell, had fought to preserve the few remaining resources left on board the spacecraft after the explosion. Separately, the ground crew in Houston, led by flight director Eugene Kranz, had worked to ensure that the astronauts found the resources necessary for re-entry into the Earth's atmosphere. Together, their combined leadership of the flight team and ground crew produced one of the golden moments in American space-flight history, the safe return of the *Apollo 13* astronauts (Kluger and Lovell, 1994; Useem, 1998; Kranz, 2009).

In the miners' rescue an additional tier of leadership alongside that of the shift supervisor and the mining minister would prove vital as well. The third tier would be exercised by Golborne's superior, the President of Chile. Sebastián Piñera had been inaugurated less than five months earlier on 11 March. Before taking office, he had acquired a personal fortune by finding risky opportunities in business and making the most of them, thriving where major opportunities and risks coexisted.

Extreme risks and opportunities would certainly come into sharp focus during the days ahead, and as a result, so too would Piñera's leadership in concert with that of Golborne and Urzúa. All three would have to work together to overcome a host of urgent and complex challenges in the days ahead if each was to succeed.

In examining the multi-tiered leadership that did emerge to achieve the golden moment in Chilean mining rescue history, we seek to extract essential principles for multi-tiered leadership during exceptional times. For reasons of space, we focus in this chapter on the top tier and its relationship with the middle tier, leaving the role of the middle tier itself and the front-line tier for elsewhere (see, for instance, Franklin, 2011; Pino, 2011; Useem et al., 2011a, 2011b).

MULTI-TIERED LEADERSHIP

The impact of tiered leadership is likely to be particularly important in periods of uncertainty, urgency and complexity. It is then that leadership decisions are likely to be stronger if they are shaped by guidance from multiple levels, and it is also then that essential resources are more likely to be mobilized if several tiers of leadership are simultaneously engaged. Building on March and Simon's (1958) work on organizations, Thompson for instance has argued that 'coordination by mutual adjustment may involve communications across hierarchical lines', and that the more uncertain the situation, the greater an organization's reliance on that vertical coordination (Thompson, 1967, p. 56).

The importance of hierarchical coordination can be seen in Klein et al.'s (2006) study of 'extreme action' medical teams in emergency trauma centers that face complex, fast-changing and time-sensitive tasks. The researchers found that teams worked to achieve their overall goals through a vertical system of 'shared leadership' that entailed frequent delegation of specific leadership roles to subordinate members of the trauma teams.

Writing in the same conceptual vein, Küpers and Weibler (2008) have argued for viewing leadership as less 'person-centered' and more a 'relational' and 'collective phenomenon' that entails 'multiple levels' of working collaboration. Others have similarly pressed for appreciating that leadership is often exercised through the collaboration of several levels (Berson et al., 2006; Hannah and Lester, 2009; Yammarino et al., 2005; Yukl, 2012).

The value of examining leadership across vertical tiers of authority, one of several multiple-level dimensions, can be seen for instance in a study of product innovation among 15 large US firms. The authors found product innovation to be facilitated when leaders of the innovations maintained effective upward relations with senior company leaders and secured essential resources from them (Dougherty and Hardy, 1996).

Drawing on these concepts and concerns, this chapter seeks to identify the components of what is critical to the multi-tiered exercise of leadership in a period of high uncertainty and great complexity. The rescue of the miners in Chile offers an opportunity to flesh out the dynamics of tiered leadership in the extreme. We seek to identify the mission-critical principles that underlie the exercise of multi-tiered leadership when it is likely to have large impact.

INFORMATION SOURCES

With an estimated 1400 journalists descending on the San José mine in northern Chile, publicly available accounts of the rescue steps would become extensive and serve as a valuable source. Much of the president's leadership and that of the mining minister would be conducted behind closed doors, however, and we have of necessity conducted more than 15 hours of interviews and meetings with those directly involved in the top and middle tiers of the rescue. While some of these private sources requested anonymity, those that did not are identified in Table 10.1. Except where otherwise indicated, quoted material is drawn from these interviews.

Table 10.1   Private information sources

Leader	Title	Date
René Aguilar	Head of Safety, El Teniente mine, Codelco; Deputy Chief of Rescue	22 December 2010; 14 March 2012
Cristián Barra	Cabinet Chief, Ministry of the Interior	5 January 2011
Laurence Golborne	Minister of Mines; Chief of Rescue	1 November 2010; 22 June 2011
Luz Granier	Chief of Staff, Minister of Mines	1 November 2010
Roberto Matus	Deputy Chief of Mission, Embassy of Chile, Washington, DC	23 February 2012
Sebastián Piñera	President, Republic of Chile	15 March 2012
André Sougarret	Manager, El Teniente mine, Codelco; Chief Engineer for the Rescue	5 January 2011

TAKING CHARGE

The day after receiving the smartphone message about the cave-in, Golborne deliberated on his response:

When I woke up at 7 in the morning, I was wondering whether I should go or not. We did not have a good assessment of the situation. Also, you have to consider that I did not come from the world of mining and I did not know what had to be done. From 5000 kilometers away, I didn't know much, but I did understand the magnitude of the problem.

Despite the ambivalence, Golborne quickly concluded he should fly to the site of the disaster. 'Mining is my subject in the government', he explained. In doing so, however, he would likely commit the government to resolving the crisis and perhaps even running the rescue, with all the political risks that that entailed. Though a disaster not of the government's making, as soon as Golborne reached the site, his government would begin to own the rescue. But when Golborne asked the president over breakfast for permission to return, Piñera did not hesitate: 'Yes, yes, go!'

Upon reaching the stricken mine at 3.30 a.m. the next day, 7 August, Golborne noted that CNN and other channels were already broadcasting live, early signs of a media deluge soon to follow. The mining minister briefed the president by satellite telephone at dawn and several more times during the morning hours. The news was not encouraging. The miners, if still alive, were far below the surface, the shafts leading to them were blocked or too unsafe to use, and any solution seemed far beyond the operator's capacities. Golborne privately concluded that the miners would likely never even be found, let alone located alive. Though Chile's president was by then in Colombia for the inauguration of its new president, he broke off his official visit to return home.

The paths and intentions of the president and mining minister converged as events unfolded on 7 August. Golborne joined an emergency meeting with the mine owner and his rescue team, but the mining minister soon realized that confusion prevailed. Even elemental facts such as the number of trapped miners – estimates ranged from 33 to 37 – could not be verified. As a result, Golborne asserted control of the emergency gathering and, by unspoken implication, control of the rescue plan and organization that would have to follow.

Flying back to Chile at the same time, Piñera called mining officials, foreign companies, even country leaders. Knowing that the presidential aircraft would be passing over the site of the disaster on its way to Santiago, the president ordered an unscheduled stop at Copiapó. By time his flight landed at 10 p.m. that evening, his resolve pointed in the same direction as Golborne's. 'When I was informed that the company that owned the mine was not capable to do the search operation', the president said, 'I made a simple decision: it was the government or nobody.' As the president told Cristián Barra, a senior official who met the aircraft on the ground: 'We are not going to rest until we find them and bring them out.'

By now, Golborne realized that he would be expected by many in Chile to take responsibility for the crisis and for the rescue, given his title and given that the miners' lives and country's reputation were at stake. With the resources of the national government at his disposal, he was arguably the best-positioned individual in Chile to manage the effort. Still, the odds would be long. The team leader of the failed search had already informed Golborne, 'They must be dead', and, 'if they are not dead, they will die'.

Then, a tumultuous meeting with the victims' relatives moved Golborne toward fuller ownership of the rescue. When his voice faltered, the wife of one of the miners shouted, 'Minister, you cannot break down. You have to give us strength!' It would be difficult to explain to the relatives, or anybody in Chile, he concluded, if he did not stay composed – and especially if he did not take charge. 'Although I do not come from the mining world and was questioning myself [on] what I could do in the mine,' he said, 'I understood I had to be there.'

When the president joined the families with the mining minister, the relatives complained about the tepid response and failed effort so far. Many came from a mining tradition and knew well the technical issues confronting the rescue. They demanded that the mine's management be pushed aside. They insisted on the inclusion of a local geologist who had been urging boreholes to locate the miners. The president agreed on the spot to include the geologist, but then far more. 'We are going to search for them', the president avowed, 'as if they were our children.'

Two formalities followed. The interior minister decreed that the government controlled the mine, and the president declared that the mining minister was in charge. In doing so, reported informed observers, President Piñera drew on his confidence in Golborne that had already been established during the regime's short time in office. They had not worked together before 11 March 2012 when President Piñera had taken office, but Golborne had quickly distinguished himself in the president's eyes. 'Piñera learned to trust Golborne', explained one government official, 'because his handling of the tasks at the mining ministry had been outstanding.'

DEFINING THE MISSION

Golborne had warned the president against making the unscheduled stop at Copiapó on 8 August, fearing that a presidential visit would make it even more compromising for the government if the crisis worsened. *Newsweek* magazine publicly expressed what many around the president were saying privately:

> Disaster and politics make a volatile cocktail, as risky as it is tempting. A successful rescue can create an instant hero, bathing a leader in glory before a global audience. But a bungled operation, an outright tragedy, or even dubious behavior by a national leader while the world is watching can just as quickly cripple a government and bury a political career. (Margolis, 2010)

But the president had already made up his mind to define the government's mission as a full-throttled rescue, a choice that was well in keeping with his decisive temperament, as captured in the words of one senior official: 'President Piñera does not appear to have second thoughts. He does not show doubts. Maybe he internally has second thoughts and doubts, but he never shows them.' The president became fixed on a goal until new data dictated otherwise: 'He looks for information, forms an opinion, and then decides until new information is available.' Applied in this instance, said the official, 'it was a clear cut decision to search for the miners'.

Still, the commitment came with significant risks, and the president's inner circle was already working on 'damage control' in case the rescue failed. 'If things went well,' said one advisor, 'it would be great, but, the downside – if things went bad – was enormous.' Golborne repeatedly cautioned against presidential visits, warning that a worsening crisis could impose irreversible damage on the presidency.

The president himself appreciated the perils. 'We took a lot of risks', he said. 'What if we never found them or if we found them all dead?' But in his risk-and-opportunity calculus, the latter offset the former. 'President Piñera was aware of the risks', recalled Golborne. 'But he is trained in weighing costs and benefits of actions. He is not irresponsible. He weighs every decision, costs and benefits, and then decides.' The president later explained his decision to embrace the mission:

> When I returned from Colombia, my staff was telling me, 'Don't get close to the San José mine because it is going to end in a tragedy.' I told them, 'Even if there is one probability in one million of finding them alive, I shall do whatever is necessary to rescue them because it is my duty as president of

Chile, and I believe that, with God's help, with the help of many, with technology, and an unshakeable faith, we will achieve a miracle.' (*El Tiempo*, 2010)

The president had made it clear both privately and publicly that the miners must be located whatever the hazards or costs. As recalled by another top official, 'Piñera was telling Golborne, once and again: "you have to find them, you have to find them!" The "mission impossible" message never got to Piñera.'

The president's ownership of the rescue mission aligned and emboldened the large rescue team that Golborne would assemble in the days ahead. The unambiguous backing by the nation's chief executive steadied the hand of those on the ground who themselves were deeply affected by the crisis. René Aguilar, a key member of the team, recalled the stress of the moment: 'I felt anguish every night, as we did not know whether the men were alive. Every night, when leaving the mine, I had to walk through the camp; I would see the banners saying: "Daddy, we are waiting for you" and "Son, we are here".'

The president's embrace of the recovery helped Golborne's team focus on the task at hand and sustain its equanimity. 'If you are not conscious of why you have to stand the pressure, it is difficult', said Aguilar. 'We had a mission: to rescue the men!' Despite deep doubts on whether they would find anybody alive, the rescuers did not doubt the top tier's resolve to reach them.

EFFECTING THE RESCUE

President Piñera flew to Santiago on 8 August but returned the next day with two individuals who were to be added to Golborne's rescue team: André Sougarret, who would direct the engineering, and René Aguilar, who would work with the miners' relatives. Barra, already on site, would manage the rescue team's relations with the national government.

The decision to bring Sougarret onto the rescue team was indicative of the president's swift and deep commitment to the rescue. The president asked Gerardo Jofré, chair of the state-owned copper enterprise, National Copper Corporation of Chile (Codelco), for a top-flight mining engineer to direct the rescue's engineering, and the company singled out Sougarret, then manager of El Teniente, the largest of the state-owned mines and one of the largest underground copper mines anywhere.

Soon after the cave-in, the board chair called Sougarret: 'This is a thing at the highest level', he said. 'You have to show up at La Moneda', the presidential palace. With no further information and no more than a hard hat and a small backpack, Sougarret was dispatched to the president's aircraft which was being readied for a flight to the stricken mine. Once airborne, President Piñera called Sougarret forward to his private cabin.

The president explained what he knew of the disaster and then told Sougarret that his mission now was to rescue the miners – and that he could count on all necessary resources from the president. Sougarret knew too little about the situation to offer any real response, and he soon he found himself with the president in a tent with 50 of the lost miners' relatives. Their faces spoke of desperation. The president explained that he had come with the experts, including those at his side, and he would provide them with all the resources they would need. Only then did Sougarret fully appreciate that 'I would have to take charge of the operation'. The president departed, leaving Sougarret on the spot, and that, he recalled, 'was a key moment for me, the start of everything' (Rojas, 2010).

Fourteen days later the team's borehole under Sougarret's guidance pierced a cavity 688 meters below. Not sure what a camera later to be lowered would reveal, Piñera nonetheless immediately flew back to the mine. 'We have to learn to be visible in the good times,' he explained to Barra, 'and the bad ones.' This time it proved better than good. On 17 August, President Piñera held up a note which had been taped to the bottom of a retracted drill head: 'Estamos bien en el refugio, los 33' – 'We are well in the shelter, the 33.'

The president publicly praised the 'strength, bravery and courage' of the miners, the relatives 'who never lost hope', and the rescue team 'who spared no effort to find the miners'. Several days later he reiterated the mission yet again, and now fixed a date for its completion: 'We will continue doing whatever is humanly possible to rescue the miners', and, 'they will be with us for Christmas and the New Year' (Government of Chile, 2010).

The president telephoned country leaders around the world for technology and assistance, including the US president. The White House called back an hour later with help. NASA joined the rescue, along with US companies including Aramark, Center Rock, Schramm and UPS.

In the days that followed, Golborne led the rescue on site, but the president remained directly engaged, following daily developments and arranging for additional resources. 'Piñera was always saying the government is here', reported one of the rescuers. And he himself was frequently there, making six trips to the mine in the weeks ahead.

On 12 October the rescue team began winching the miners one by one up an enlarged shaft in a capsule designed with the help of NASA. At 8.55 p.m. on 13 October, shift supervisor Luis Urzúa, the last of the lost, emerged on the surface. He announced to Piñera, 'I've delivered to you this shift of workers, as we agreed I would.' The president replied, 'I gladly receive your shift because you completed your duty, leaving last, like a good captain', adding, 'You are not the same after this, and Chile won't be the same either.' Several rescue paramedics still underground held up a sign a live telecast: 'Misión cumplida Chile' – 'Mission accomplished Chile'.

Urzúa's team leadership in the cavity was credited for sustaining the 33 miners throughout their ordeal. Golborne's organized leadership on the surface was credited for rescuing the miners. And Piñera's sovereign leadership from the capital was credited for focusing the country's resolve and resources to bringing up the 33.

The president had authorized the mining minister to take charge of the rescue at a mine that the government did not own or control; he committed his government to backing the rescue, a risky endeavor opposed by many in his own administration; he recruited technical experts and specialized equipment from home and abroad; and he publicly and privately expressed unvarying support for Golborne's leadership initiatives throughout the ordeal, all in a race against time. In the summary observation of one journalist, 'Piñera oversaw the rescue of the 33 miners like a field marshal on the front' (Margolis, 2010).

TIERED LEADERSHIP FOR EXTREME EVENTS

'Black swans' are those low-probability but high-consequence events whose chaotic consequences are usually accompanied by a sudden leadership vacuum. Emergency responders have long followed a protocol of assigning one individual to serve as incident commander, but extreme events, such as the mining cave-in, rarely come with such pre-set templates (Taleb, 2010; Bostrom and Ćirković, 2008; Collins and Hansen, 2011; Hammond, 2000; James and Wooten, 2010; Kunreuther and Useem, 2010; Perrow, 2011).

In that void, President Piñera built the leadership required to surmount the crisis, taking charge when nobody was in charge. But in doing so, he also depended on the separate exercise of leadership at two other tiers as well. Had Urzúa failed to lead his fellow miners through their weeks of deprivation and stress, and had Golborne failed to lead his rescue team through their weeks of drilling and extraction, Piñera's leadership efforts would have been for naught.

From witnessing the exercise of multi-tiered leadership during the rescue of the 33 miners, with a special focus on the top tier and its relationship with the middle tier, we see five emergent principles for the exercise of multi-tiered leadership during extreme events. Each comes with distinct directives for those leading at the middle or upper tier, as summarized in Table 10.2.

Table 10.2   Principles of tiered leadership in extreme events

A. Upper tier	B. Middle tier
Taking charge, defining the mission and thinking strategically:	
1. Taking charge, defining the overarching mission, and thinking strategically.	1. Taking charge, embracing the level-specific mission, and thinking strategically.
Commitment and evidence:	
2. Unequivocal downward display of commitment and confidence.	2. Consistent upward conveyance of information and forecasts.
Resources and credit:	
3. Provision of resources to the middle tier and explicit sharing of credit with it.	3. Deliberate upward sharing of visibility and credit for milestones in surmounting the crisis.
Decision-making:	
4. Clear expression of strategic intent without micromanaging the middle tier's decisions.	4. Taking major decisions upward for review and approval by the higher tier.
Risk-taking:	
5. Recognition and management of the risks faced by both the upper and middle tiers.	5. Recognition and management of the risks faced by both the upper and middle tiers.

By way of brief illustration, consider principle B3, the middle tier's upward sharing of visibility for milestones in surmounting an extreme event. Since 1400 journalists had assembled at the mining site, virtually every utterance and decision by officials became nationally and globally newsworthy. The minister of mines, as a result, gave careful thought to the timing of presidential visits to the rescue site to ensure that the president received proper recognition for his leadership behind the scenes.

Or consider the exercise of principle A5, appreciating and acting on the professional risks faced by both oneself and one's counterpart at the other tier. In deciding to authorize the rescue and assign the mining minister to direct it, the president understood and accepted that he was placing his political capital at substantial risk. At the same time, he would also have to appreciate that his mining minister would be burdened with the prospect of a career-ending political disaster if he failed to execute the rescue.

CONCLUSION

From our study of the exercise of leadership during an event while 33 miners waited and much of the world watched – more than 1 billion people were estimated to have viewed the rescue live – we have seen the special value of multi-tiered leadership. As also witnessed during the rescue of *Apollo 13*, each tier's leadership worked in ways that were mindful of the other's leadership imperatives, and neither tier could succeed without the other's distinctive actions. While the middle tier was the most visible party in leading the miners' rescue in Chile, that tier would likely not have succeeded without the coordinated actions of the upper tier as well.

We have also seen how March and Simon's (1958) and Thompson's (1967) stress on vertical coordination in periods of uncertainty and complexity has been mindfully enacted by the central figures in the miners' rescue. And as expected from the findings of Dougherty and Hardy (1996), we have found specifically in this case that the middle tier had built relations with the upper tier to help secure resources, and that those relations proved essential for the rescue, as captured in principles A3 and B2 in Table 10.2. Less anticipated from prior research, but instructively emergent from the present study, the upper tier also conveyed strong downward commitment to and confidence in the middle-tier leader – and the middle tier reciprocated by sharing visibility and credit with the upper tier for achieving both the intermediate and final steps, as characterized by principles A2 and B3.

We conclude by suggesting that a fully elaborated model for multi-tiered leadership in extreme circumstances would include the five upper- and middle-tier principles in Table 10.2 along with their equivalent for the lower tier. We also believe that this model is not complete and that additional principles can and should be drawn from the grounded studies of extreme leadership reported in this book and elsewhere.

By building on repeated close-in examinations of leadership in a range of extreme moments, we can construct a more complete model, we believe, and that model will be particularly important for periods of uncertainty that help define when extreme leadership is most essential. It is then, as Gawande (2009) and others who have focused on surgical teams have argued, that a complete list of decision principles becomes particularly important (Brinkmeyer, 2010; de Vries et al., 2010; Haynes et al., 2009; Useem, 2011).

Failure by any of the tiers to embrace all – not just some – of their level-specific mission-critical leadership principles can prove impairing or even catastrophic. Conversely, as we have seen in Chile, their full embracement by two tiers working together produced a life-saving outcome for all.

NOTE

* Includes some ideas from *Developing Global Leaders* by Bob Johnson and Rob Oberwise, Palgrave-Macmillan, 2011.

REFERENCES

Berson, Yair, Louise A. Nemanich, David A. Waldman, Benjamin M. Galvin and Robert T. Keller (2006). Leadership and organizational learning: a multiple levels perspective. *Leadership Quarterly*, 17, 577–94.

Bostrom, Nick and Milan M. Ćirković (2008). *Global Catastrophic Risks*. Oxford: Oxford University Press.

Brinkmeyer, John D. (2010). Strategies for improving surgical quality checklists and beyond. *New England Journal of Medicine*, 363, 1963–65.

Collins, Jim, and Morten T. Hansen (2011). *Great by Choice: Uncertainty, Chaos, and Luck – Why Some Thrive Despite Them All*. HarperCollins.

de Vries, Eefje N., Hubert A. Prins, Rogier M.P.H. Crolla, Adriaan J. den Outer, George van Andel, Sven H. van Helden, Wolfgang S. Schlack, M. Agnès van Putten, Dirk J. Gouma, Marcel G.W. Dijkgraaf, Susanne M. Smorenburg and Marja A. Boermeester for the SURPASS Collaborative Group (2010). Effect of a comprehensive surgical safety system on patient outcomes. *New England Journal of Medicine*, 363, 1928–37.

Dougherty, Deborah and Cynthia Hardy (1996). Sustained product innovation in large, mature organizations: overcoming innovation-to-organization problems. *Academy of Management Journal*, 39, 1120–53.

El Tiempo (2010). Empresarios colombianos no deben temerle a la competencia: Piñera. 27 November.

Franklin, Jonathan (2011). *33 Men: Inside the Miraculous Survival and Dramatic Rescue of the Chilean Miners*. Putnam.

Gawande, Atul (2009). *The Checklist Manifesto: How to Get Things Right*. Holt.

Government of Chile (2010). http://www.gobiernodechile.cl/cronologia-los-hitos-del-rescate-de-los-33-mineros, October 12.

Hammond, Kenneth R. (2000). *Judgment Under Stress*. Oxford: Oxford University Press.

Hannah, S.T. and P.B. Lester (2009). A multilevel approach to building and leading learning organizations. *Leadership Quarterly*, 20, 34–48.

Haynes, Alex B. et al. (2009). A surgical safety checklist to reduce morbidity and mortality in a global population. *New England Journal of Medicine*, 360, 491–99.

James, Erika Hayes and Lynn Perry Wooten (2010). *Leading Under Pressure*. Routledge.

Klein, Katherine, Jonathan C. Ziegert, Andrew P. Knight and Yan Xiao (2006). Dynamic delegation: hierarchical, shared, and deindividualized leadership in extreme action teams. *Administrative Science Quarterly*, 51, 590–621.

Kluger, Jeffrey and James Lovell (1994). *Lost Moon: The Perilous Voyage of Apollo 13*. Houghton Mifflin.

Kranz, Eugene (2009). *Failure Is Not an Option: Mission Control from Mercury to Apollo 13 and Beyond*. Simon and Schuster.

Kunreuther, Howard and Michael Useem (eds) (2010). *Learning from Catastrophes*. Pearson.

Küpers, Wendelin and Jürgen Weibler (2008). Inter-leadership: why and how should we think of leadership and followership integrally? *Leadership*, 4, 443.

March, James G. and Herbert Alexander Simon (1958). *Organizations*. Wiley.

Margolis, Marc (2010). *Newsweek*, October 13. www.thedailybeast.com/newsweek/chilean-president.

Perrow, Charles (2011). *The Next Catastrophe: Reducing Our Vulnerabilities to Natural, Industrial, and Terrorist Disasters*. Princeton University Press.

Pino, Manuel (2011). *Buried Alive: The True Story of the Chilean Mining Disaster and the Extraordinary Rescue at Camp Hope*. Palgrave.

Rojas, Rocío Montes (2010). Chile – rescate de mineros: entrevista a André Sougarret – rescate de mineros. *El Mercurio*, 17 October.

Taleb, Nassim Nicholas (2010). *The Black Swan: The Impact of the Highly Improbable*. Random House.

Thompson, James D. (1967). *Organizations in Action, Social Science Bases of Administrative Theory*. McGraw-Hill.

Useem, Michael (1998). *The Leadership Moment: Nine True Stories and Their Lessons for Us All*. Random House.

Useem, Michael (2011). *The Leader's Checklist: Fifteen Mission-Critical Principles*. Wharton Digital Press.

Useem, Michael, Rodrigo Jordan and Matko Koljatic (2011a). How to lead during a crisis: lessons from the rescue of the Chilean miners. *MIT Sloan Management Review*, 53 (Fall), 1–7.

Useem, Michael, Rodrigo Jordan and Matko Koljatic (2011b). Leading the rescue of the miners in Chile. Case, Wharton School, University of Pennsylvania, and School of Business Administration, Pontifical Catholic University of Chile. Http://kw.wharton.upenn.edu/wdp/files/2011/07/Leading-the-Miners-Rescue.pdf.

Yammarino, Francis J., Shelley D. Dionne, Jae Uk Chun and Fred Dansereau (2005). Leadership and levels of analysis: a state-of-the-science review. *Leadership Quarterly*, 16, 879–919.

Yukl, Gary (2012). Effective leadership behavior: what we know and what questions need more attention. *Academy of Management Perspectives*, 26, 66–85.

11. Team leadership: the Chilean mine case

Terri A. Scandura and Monica M. Sharif

INTRODUCTION

The world watched in awe as the first of the 33 Chilean miners emerged from the transport tube. Without a doubt, the rescue of the miners in October 2010 was an impressive technological achievement. But perhaps the more enduring lessons from the mine may relate more to team leadership under what are now known to be among the most extreme conditions imaginable. Textbooks and popular books have been written on the subject of team leadership. However, the events that unfolded in the mine offer lessons for both students and managers alike on how to build and sustain a team that can survive hardships and change.

This exploratory chapter will first present a summary of the Chilean mine incident. It will then present well-known frameworks for team leadership in organizations and reflect upon how the Chilean miners' experience both illustrates and informs these frameworks. The goals are to advance a viewpoint that may be used to teach team leadership to students in an interesting and relevant way, and to offer some new ideas for theory and research on team leadership in organizations. It is important to note that the Chilean mine disaster represented a multi-team system (DeChurch and Marks, 2006). There was a team working on the rescue above the surface, and a team of trapped miners below the surface. Our discussion will draw from examples of each team, and also the interplay between them after contact was made with the miners with the drill. While our review is not exhaustive with respect to the literature on team leadership, it will be representative of the most commonly discussed issues in leadership in team contexts, including multi-team systems. Therefore, this chapter will increase knowledge on leadership by integrating previous research on teams to describe the success of team processes in this extreme scenario. This chapter will also add to the literature on rare events (that is, Baker et al., 2006; Ciborra, 1999;

Crossan et al., 2005) by presenting another scenario where improvisation is crucial to team processes.

THE CHILEAN MINE CASE

Prior to the accident, the Chilean mine team was most similar to a functional work team in which the members had moderate authority to determine work procedures and a strong leader. The team was cohesive, and accustomed to taking direction from their leader, shift foreman Luis Urzúa. Further, they had a history of working together, membership was stable and diversity was low. In terms of skills, the miners had minimal supplies to survive. There was a storeroom with two tanks of oxygen, and a limited amount of food and water (Franklin, 2011). The following quote from one of the miners describes the onset of the collapse:

> At about two o'clock in the afternoon, we were suddenly overwhelmed by the powerful thundering of rocks. The explosion of rocks was like a rolling wave that left us covered with dirt. There was a dense cloud of dust that would take four long hours to dissipate. The human soul tends to perceive these events in terms of their own story, but the first thing we all thought to do was to stand very still several seconds until we could get a better sense of the danger that had so abruptly interrupted our routine. (Henriquez, 2011, pp. 55–6)

Accounts of the Chilean miners' social system during the days trapped under the ground reveal that the leader established priorities and that a democratic style of decision-making emerged (Franklin, 2011; Henriquez, 2011). Alex Vega, mechanic, noted, 'The hierarchy was lost almost immediately ... The thirty-three of us were one and we began a democratic system; the best idea that made the most sense was the idea that ruled' (as reported by Franklin, 2011, p. 61).

The Chilean miners clearly stayed focused on a goal, which was that all 33 men would survive. Urzúa reinforced this goal by insisting that he would be the last miner to leave, and he followed through on this promise. During the days and nights in the mine, the miners remained focused on small tasks, such as food rationing – cookies, milk, cans of tuna and a can of peaches. They would each eat small portions every 48 hours, knowing that rationing was necessary because the food needed to last at least three weeks.

Miners had a high degree of role clarity related to their skill sets and there was a complementary skill set within the team (Klimoski and Jones, 1995). In the mine, there were electricians (one of whom was a medical worker), machine operators, drillers, mechanics, drivers, a hydraulic engineer, a topographer (also the shift foreman), a manager and a supervisor (Henriquez, 2011, pp. 115–16). Urzúa's skills as a topographer were key, as he made a rough sketch to determine where they were located as one of his first tasks (Franklin, 2011). The medical worker's skill set was very important as the physical condition of the miners deteriorated while waiting for rescue, due to dehydration, starvation and lack of sleep. Problems started emerging immediately, especially with regards to urinary tract obstruction, that had to be treated without medication (Fraser, 2010). He monitored each miner's condition, and while scratched and bruised, there were no serious injuries from the blast. Some other miners monitored environmental conditions and others drilled for water (Fraser, 2010). All of the miners knew how to operate equipment, and used the equipment to make loud noises, hoping someone would hear them.

On 22 August 2010, at 5.50 a.m., there was a key transition for the functioning of both teams. At first, the drill missed the miners. The miners heard it pass them, and then realized it was below them. The miners struck the drill with metal, and then painted it orange with spray paint they had in their mining supplies. They attached plastic bags with notes in them. The drill was drawn back up to the surface. At first the rescue team was not sure if they had found the miners on that try. But then they saw the orange paint and knew it was a signal. From that moment of transition, the multi-team system worked together to gather information from below through the notes and a camera, to determine what supplies were immediately needed for survival while a plan was implemented to send the rescue capsule to them. The ordeal of starvation and fear had come to an end. The next task became one of rescue and coordination with the rescue team above.

The team leader divided the miners into three shifts, organized around their living arrangements. After contact was made with the rescue team, he followed the advice of experts on the surface and created a dark area for sleeping, a light one for community activities, and a dim area for work activities to simulate normal awake and rest periods. One of the first items sent down the tube created to send essentials to the team was a questionnaire to assess the health of each miner (Fraser, 2010). This was followed by glucose, electrolytes and high-protein liquids before solid food was sent.

Urzúa maintained control of his team in the most challenging of circumstances. He created a shared vision, used ceremonies and rituals (they held church services, prayed and sang Elvis Presley songs to pass the time). His symbolic gesture to be the last one to leave the mine was a motivating force, and they celebrated the small achievements such as the moment when they first saw the rescue capsule. Urzúa adapted his leadership style from the military-type style typical of mining operations to a style where decisions were made in a democratic way; the miners reported that they each had a vote on important decisions after they were discussed. After all of the 33 miners were rescued, Diaz, head of the medical team that monitored the miners, reflected, 'This has practically been a complete rescue ... We have learned how important it is to have a cohesive group of workers' (Fraser, 2010, p. 1379).

TEAM LEADERSHIP IN EXTREME SITUATIONS

Most treatments of teams and team leadership begin with definitional matters relating to the type of team being considered. These types range from functional work teams and cross-functional teams to self-managed teams and top executive teams (Yukl, 2010). Teams have been defined as groupings of individuals who are interdependent and have a common purpose (Katzenbach and Smith, 1993). The Chilean mine team was a functional work team and members had some authority to determine work procedures. They also had a strong leader and a history of working together. It is important to consider these initial inputs to the team process since it is clear that they are related to how the team survived as the crisis unfolded. More importantly for this analysis, the mine disaster meets all of the criteria discussed in the literature on extreme or disruptive team contexts (Hannah et al., 2009).

This case illustrates the importance of the relationship of team inputs to the team process. The miners' ultimate survival depended upon how they put both material and human resources to use by setting up a cooperative behavioral system. Additionally, it was clear that dynamic adjustment and improvisation was necessary for the rescue team to locate and save the miners. Our analysis will demonstrate the pivotal role of team leadership and the key process variables identified in research on teams that contributed to the survival of the miners.

TEAM LEADERSHIP IN THE CHILEAN MINE CASE

Theory and research on leadership in extreme contexts is in its nascent stage. However, there has been increasing interest in the subject. Hannah et al. (2009) developed a framework for the examination of leadership in extreme contexts. They defined extreme contexts as those that have physical and/or psycho-social consequences for members that are 'unbearable', and these circumstances challenge the organization's ability to prevent them. The collapse of the mine is clearly an extreme context. According to Hannah et al., the role of leadership in such contexts must be adaptive, and characterized by 'competence, support, structures, priorities, role clarity, effective communication, coordination, maintains cohesion, focus, calm, a sense of humor' (p. 912).

Klein et al. (2006) examined extreme action teams in an emergency trauma center. Their qualitative research showed that leadership was shared. Leaders engaged in a pattern of rapid and repetitive delegation; however, active leadership was practiced by junior members of the team. These authors emphasized the importance of improvisation in the leadership role. They reported leadership functions of providing strategic direction, monitoring, providing hands-on treatment and teaching the team members. They conclude, 'Dynamic delegation of the active leadership role fosters learning and reliability ... The hallmark of dynamic delegation is the rapid and repeated transfer of the active leadership role up and down the leadership hierarchy' (p. 613). The Chilean miners' decision-making tactics indicate a democratic style (Franklin, 2011; Henriquez, 2011). For example, all of the members were allowed to suggest ideas, and the idea that made most logical sense was chosen. Therefore, a pattern of dynamic delegation described by Klein et al. is similar to the leadership style in the extreme situation encountered in the mine. It differs in that there was one central leader (Urzúa) who coordinated all inputs from team members and the delegation of tasks.

Rico et al. (2008) discussed team-level knowledge structures and articulated a model of 'team situation models' (TSMs), which they defined as 'dynamic, context-driven mental models concerning key areas of the team's work such as the objectives or the roles of colleagues' (p. 164). Their model incorporates two elements: anticipation and dynamic adjustment. Interestingly, they use an example of firefighters engaged in fighting an apartment building fire to illustrate these two components. In this example, firefighters had to plan for the length of hose needed (anticipation) and then adjust to ensure the hose was not caught on the stairs (dynamic adjustment). The firefighter example is an extreme situation, and their model appears to be relevant for team leadership in extreme contexts. The rescue team in the Chilean mine incident exemplified the element of anticipation. They had the training and experience needed for rescues. However, as with every unique situation, dynamic adjustment was necessary to locate the miners. As noted in the case above, at first the drill missed the miners but the rescue team continued the trial and error process. This search process provides a vivid illustration of the process of dynamic adjustment. The drill locations were changed until the miners were ultimately located.

Once the miners were located, a transition occurred in the multi-team system. In a meta-analysis of research on teamwork processes, LePine et al. (2008) proposed that three intermediate-level teamwork processes may be employed to summarize the relationship of team processes and effectiveness. They found support for a second-order model, which included transition processes, action processes and interpersonal processes, moderated by task interdependence and team size. Transition processes are important drivers of multi-team systems as they will activate within-team as well as cross-team action processes (Marks et al., 2005). Further, performance is dependent upon goal hierarchies that are interdependent. The role of team coaching during transitions has been articulated by Hackman and Wageman (2005). Using examples of briefings of flight crew members, the authors discussed the importance of team coaching at the beginning of events. Strategic intervention may be needed at the midpoint and at the ending because it presents an opportunity for reflecting on task accomplishment. Examining critical incidents using historiometric analysis of hurricanes and post-war stability operations, DeChurch et al. (2011) reported that leaders play a critical role in the aftermath of critical contexts. Using an inductive method, they developed a framework for multi-team leadership functions involving strategic and coordinating behavior. Throughout the 17 days in which the rescue team searched for the miners, there was clearly an interdependent goal of rescue and survival on the part of both the miners and the rescue team above. Coordinating behavior was essential for both teams to succeed, and after 17 days, when the drill bit pierced a tunnel near the miners' shelter, coordination between the rescue team and the miners became essential.

LEADERSHIP LESSONS: KEY TEAM PROCESSES

Goal Commitment

Commitment to goals and related specific tasks is essential. The Chilean miners had a specific goal: all 33 men would survive. The leader, Urzúa, emphasized this goal and made it clear that he would be the last miner to leave. As mentioned in the case, the miners focused on small tasks such as food rationing and kept a strict schedule. This level of attention to detail was important to keep the team focused on the essentials. The interplay of goals and commitment was clear, as Urzúa was able to maintain his leadership role. We believe that the Chilean mine case offers new insight into team leadership in extreme situations. Research is needed to examine both the members' and leader's challenges and the process by which a leader maintains control of the team.

Member Skill Sets

Team skills are a second important team process. All of the miners had a clearly defined role that was suitable to their skills (Klimoski and Jones, 1995). As described in the case above, the medic's skills were essential for immediate emergency situations. Another key skill set was Urzúa's skills as a topographer (Franklin, 2011). Creativity was needed to take inventory of the tools and equipment they had on hand, and think of new ways in which they could be used. Their ingenuity contributed to their survival and each skill set contributed to the process. The role of creativity and innovation in extreme contexts appears to be an area that requires more attention with regards to both theory and research.

Internal Coordination

Urzúa, the team leader, coordinated the teams by separating the miners into three shifts that were organized around their living arrangements. He also followed the recommendations of the rescue team by creating different areas for the normal awake and rest periods for the team. This degree of internal organization and coordination has been shown by team research to be essential, especially under rapidly changing conditions as members must adjust their behavior to the situation (Rico et al., 2008). The creation of smaller teams from the larger team of 33 enhanced cohesiveness and was a key process in the mine. Maintaining cohesion and cooperation was an essential strategy for their survival.

External Coordination and Resource Acquisition

Seeking resources and support from external sources is another key process for leadership with regards to effective team performance (Marks et al., 2005). The collection of accurate information was a key aspect of determining the resources needed. As mentioned in the case, a question-naire was used to assess the miners' health (Fraser, 2010). This is an example of the need for accurate information prior to resources being obtained; in the case of the miners, this might have meant life or death since many could not tolerate solid food right away (despite their dreams of eating *empanadas*). The team leader maintained control of his team by instilling a shared vision and organizing ceremonies and rituals. He led in a democratic fashion so that all decisions accounted for the miners' different opinions. The miners also made an effort to celebrate the small achievements (such as the first sight of the rescue capsule).

Cohesion and Conflict Management

Gupta et al. (2010) showed that team leadership was related to perform-ance; however, team cohesion and conflict mediated this relationship. Research in the management literature has repeatedly found cohesion (Beal et al., 2003; Gully et al., 1995; Gully et al., 2002) and conflict management to be two of the most fundamental team-level variables that influence team effectiveness (Tekleab et al., 2009). In the case of the Chilean mine, the goal was never in doubt: survival and rescue was the goal. As mentioned previously, the miners worked together to define clear roles and develop a shared vision. They made all of their decisions collectively and democratically handled differences of opinion. When differences of opinion occurred, they discussed the best option for the ultimate survival of all of the members. These strategies demonstrate the miners' strong cohesion and conflict management skills. What makes the case of the Chilean mine so fascinating is that the inputs and processes were the key to developing a sense of cohesiveness and effective conflict management that ultimately led to a positive outcome. As noted by Scandura (2010), 'Teaming is so inherently natural that in times of crises, human beings intuitively know it is the pathway to their survival' (p. 7G). Reflection on the processes in the mine may hold much value in how we teach and conduct future research on teams in organizational settings.

CONCLUSION

We have much to learn from this case of extreme leadership and the insights that it offers for future research on teams. For team leadership to be effective in crises, there are key team processes that must be mobilized quickly and effectively. These processes have been identified in organizational research as noted above, and may be critical to the effectiveness of team leadership in a variety of situations (Yukl, 2010). While these processes are comprehensive and explain much of the processes in the Chilean mine extreme leadership situation, it is clear that the literature needs to pay more attention to the roles of spirituality and humor, which played key roles in the survival and well-being of the team in an extreme situation.

Our brief review of the literature on team leadership in extreme situations indicates that research has shown the importance of this topic. The Chilean mine disaster provided a case study through which the research findings were illustrated. Team leadership played a pivotal role in the ultimate successful outcome for the miners and all involved. Failure was possible in this extreme incident. Negative consequences could have surfaced if leadership was ineffective or if group processes were not in place. The situation provided an example of a multi-team extreme context where there was a need for coordination both within the team and with teams outside. Lastly, it is also important to consider that although team leadership affects performance, key team processes must be considered including goal commitment, internal and external coordination, resource acquisition, cohesion and conflict management. This discussion of the Chilean mine disaster and rescue illustrates concepts from the literature on extreme situations and team leadership and indicates some areas that are in need of further research. This case study provides an interesting extreme context that may be used in teaching concepts from team theory and research. The rescue was no doubt a technological marvel. However, the leadership and team processes offer lessons that we can bring to the classroom and to our research agendas.

REFERENCES

Baker, D.P, R. Day and E. Salas (2006). Teamwork as an essential component of high-reliability organizations. *Health Services Research*, 41 (4), 1576–98.

Beal, D.J., R.R. Cohen, M.J. Burke and C.L. McLendon (2003). Cohesion and performance in groups: a meta-analytic clarification of construct relations. *Journal of Applied Psychology*, 88, 989–1004.

Ciborra, C.U. (1999). Notes on improvisation and time in organizations. *Accounting, Management and Technology*, 9 (2), 77–94.

Crossan, M.M., M.P.E. Cunha, D. Vera and J. Cunha (2005). Time and organizational improvisation. *Academy of Management Review*, 30 (1), 129–45.

DeChurch, L.A., C.S. Burke, M.L. Shuffler, R. Lyons, D. Doty and E. Salas (2011). A historiometric analysis of leadership in mission critical multiteam environments. *Leadership Quarterly*, 22 (1), 152–69.

DeChurch, L.A. and M.A. Marks (2006). Leadership in multiteam systems. *Journal of Applied Psychology*, 91 (2), 311–29.

Franklin, J. (2011). *33 Men: Inside the Miraculous Survival and Dramatic Rescue of the Chilean Miners*. New York: Putnam.

Fraser, B. (2010). Chilean miners see the light at last. *Lancet*, 376, 1379–80.

Gully, S.M., D.J. Devine and D.J. Whitney (1995). A meta-analysis of cohesion and performance: effects of level of analysis and task interdependence. *Small Group Research*, 26, 497–520.

Gully, S.M., K.A. Incalcaterra, A. Joshi and J.M. Beaubien (2002). A meta-analysis of team-efficacy, potency, and performance: Interdependence and level of analysis as moderators of observed relationships. *Journal of Applied Psychology*, 86, 819–32.

Gupta, V.K., R. Huang and S. Niranjan (2010). A longitudinal examination of the relationship between team leadership and performance. *Journal of Leadership and Organizational Studies*, 17 (4), 335–50.

Hackman, J.R. and R. Wageman (2005). A theory of team coaching. *Academy of Management Review*, 30 (2), 269–87.

Hannah, S.T., M. Uhl-Bien, B. Avolio and F.L. Cavarretta (2009). A framework for examining leadership in extreme contexts. *Leadership Quarterly*, 20, 897–919.

Henriquez, J. (2011). *Miracle in the Mine: One Man's Story of Strength and Survival in the Chilean Mines*. Grand Rapids, MI: Zondervan.

Katzenbach, J.R. and D.K. Smith (1993). *The Wisdom of Teams*. New York: Harper Business.

Klein, K.J., J.C. Ziegart, A.P. Knight and Y. Xiao (2006). Dynamic delegation: shared, hierarchical, and deindividualized leadership in extreme action teams. *Administrative Science Quarterly*, 51, 590–621.

Klimoski, R. and R.G. Jones (1995). Staffing for effective group decision making: key issues in matching people and teams. In R.A. Guzzo and E. Salas (eds), *Team Effectiveness and Decision Making in Organizations*. San Francisco, CA: Jossey-Bass, pp. 291–332.

LePine, J.A., R.F. Piccolo, C.L. Jackson, J.E. Mathieu and J.R. Saul (2008). A meta-analysis of teamwork processes: tests of a multidimensional model and relationships with team effectiveness criteria. *Personnel Psychology*, 61, 273–307.

Marks, M.A., L.A. DeChurch, J.E. Mathhieu, F.J. Panzer and A. Alonso (2005). Teamwork in multi-team systems. *Journal of Applied Psychology*, 90, 964–71.

Rico, R., M. Sanchez-Manzanares, F. Gil. and C. Gibson (2008). Team implicit coordination processes: a team knowledge-based approach. *Academy of Management Review*, 33, 163–84.

Scandura, T.A. (2010). Leadership lessons from the Chilean mine. *Miami Herald*, 25 October, p. 7G.

Tekleab, A.G., N.R. Quigley and P.E. Tesluk (2009). A longitudinal study of team conflict, conflict management, cohesion, and team effectiveness. *Group Organization Management*, 34, 170–205.

Yukl, G. (2010). *Leadership in Organizations*, 7th edn. Upper Saddle River, NJ: Prentice-Hall.

12. Where pure leadership is revealed: our police in harm's way

Mark D. Bowman and George B. Graen

INTRODUCTION

> As the Personal Security Officer to Generals David Petraeus and John Allen
> in Iraq and Afghanistan and 28 years in state and federal law enforcement, I
> have seen up close and personal what having proper training and leadership
> means under the most stressful and perilous scenarios. Never in our history
> has the battle space of not only the soldier, but also the first responders at
> home, been so dangerous as it is today. Dr Graen has recognized the great-
> est asset we can offer to our heros [sic] at home and abroad is the proper
> advanced training, equipment, and technology to be prepared to face the
> challenges presented by the post 9/11 world.
>
> Mark A. Howell (2012)

Organizations are designed for stability and possess established defenses
against disruptive changes in their environment. However, disruption
happens often without warning. Adaptation to such events is handled by a
damage control team rather than an executive leadership team. Change in
and of organizations is contrary to its design and purpose and will be
resisted. Change too often is poorly managed and results in damage to or
even demise of an organization. In this chapter, examples of creating
gradual change in our police practices in harm's way is presented and
analyzed, searching for an understanding of the process. First, the
improvements suggested by the International Association of Chiefs of
Police (IACP) and by management of team leadership in extreme
contexts (Graen and Graen, 2013) protecting our first responders are
reviewed. Next, examples of doing police work with teams of officers is
presented and analyzed for needed improvements. After this, the police
context and the police organization are described and analyzed. Finally,
implications for the field of extreme contexts are discussed.

The IACP has identified leader development as one of the principal
challenges for police organizations in the twenty-first century (IACP,

1999). The IACP and others have adopted a curriculum based on the third-year leadership course that every cadet must take at the US Military Academy at West Point, NY (McNally et al., 1996). That curriculum is essentially a pragmatic micro- and macro-organizational behavior course that examines individual, leadership and organizational theories within the context of a police organization. One of the leadership theories that students learn is leadership-motivated excellence (LMX) (Graen, 2013a).

Mark Bowman had the good fortune of being assigned to the Professional Development and Training Bureau in his city police department for three and a half years. He was responsible for developing and implementing leader development programs. The police adaptation of the West Point leadership curriculum figured prominently in his department's leader development efforts (Jacocks and Bowman, 2006). Bowman also served as an instructor for the IACP on its version of the course. Some students on this course had been leaders for many years, some for a short period of time, and some would soon become formal leaders. Almost all of the more than 300 students in those courses easily recognized the implications of LMX strategy in police work. They had all experienced the consequence of the theory but had not necessarily recognized the prescriptive nature of high-quality relationships.

The course is becoming more available to police leaders throughout the United States. Bowman is currently providing this course to police leaders through his university (Methodist University) and will be helping police leaders. If we expect police leaders to lead well, then police organizations have a clear duty to educate and train their leaders. Learning how to improve the quality of relationships between leaders and those they lead is only the first step in improving performance in both routine and dangerous circumstances.

If any protocol is to be of greater value in dangerous circumstances in police organizations then how it is enacted must be consistent at leadership levels. Most policing activity is undertaken by individual police officers at the bottom of the organizational hierarchy. Police sergeants lead almost all policing accomplished in the US and lead in almost all dangerous circumstances. Not only must police sergeants know about leadership theory, but they as a group must also reach consensus as to how it will be enacted at their level in police organizations. This will require thoughtful action beyond simple education and training. Police sergeants must come together to discuss and agree on how they will develop higher-level relationships with members. In particular, they must reach consensus on how they will consistently define and assign member roles in dangerous circumstances. This will not only improve performance within each police squad but it will also ease the difficulties experienced when individuals must face danger when working with another groups of first responders.

This trust is most critical when police leaders must lead in dangerous circumstances. If police sergeants define and assign roles differently, as is now often the case, then members of that ad hoc team who must face danger together cannot leverage role clarity and consensus to develop 'swift trust'. While trust developed over time is much preferred, reality forces leaders to sometimes rely on assumed trust. Police are more likely to improve leadership and the consistency with which it is enacted than they are to change entrenched bureaucratic realities, such as internal transfers, new promotions, etc.... and operational realities, such as what leaders and followers may be available to respond to critical incidents. Police sergeants must reach consensus on how they will define and assign roles so that any police officer will be able to quickly assume a role in and be assured of a strong alliance.

NEEDED CHANGES FOR POLICING

Rapid improvements in equipment are being made for protection from physical wounds of police in 'harm's way', but improvements to shield the cognitive and emotional functions lag far behind. Historically, what is now called post-traumatic stress (PTS) has existed since humans first ventured into harm's way. Only recently has it been recognized that it has become a pandemic and out of control as a serious disorder, that can be reduced in severity and incidence by new and available technology. Today, despite the recent improvements, too many young people with outdated training, naive expectations of harm's way and motivated by a mixture of adventure, duty and promises of benefits are being delivered into harm's way. They become easy victims of assault snipers, human bombs, hidden explosive devices and the extreme stress of unknown dangers. They may witness horrors that leave many physically sick and emotionally crippled. They need a heavy dose of defensive team training and rehearsal.

Today, they need to be better prepared for the unthinkable gut-wrenching sickness from the increased dangers since the US's 9/11. Graen (2013b) recommends the following, based on research on first responders who work in police and fire departments, the Army, Navy, Air Force and Marines.

First, find the 'right stuff'. Selecting the best candidates needs to involve, in addition to the current standards of placement, using the new heart rhythm standards and team compatibility criteria. Those failing to meet these criteria should not be placed in harm's way. Team leadership requires that team mates are convinced that all have competence, can be respected, can be trusted to honor bodyguard alliances, and that they commit to the welfare of the team and the success of the mission. Team members should be cross-trained and do double duty for short periods. Replacements should be trained to achieve 'quick' respect, trust, commitment and become dependable participants in a team.

Second, present 'realistic previews'. Throughout the entire developmental process, realistic previews should be presented. These should include what to expect in the two worlds of safe and unsafe work life, compared to that of the well-known world of civilian life. This may include giving up specified civilian rights and privileges, taking oaths, becoming subject to a different code of conduct, and the realities of being assigned to work in harm's way for extended periods. Overall, the objective is to gradually prepare a civilian to be prepared to face both worlds of the first responder's work with an authentic view of the opportunities and challenges.

Third, train 'team-leadership motivated excellence'. The heart and soul of a Special Weapons and Tactics (SWAT) team lies in the mature development of mutual bodyguard-to-bodyguard alliances inside of the team. (These alliances are 'life and death' agreements to reciprocally watch each other's back and requisition whatever is needed to keep each other alive and well.) Although some of these interpersonal alliances emerge naturally when a team must face harm's way, the process of developing super-strong mutual alliances can be trained, given the proper control of emotions. These alliances are seen as strategic to those involved. They can form the armor for both mind and body that produces the sought-after resilience in harm's way. Alliance members also brief and debrief one another and help each other cope with experiences that, if left unshared, may eat away at them, such as concerns about their fears that their world is shattered. The characteristics of naturally developing mate-to-mate alliances produce a number of interesting outcroppings. These alliances when shared completely throughout the team and with other interdependent teams improve teamwork. New police officers who cannot pass the test for the teams that work in harm's way should be removed from such a context (Graen, 2013c).

Fourth, train with 'authentic' field problems. Training protocols should be developed and patterned after the SWAT simulations using realistic structures and local processes experienced in actual situations. These field problems are designed to train proper team actions and the value of alliances before, during and after the severe stress of quickly solving life-or-death problems as a team (Waller and Uitdewilligen, 2013). These field problems are best held at night with physically exhausted teams. Performance of teams should be evaluated and they should be debriefed when their emotions are aroused. Repetition in different field problems requiring the use of similar protocols is employed until the team has learned to apply the new protocol. The reward for team success is increased cohesion that comes from facing and overcoming a challenge as a group.

Fifth, give 'special PTS prevention training'. As part of authentic field problems, teams can be trained in behavior control over emotional reactions. Teams can be trained in what we know about the causes and protective actions to reduce emotional shock, and to help alliance partners who show tell-tale signs by safely and later initiating team debriefing. If signs persist, teams will be responsible to get their affected member to engage treatment. Prevention of PTS needs to be upgraded, and we know how to achieve this. Finally, let us stop calling PTS a 'disorder', because it unfairly handicaps our heroes in obtaining civilian employment.

Leadership often has been separated into those leaders who concentrate on structuring the work for their followers and those who emphasize consideration of their followers' needs. As presented in this chapter, a radically different kind of teamwork leadership is called for in harm's way. This new model is described herein. In our research, more effective leaders at all levels offer 'mateship' by developing an excellent unique strategic alliance in which the leader's number one job is to watch the follower's back and make them as successful as they want to be. The follower's number one job is to do the same for the leader. These interpersonal strategic alliances are then linked to networks of such alliances and produce functional team leadership which is an additional source of power for an organization. In harm's way, this team leadership can assume the mission of both defending our homeland and protecting our first responders. Moreover, in turbulent environments team leadership can improve the speed of adaptability and hence overall effectiveness. As a byproduct, we recommend more leadership studies of harm's way environments as a way of learning more about adaptability and change in less dangerous environments.

CALL THE PUBLIC SAFETY SERVICES EMERGENCY TELEPHONE NUMBER

We next illustrate how executive leadership emerges in dangerous contexts, using Bowman's critical incidents as a commander of police in 'swift trust' situations. Patrol Sergeant Bowman was responsible for leading a squad of ten police officers in a large southern police department assigned to the late evening shift (7 p.m. to 3 a.m.) in an 'active' (high-crime) precinct. This shift period is much more active than other police shifts and it was common for officers to become involved in dangerous circumstances. Danger in policing most frequently arises in evolving events, but on occasion, the police have the advantage of planning for danger. On this particular night shift, two detectives had approached Bowman concerning a pattern of rapes and attempted rapes that had emerged in an area of the precinct. The crimes had been occurring in the early morning hours of Saturdays and Sundays in a subdivision that was usually accessed through only two streets off a major thoroughfare. Bowman developed a plan based on the analysis of the crime pattern. The personnel assigned to this planned patrol were eight of Bowman's direct reports, two case detectives, a dog handling (K9) team and the helicopter unit. Bowman's previous military experience had taught him the difficulty of temporarily integrating external personnel into a unit, but he thought that he could plan for contingencies and coordinate the activities of all the officers.

Bowman prepared an operations protocol and briefed his team on Friday at the beginning of the first night of the operation. On that first night of the operation, none of his personnel encountered the suspect and there were no reported crimes in the area. He was pleased though that the hastily formed team had an opportunity to practice their signals, as several suspicious individuals on foot and in vehicles were spotted, monitored and confronted. He was confident that this performance was adequate to meet the challenge should they discover the suspect on Saturday night.

At the beginning of the shift on Saturday night, all personnel again met to review the plan order and begin the operation. At about 3 a.m. two of the officers in an unmarked vehicle spotted a suspicious car and followed it for a short distance. The driver of that car turned off the car's headlights and attempted to evade the officers. The officers found the car parked in front of a townhouse. The officers approached the vehicle and discovered the driver slumped in the seat to avoid detection. The driver matched the description of the rape suspect and the officers notified Bowman of their discovery and that the suspect refused to exit the car. Bowman called the two case detectives and additional officers to respond to the suspect's location with him.

When he arrived at the suspect's location, the officers who had originally confronted the suspect again told Bowman that the suspect refused to exit the car. The suspect very closely matched the description of the rapist who had victimized several women in that area. Bowman discussed the situation with the case detectives and it was decided that if they could not convince the suspect to exit the car they would forcibly remove him from the car and arrest him. Bowman asked the suspect to exit the vehicle and warned him that he would be forcibly removed should he again refuse. He again refused.

Bowman positioned an officer to observe the suspect from the front of the car while two officers broke out the rear driver's side window to gain access to the rear seat and physically restrain the suspect. Two officers were positioned to remove the suspect through the driver's side door. As the window was broken, the officer at the front of the car warned that the suspect was reaching for a silver object in his waistband. Bowman ordered all officers to take cover behind cars parked near the suspect's car.

As Bowman and the officers took positions behind cover and drew their handguns the suspect removed a silver semi-automatic handgun from his waistband and held it to his head. The suspect then exited the car and continued to hold the handgun to his head. He had the capability of using deadly force but was not an imminent threat. Bowman and the team of officers had few viable force options available. The reality of the situation was that the suspect was holding the officers hostage. The suspect ignored orders to drop the handgun and then ran away with the team of officers pursuing.

As officers began the foot pursuit, the K9 team arrived in a vehicle which forced the suspect to run toward another set of nearby townhouses. Officers caught up with the suspect and confronted him as he was attempting to open the front door to one of the townhouses. The suspect again turned toward the officers and held the handgun to his head. Bowman instructed the K9 officer to use his dog to subdue the suspect but the K9 officer refused to do so. The suspect again began to run with Bowman and the officers again pursuing.

The suspect ran about another block through an alley and made his way to his townhouse and entered that through the rear door. Bowman positioned officers to establish an inner and outer perimeter and initiated a SWAT and crisis negotiator call-out. At about 11 a.m. SWAT made entry into the suspect's townhouse and discovered him hiding in the attic. The suspect was subsequently identified by victims and through DNA evidence as the serial rapist. He was subsequently convicted and sentenced to a lengthy prison sentence.

The final outcome was certainly acceptable, but the process was not. Bowman could have made use of a positive outcome bias and declared 'no harm no foul'. He realized that no one being hurt was just as likely a function of good fortune. In the after-action review, the members of Bowman's squad voiced their belief that the K9 officer had failed to perform adequately and put them and perhaps innocent citizens at risk. As a leader, Bowman pondered what he could have done to better integrate the K9 officer into the operation. Team members cannot refuse to cooperate at critical moments, or they place others in unnecessarily danger.

AN EXTREME CONTEXT

Police Organizational Context

Avolio (2007) called for greater integration of context into leadership research. Some context in which police leaders and followers interact is very much like that found in most hierarchical organizations, but some context in police organizations is unique. A key feature of focus is how police organize and respond to those challenges and how that interplay creates a unique environment in which police organizations operate.

In 2004 there were 17 860 state and local law enforcement agencies and those agencies employed 732 000 sworn law enforcement officers (Reaves, 2007). The most common form of police organizational design is the hierarchical pyramid with rigid lines of command and control (Swanson et al., 2005). A random viewing of police websites, which often contain organizational charts, will reveal the common block and line charts that depict a hierarchical organization. What is unique about police organizations is what happens at the bottom of the organizational chart where policing occurs.

Almost all policing is accomplished by patrol officers and detectives who are organized into small groups which are found at the bottom of the organizational chart. These groups may have a variety of titles such as squad, team or shift. A group is typically led by an individual most commonly given the rank title of Sergeant (Swanson et al., 2005). The ideal span of control is generally accepted to be one leader to seven followers, which may be difficult for every police organization to achieve on paper, much less in practice. As a sergeant, Bowman has found himself responsible for leading up to 20 police officers during a shift due to personnel turbulence such as promotions, leave, training or temporary assignments. This characteristic of organizing is much like that of any other hierarchical organization. What makes the operational context unique in policing is how the police officers and detectives generally conduct their work.

Much police work is accomplished by solitary police officers or detectives out of the view of a formal commander (Champion and Hooper, 2003). The most common form of work within patrol and detective groups would be classified as a form of unilateral inter-dependence (Forsyth, 2006). Each patrol officer performs work independently and answers to the group's leader. Some challenges may require a form of interdependence. This form of interdependence most commonly occurs in the patrol function on calls for services which have historically presented greater hazard for officers. Typically, more than one patrol officer is dispatched to calls such as burglaries or robberies in progress or domestic disputes. The officers who are assigned to such a call work closely together only for the duration of that call and then return to solitary patrol work. The groups in which these officers work are also loosely coupled.

Most police groups work independently (Ivancevich et al., 2008) to achieve the goals of the next-higher unit on the organizational chart. Patrol groups may work on different shifts or in different geographic areas and their group outputs are simply pooled to account for the performance of the higher unit. Some patrol work, such as preliminary criminal investigations, may be passed along to a detective group for a follow-up investigation. This sequential interdependence is generally carried out in an administrative environment rather than an operational environment. Preliminary investigations by patrol officers are typically passed along to detectives in paper or electronic form and there is little actual interaction between the group members. Reciprocal inter-dependence between police groups is very rare and usually only occurs in extreme events such as hostage situations or natural disasters.

The operation in which Bowman and his team searched for and eventually captured a serial rapist is a good example. The reciprocal interdependence between detectives and patrol groups was uncommon. Patrol groups usually pass work along to detective groups. In this case detectives turned to a patrol group to help them identify and capture a serial rapist. The short-term group that Bowman formed to conduct the operation was assigned the singular goal of identifying and capturing the serial rapist. When the SWAT Team and Crisis Negotiation Team arrived there was coordinated action between those groups and the patrol personnel as the serial rapist's townhouse was isolated and the rapist was eventually captured. This activity would also be classified as reciprocal interdependence. In this instance many individuals and groups were able to come together to accomplish a very important goal under dangerous circumstances. Another advantageous characteristic of this operation was that much of it was planned, and Bowman played a role in choosing those who participated in the operation.

For police organizations the most common form of organizing in dangerous circumstances is very much like how people organize for an informal basketball game. At the neighborhood ball court the population of individuals who routinely play ball is usually relatively constant. For a variety of reasons each game may consist of a different mix of that population and how the individuals organize into teams will also vary. Each of the players knows the other players and has likely played with and against most of the members of the population. Like any population, people will enter and leave for a variety of reasons. Some new players may be new entrants to the population or may only be transients visiting or passing through the area.

These same dynamics apply to police patrol response to dangerous circumstances. Each patrol group is relatively stable for short periods of time and the group members will have varying levels of knowledge of one another and experience working together. Each group will change over time with some members leaving and new members entering the group. Often a different mix of group members will work together in responding to dangerous circumstances that require the effort of more than one officer. Some dangerous circumstances may require only two officers, whereas others may require a larger group. In organizations large enough to organize patrol groups geographically, officers who have never worked together and may only have passing knowledge of one another may be required to work together. Dangerous calls for service are dispatched to the nearest units and those units can be from different subunits of their parent police organization if the call is near a geographic boundary. The nature of dangerous circumstances will always vary as will the police response to those circumstances (Faggiano and Gillespie, 2004). The range of possible leader–follower mixes would be: a leader and only direct subordinates; a leader and direct and other subordinates; and a leader and subordinates who do not report to the leader. In Bowman's almost 30 years of police experience all three categories commonly occur.

The context in which police organizations must operate is usually much like that of any other hierarchical organization but sometimes police organizations are faced with especially dangerous circumstances. Leading in these contexts presents challenges that are familiar to many leaders; some are unique to police organizations. Next, we will explore the nature of relationships between leaders and followers in these routine and dangerous contexts.

Police Organization

Implicit in the concept of leadership style is that the leader and follower groups are relatively stable. From an administrative perspective, police groups may appear to be stable, but as a practical matter, the leadership of police groups that operate in the field at any given time will vary considerably. For that reason (Graen, 2013a) the leader-motivated excellence (LMX) theory of hierarchical strategic alliances is a good theory to both account for and improve leadership in police organizations.

Teams of leaders and followers will change in police patrol and detective groups. Simply by virtue of passing time each new leader–follower dyad will progress through the stages of 'leadership-making', beginning with the stranger stage, advancing to the acquaintance stage, and some reaching the mature stage (Graen and Uhl-Bien, 1995). Many positive outcomes of this strategy, such as increased job satisfaction, increased organizational commitment and reduced turnover, were found in three meta-analyses (Gerstner and Day, 1997; Dulebohn et al., 2011; Ilies et al., 2007). In a recent study of a large police organization, LMX strategy was found to be positively related to increased job embeddedness and negatively related to turnover intentions and job search behaviors (Bowman, 2009). While individual differences will affect the number of dyads that can achieve the highest level of maturity, much research provides substantial support for leadership development that emphasizes LMX strategy.

Previous research has found many positive organizational and individual outcomes from improved use of LMX strategy. Moreover, much research provides logical connections to factors that have been found to influence performance in dangerous circumstances. In particular, it has been found to be related to mutual trust, which is critical to performance in harm's way. Police teams must watch each other's backs at all times in harm's way.

There are obvious limitations in researching performance in dangerous environments (Kolditz, 2007). Many researchers might be reluctant to enter those environments along with participants. There are ethical constraints that limit the potential for quasi-experimental and experimental methods in dangerous environments. In crime in particular, the criminal gets a vote on the performance variable. For those reasons most research on performance in harm's way has been qualitative and retrospective in nature; however, many things can be measured and analyzed by the creative scientist.

The relationship between an officer's conduct and LMX strategy has been clearly established (Gerstner and Day, 1997). Role conflict is negatively related to it and role clarity is positively related. This is not surprising in that the theory's strategy part starts with role-finding, proceeds to role-making, and finally arrives at role-implementation at its highest level (Graen and Uhl-Bien, 1995). Jobs have consequences in routine organizational contexts and more dire consequences in dangerous contexts. In dangerous contexts assigned roles define individual perform-ance responsibilities and define interdependence between jobs. Regard-less of whether the required interdependence is unilateral, sequential or reciprocal (Forsyth, 2006), lack of role clarity will limit cohesive action or aggregation of individual actions. Clearly, the lack of role clarity and increased role conflict increases the risk in dangerous circumstances.

Risk occupies a central theme in the trust literature (Burke et al., 2007). Without risk, trust is of little consequence. Risk and trust are also central themes in the growing body of literature on performance in dangerous circumstances. In 2007 Kolditz (p. xvii) defined 'In-Extremis Leadership' as 'giving purpose, motivation and direction to people when there is imminent physical danger and where followers believe that leader behavior will influence their physical well-being or survival'. Of course in dangerous circumstances risk is inherent in the context. The amount of risk may vary due to circumstances beyond anyone's control, but mutual trust is a factor over which pairs of people have a great deal of control.

Kolditz (2007) found that effective combat leaders were respected for competence and trusted for motives by their troops. In combat, faith in leadership is based largely on competence in combat and caring for troops. There are also social, bureaucratic and training actions that influence trust and those are the only actions subordinates see prior to combat. It has been found that leader trust earned in peacetime transfers to combat operations but that soldiers do re-evaluate trust when tran-sitioning from peacetime to combat operations (Sweeney, 2010). Social, bureaucratic and training actions are the grist of the organizational environment in which LMX strategy operates. It should not be surprising then, that LMX strategy was found to be highly and positively related in a meta-analysis of trust and leadership outcomes (Dirks and Ferrin, 2002). Those who go in harm's way usually do not do so alone, which should raise the question about the importance of trust in peers to watch one's back.

Alliances and their quality are critical in developing and sustaining trust, respect and commitment among those who must go in harm's way. Each follower must trust his or her leader and the quality of that alliance. Peers must trust one another and their alliances as well. Leaders can grow a trust environment in their groups by consciously attempting to achieve the highest-quality alliance possible with each subordinate and between peers on the team.

New officers form a professional alliance with a leader as a stranger. In routine circumstances taking time to find, make and implement a healthy alliance is not only acceptable but is also wise. A police leader does not have the luxury of taking time when confronted with a dangerous circumstance to integrate a stranger into an operation. How then can leaders and followers quickly develop trust? A recent stream of research in the trust literature has examined developing 'swift trust' in hastily formed networks (Tatham and Kovacs, 2010). Hastily formed networks (HFNs) are temporary work groups, sometimes collocated but sometimes distributed, in which some or all of the members have not previously worked together. A police group that forms temporarily to confront dangerous circumstances is a type of hastily formed network. The literature on swift trust provides reason to believe that mutual trust can be improved in a hastily formed police network. As Hackman (2012) noted, over 80 percent of all airline incidents involve at least one new crew member.

Swift trust has been found to be related to a variety of factors (Tatham and Kovacs, 2010). When members of an HFN operate using similar rules, processes or procedures then it is much easier for them to trust one another. Police officers, especially within the same agency, operate in a bureaucratic organization with many rules, processes and procedures. When members of an HFN are of the same group category then it is much easier for them to trust one another. Typically in police HFNs, the members who form the networks are similarly situated in the organization. Usually patrol officers would form HFNs with other patrol officers and detectives would more readily form HFNs with other detectives. Finally, having knowledge of another's role in the HFN makes it easier to trust that person. Rules, processes and procedures are universally defined in police organizations. First-line leaders may have limited control over the category of personnel they must lead in dangerous circumstances. As has been previously discussed, the quality of interpersonal alliances is critical in increasing role clarity and reducing role conflict.

After Bowman learned about LMX strategy he spent considerable time reflecting on how the varying levels of relationships influenced outcomes. He thought about the speed at which relationships moved through the levels and what might have influenced that speed. Not surprisingly he found that relationships reached the highest level and moved through the levels fastest with members who were most like him (homogeneous). Bowman developed the strongest relationships with members who policed assertively but thoughtfully. Most of those members were like Bowman, college-educated and physically fit. As he reflected on his experiences he found that race and gender did not play a role in the relationships. Instead, competence and trust were the coins of the realm. Those of course are Mark's reflections, and like all humans he is susceptible to self-serving bias.

Confirmation

What has convinced Mark of the value of LMX strategy beyond his own reflections has been the conversations he had with former members. As a lieutenant he had the good fortune to serve with another lieutenant who had years earlier come to his squad (Mark was a sergeant then) as a new police officer fresh from the police academy. This new officer was college-educated and physically fit. He sought out opportunities to police assertively and thoughtfully. This officer quickly moved through the levels of relationships as he quickly learned the job, and Mark became increasingly comfortable with expanding the officer's boundaries. Mark did not realize the influence their professional alliance had on the officer until they discussed one dangerous incident years after it happened.

One night Bowman and his squad faced an unruly crowd of about 100, mostly drunken, individuals at an alcohol establishment at closing time. It became necessary to disperse the crowd as many were throwing rocks and bottles at officers and passing cars. Bowman quickly formed a skirmish line of about eight officers and dispersed the core group of rioters. Bowman's former subordinate related how he felt during the incident. He said that like all police recruits he had gone through crowd control training in the academy but that the small wooden blocks that had been thrown in academy training did not simulate the same level of fear as did rocks and bottles. He said what gave him confidence to face a crowd ten times larger than the squad of officers was the level of trust he had in Bowman as a leader. Had their relationship not quickly evolved, the officer's confidence and subsequent performance in a small riot might have been less than adequate.

As Bowman thought about LMX strategy as a leader he recognized that it was critical to improve the quality of the professional alliance he had with each of his members to the greatest extent possible. Regardless of his attempts to move his subordinates through the levels of alliance thoughtfully and quickly, he still found himself leading police officers into danger when their levels varied between stranger, intermediate and mature. As previously related, bureaucratic and operational realities conspire to limit the ability of any one leader to always have a high-quality alliance with each member. It is critical that police organizations recognize and limit the potential for these bureaucratic and operational realities to produce failure.

WHY STUDY EXTREME CONTEXT?

Overall, the study of extreme context researches executive leadership in situations in which events are likely to occur that may result in intolerable physical, psychological or material damage (Hannah et al., 2009). A good example of this approach is Graen and Graen (2013) in which researchers in the fields of harm's way in fire, police, emergency and branches of the military reviewed the data in their respective area and assembled a set of recommendations to defend the US homeland and protect first responders. Clearly, leadership can make its greatest contributions in extreme contexts. Graen and Graen's chapter reviews theory and research aimed at improving team leadership in such foreboding environments. They conclude that 'Team leadership in its greatest influence separated from administration can be demonstrated in harm's way'. This display of selflessness, taking care of one's alliance buddies, appears to be a survival mechanism from our hunter-gather history. Without such a mechanism our ancestors may not have survived the hunt of wooly mammoths.

What is learned by team leadership in harm's way may help us understand how leadership emerges in times of extreme stress in corporations and other organizations. Administration methods are well understood by professional technocrats and they work satisfactorily for business as usual. But, when the beehive hits the fan, team leadership is needed to augment administration. Clearly, both mechanisms are double-edged swords and must be carefully developed and used.

Preparing team leadership to venture into harm's way needs to be studied and understood. The rates of PTS, hard drug use, fragging and unnecessarily human and material damage are much too high. We can and must do better. In a special issue of *Military Psychology*, Campbell et al. (2010) ask three questions: (1) What is leadership in harm's way? (2) What does harm's way do to leadership? (3) What distinguishes effective leadership in harm's way? These are relevant questions and require special research designs to answer. On the positive side, US Air Force Academy researchers have outlined a new career path for those who would practice modern team leadership in harm's way (Jackson et al., 2013). This path for those seeking to become professionals begins with the study of the areas of physical stamina, psychological resilience and humble self-efficacy, a cognitive core, an interpersonal core, and spanning boundaries and forging interpersonal strategic alliances. In addition, new postgraduate experiences in professional military education (PME) and predeployment training with intact teams is proposed. Finally, graduate schools could counsel students to seek opportunities for team leadership by applying Day's (2000) concept of action learning. Clearly, team leadership's contribution to those who go in harm's way can and should be enhanced by focusing research on this critical environment (Helmreich and Schafer, 1994).

In harm's way, teams need effective executive leadership development to improve 'sense-making' and proper action in crisis. 'Everyone for themselves' is an often deadly order in harm's way. Teams must be developed and trained to think fast and correctly assess situations. Protocols of survival are often written in blood and sacrifice and need to be practiced religiously. Alertness to clues of an impending perfect storm need to be overlearned and rehearsed regularly (Weick, 1995). This approach focuses on learning from actual tragedies (e.g., Mann Gulch (Weick, 1993) and South Canyon fires (Useem et al., 2005), Indian Ocean tsunami (Athukorala and Resosudarmo, 2005; Rodriquez et al., 2006), Bhopal chemical release (Bowman and Kunreuther, 1988; Shrivastava, 1987; Union Carbide, 1985), Three Mile Island meltdown (Hopkins, 2001; Perrow, 1997), Columbia Space Shuttle explosion (Heimann, 1993; Starbuck and Miliken, 1988; Vaughan, 1996), Westray mine disaster (Hynes and Prasad, 1997), Mount Everest climbing incidents (Kayes, 2004; Tempest et al., 2007), hurricane Katrina (Comfort, 2007; Gheytanchi et al., 2007; Kapucu and VanWart, 2006; Rego and Garau, 2007), Tenerife airplane collision (Weick, 1990), Chernobyl (Hohenemser et al., 1986)), numerous military leadership and combat studies (e.g., Cosby et al., 2006; Morath et al., 2006; Leonard et al., 2006; Department of the Army, 1950, 2008; Scales, 2006; Snook, 2000; Ulmer et al., 2004; Wong et al., 2003)) and organizational doctrine such as the US Army (Department of the Army, 2006) and National Wildfire Service (National Wildfire Coordinating Group, 2007) leadership manuals. As a recent example, the BP oil rig blow out in the Gulf may have been prevented according to trial testimony (New York Times, 2013).

CONCLUSION

Context matters in the contributions of administrative hierarchal authority, executive leadership and other influences. When organizations are first designed as systems, the architects work within parameters that are fixed and assume relatively stable and manageable environments (calm). But, as shown in Figure 12.1, environments may change over time from calm to turbulent to harm's way, and the mix of sources of influences produce the perfect storm. As an organization's context become more extreme, executive leadership tends to emerge and at the extreme may dominate what actions are taken. In this chapter we have given a glimpse into the critical incidents of a police commander directing his team in harm's way. The lessons learned from such experiences suggest that what is necessary in extreme contexts may be useful in making changes in less extreme contexts. We recommend this course for future research.

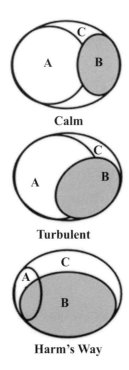

Figure 12.1   Proportion of total influce in a business unit contributed by (A) unit administration; (B) team leadership; and (C) other

REFERENCES

Athukorala, P. and B.P. Resosudarmo (2005). The Indian Ocean tsunami: economic impact, disaster management, and lessons. *Asian Economic Papers*, 4, 1–39.

Avolio, B.J. (2007). Promoting more integrative strategies for leadership theory-building. *American Psychologist*, 62 (1), 25–33.

Bowman, M.D. (2009). A test of direct and partially mediated relationships between leader–member exchange, job embeddedness, turnover intentions, and job search behaviors in a Southern police department. Unpublished doctoral dissertation. Old Dominion University, USA.

Bowman, E. and H. Kunreuther (1988). Post-Bhopal behaviour at a chemical company. *Journal of Management Studies*, 25, 387–402.

Burke, C.S., D.E. Sims, E.H. Lazzara and E. Salas (2007). Trust in leadership: a multi-level review and integration. *Leadership Quarterly*, 18, 606–32.

Campbell, D.J., S.T. Hannah and M.D. Matthews (2010). Leadership in military and other dangerous contexts: introduction to the special topic issue. *Military Psychology*, 22 (1), 1–14.

Champion, D.H., Sr and M.K. Hooper (2003). *An Introduction to American Policing*. New York: McGraw-Hill.

Comfort, L.K. (2007). Crisis management in hindsight: cognition, communication, coordination, and control. *Public Administration Review*, 67 (Supplement 1), 189–97.

Cosby, N., J. Madden, R. Jacobs, F. Flynn, J. Sellars, G. Brown, et al. (2006). Generalized non-kinetic operations (GNKO) straw man task list. A report by Booz Allen.

Day, D.V. (2000). Leadership development: a review in context. *Leadership Quarterly*, 11, 581–613.

Department of the Army (1950). *Pamphlet 600-2: The Armed Forces Officer*. Washington, DC: Defense Printing Service.

Department of the Army (2006). Army leadership: competent, confident, and agile. Washington, DC: Defense Printing Service.

Department of the Army (2008). TRADOC pamphlet 525-3-7-01: The human dimension in the future 2015–2024. Fort Monroe, VA.

Dirks, K.T. and D.L. Ferrin (2002). Trust in leadership: meta-analytic findings and implication for research and practice. *Journal of Applied Psychology*, 87 (4), 611–28.

Dulebohn, J.H., W.H. Bommer, R.C. Liden, R.L. Brouer and G.R. Ferris (2011). A meta-analysis of antecedents and consequences of leader–member exchange: integrating the past with an eye toward the future. *Journal of Management*, pp. 17–45.

Faggiano, V.F. and T.T. Gillespie (2004). *Critical Incident Management: An On-Scene Guide for Law Enforcement Supervisors*. Tulsa, OK: K&M Publishers.

Forsyth, D.R. (2006). *Group Dynamics*. Belmont, CA: Thomson Wadsworth.

Gerstner, C.R. and D.V. Day (1997). Meta-analytic review of leader–member exchange theory: correlates and construct issues. *Journal of Applied Psychology*, 82 (6), 827–44.

Gheytanchi, A., L. Joseph, E. Gierlach, S. Kimpara, J. Housley, Z.E. Franco, et al. (2007). The dirty dozen: twelve failures of the Hurricane Katrina response and how psychology can help. *American Psychologist*, 62, 118–30.

Graen, G.B. (2013a). The missing link in network dynamics. In M. Rumsey (ed.), *The Many Sides of Leadership: A Handbook*. London: Oxford University Press.

Graen, G.B. (2013b). Defending our homeland, protecting our first responders, expert advice from those who serve. In G.B. Graen and J.A. Graen (eds), *LMX Leadership: The Series*, Vol VIII. Charlotte NC: Information Age Publishing.

Graen, G.B. (2013c). Transforming your career. http://www.youtube.com/watch?v=J6U_baWTG14&feature=youtube.

Graen, G.B. and J.A. Graen (2013). Management of team leadership in extreme context: defending our homeland, protecting our first responders. In G.B. Graen and J.A. Graen (eds), *LMX Leadership: The Series*, Vol. VIII. Charlotte, NC: Information Age Publishing:

Graen, G.B. and M. Uhl-Bien (1995). Relationship-based approach to leadership: development of leader–member exchange (LMX) theory of leadership over 25 years: applying a multi-level, multi-domain perspective. *Leadership Quarterly*, 6 (2), 219–47.

Hackman, J. (2012). OB lifetime achievement address. Academy of Management Meeting, Boston, MA, August 7.

Hannah, S.T., M. Uhl-Bien, B.J. Avolio and F.L. Cavarretta (2009). A framework for examining leadership in extreme contexts. *Leadership Quarterly*, 20, 897–919.

Heimann, C.F.L. (1993). Understanding the Challenger disaster: organizational structure and the design of reliable systems. *American Political Science Review*, 87, 421–35.

Helmreich, R. and H. Schafer (1994). *Team Performance in the Operating Room, Human Error in Medicine*. Hillsdale, NJ: Lawrence Erlbaum.

Hohenemser, C., M. Deicher, A. Ernst, H. Hofsäss, G. Lindner and E. Recknagel (1986). Chernobyl: an early report. *Environment: Science and Policy for Sustainable Development*, 28 (5), 6–43.

Hopkins, A. (2001). Was Three Mile Island a 'normal accident'? *Journal of Contingencies and Crisis Management*, 9, 65–72.

Howell, M.A. (2012). Forward in Management of Team Leadership in Extreme Context: Defending Our Homeland: Protecting Our First Responders. In G.B. Graen and J.A. Graen (eds), *LMX Leadership: The series, Volume VIII*, p. xi. Charlotte, NC: Information Age Publishing.

Hynes, T. and P. Prasad (1997). Patterns of 'mock bureaucracy' in mining disasters: an analysis of the Westray coal mine explosion. *Journal of Management Studies*, 34, 601–23.

Ilies, R., J.D. Nahrgang and F.P. Morgeson (2007). Leader–member exchange and citizenship behaviors: a meta-analysis. *Journal of Applied Psychology*, 92 (1), 269–77.

International Association of Chiefs of Police (IACP) (1999). *Police Leadership in the 21st Century: Achieving and Sustaining Executive Success*. Alexandria, VA: IACP.

Ivancevich, J.M., R. Konopaske and M.T. Matteson (2008). *Organizational Behavior and Management*. Boston, MA: McGraw-Hill.

Jackson, R.J., D.R. Lindsay and J.E. Sanders (2013). The US Air Force approach. In G.B. Graen and J.A. Graen (eds), *LMX Leadership: The Series*, Vol. VIII. Charlotte, NC: Information Age Publishing.

Jacocks, Jr, A.M. and M.D. Bowman (2006). Developing and sustaining a culture of integrity. *Police Chief*, 58 (4), 16–22.

Kapucu, N. and M. VanWart (2006). The evolving role of the public sector in managing catastrophic disasters: lessons learned. *Administration and Society*, 38, 279–308.

Kayes, D.C. (2004). The 1996 Mount Everest climbing disaster: the breakdown of learning in teams. *Human Relations*, 57, 1263–84.

Kolditz, T.A. (2007). Research in in-extremis settings: expanding the critique of 'Why They Fight'. *Armed Forces and Society*, 32 (4), 655–58.

Leonard, H.A., J.M. Polich, J.D. Peterson, R.E. Sorter and S.C. Moore (2006). Something old something new: Army leader development in a dynamic environment. Prepared for the United States Army by Rand Arroyo Center.

McNally, J.A., S.J. Gerras and R.C. Bullis (1996). Teaching leadership at the US Military Academy at West Point. *Journal of Applied Behavioral Science*, 32, 175–88.

Morath, R., C. Curnow, C. Cronin, A. Leonard and T. McGonigle (2006). Identification of the competencies required of joint force leaders. Conducted by Caliber, National Wildfire Coordinating Group (2007). http://www.nwcg.gov. ICF, for the Joint Staff.

National Wildfire Coordinating Group (2007). http://www.nwcg.gov.

New York Times (2013). BP Executive Testifies That a Rig Explosion in the Gulf Was a Known Risk. *New York Times*, 27 February 2013. Page B2, Clifford Krauss and Barry Meier.

Perrow, C. (1997). *Normal Accidents: Living with High-Risk Technologies*. Princeton, NJ: Princeton University Press.

Reaves, B.A. (2007). *Census of State and Local Law Enforcement Agencies, 2004*. Washington, DC: US Department of Justice.

Rego, L. and R. Garau (2007). Stepping into the void. Greensboro, NC: Center for Creative Leadership.

Rodriquez, H., R. Wachtendorf, J. Kendra and J. Trainor (2006). A snapshot of the 2004 Indian Ocean tsunami: societal impacts and consequences. *Disaster Prevention Management*, 15, 163–77.

Scales, R.H. (2006). The second learning revolution. *Military Review*, January–February, 37–44.

Shrivastava, P. (1987). *Bhopal: Anatomy of a Crisis*. Cambridge, MA: Ballinger.

Snook, S.A. (2000). *Friendly Fire: The Accidental Shootdown of US Black Hawks over Northern Iraq*. Princeton, NJ: Princeton University Press.

Starbuck, W.H. and F.J. Miliken (1988). Challenger: fine-tuning the odds until something breaks. *Journal of Management Studies*, 25, 319–40.

Swanson, C.R., L. Territo and R.W. Taylor (2005). *Police Administration: Structures, Processes, and Behavior*. Upper Saddle River, NJ: Pearson Prentice Hall.

Sweeney, P.J. (2010). Do soldiers reevaluate trust in their leaders prior to combat operations? *Military Psychologist*, 42 (Suppl. I), S70–S88.

Tatham, P. and G. Kovacs (2010). The application of 'swift trust' to humanitarian logistics. *International Journal of Production Economics*, 126, 35–45.

Tempest, S., K. Starkey and C. Ennew (2007). In the death zone: a study of limits in the 1996 Mount Everest disaster. *Human Relations*, 60, 1039–64.

Ulmer, Jr, W.F., M.D. Shaler, R.C. Bullis, D.F. DiClemente, T.O. Jacobs and S.A. Shambach (2004). Leadership lessons at division command level. A report prepared under the direction of the United States Army War College Carlisle Barracks, PA.

Union Carbide Corporation (1985). Bhopal methyl isocyanate incident investigation team report. Danbury, CT: Union Carbide Corporation.

Useem, M., J.R. Cook and L. Sutton (2005). Developing leaders for decision making under stress: wildland firefighters in the South Canyon fire and its aftermath. *Academy of Management Learning and Education*, 4, 461–85.

Vaughan, D. (1996). *The Challenger Launch Decision: Risky Technology. Culture and Deviance at NASA*. Chicago, IL: University of Chicago Press.

Waller, M. and S. Uitdewilligen (2013). Transitions in action teams. Management of team leadership in extreme context: defending our homeland: protecting our first responders. In G.B. Graen and J.A. Graen (eds), *LMX Leadership: The Series*, Vol. VIII. Charlotte, NC: Information Age Publishing, pp. 165–93.

Weick, K.E. (1990). The vulnerable system: an analysis of the Tenerife air disaster. *Journal of Management*, 16, 571–93.

Weick, K.E. (1993). The collapse of sensemaking in organizations: the Mann Gulch disaster. *Administrative Science Quarterly*, 38, 628–52.

Weick, K.E. (1995). *Sensemaking in Organizations*. Thousand Oaks, CA: Sage.

Wong, L., P. Bliese and D. McGurk (2003). Military leadership: a context specific review. *Leadership Quarterly*, 14, 657–92.

PART III

Extreme individual leaders

13. Glenn Miller: leadership lessons from a successful big band musician

Michael J. Urick and Therese A. Sprinkle

INTRODUCTION

When one thinks of an 'extreme' leader, Glenn Miller, the famous big band leader from the 1930s and 1940s, may not be the first person who comes to mind. Yet, Miller is famous not only for revolutionizing the music industry, but also for inspiring a fragile United States public disturbed by the effects of the Second World War; a critical period of time for the US marked by uneasiness and uncertainty. As an emblem of patriotism at home and abroad, Miller faced a unique situation that fell outside the norm of the experiences of any other musician or leader, thereby making his case an excellent example of 'extreme' leadership.

This chapter will explore Miller's leadership through the lens of Transformational Leadership Theory and Complexity Theory to analyze the role of an 'extreme' context in his effectiveness. The application of these theories suggests a new model of 'extreme' leadership that shows how success and effectiveness are related to the complex interplay of a leader's characteristics and abilities with environmental factors. In applying this new model, Miller's behaviors and successes are offered as a case study of an effective 'extreme' leader. Overall, there are two main purposes of this chapter. The first is to illustrate that the nature of an 'extreme' context drives which particular leader traits or behaviors are important for success to occur. Second, this chapter emphasizes that leaders should be considered as part of the complex interplay between 'extreme' contexts, other environmental mechanisms and success criteria such that they must have the skill and ability to understand, react to and influence an environment.

GLENN MILLER

The context in which Miller rose to success was marked by tension, instability and rapid change (Green, 1992); it was a critical juncture for the US and the music industry. For example, during his career Miller experienced racial instability in the US (Jacoby, 2008). He also witnessed the rise of Hitler in Germany in 1933 which increased the vulnerability of the US as well as the country's forced involvement (following the attack on Pearl Harbor in 1941) in the Second World War (Green, 1992). In the midst of all this change, the music industry remained unconcerned with the broader state of the world and was focused on improvised jazz solos played by individual star instrumentalists (Simon, 1974), which seemingly mimicked the increasingly disconnected society. It was in this complex context that Miller found his unique space of action to craft a more harmonious style of music in the hopes of uniting a divided society.

(Alton) Glenn Miller was born in 1904 to a poor family in America's Midwest. Young Glenn found an old trombone and began to take lessons (Lester, 1999). Instilled with a competitive nature, hardworking spirit and drive to perfection, Miller doggedly pursued the trombone despite only developing a mediocre proficiency. His interest in music compelled him to drop out of college to pursue performing as a career (Simon, 1974). After years of arranging music and touring under the tutelage of other bandleaders (for example, Ben Pollack, the Dorsey Brothers and Ray Noble), he was determined to build his own big band (Walker, 1964). Despite Miller's business acumen and ability to make decisions like a tough business executive, his first attempt was unprofitable. Miller had major personnel issues (including band members not showing up sober to performances, and low morale) and financial issues (including being forced to play shows for low pay while out-of-pocket expenses kept increasing). Ultimately, however, much of his failure was related to the lack of a unique sound that differentiated the band from other competing groups in the minds of both listeners and promoters who hired bands for performances (Simon, 1974). Miller was competing with other notable big bands led by exceptional musicians such as Benny Goodman, Duke Ellington, Tommy and Jimmy Dorsey and Harry James, each of which had a distinct sound, often because of strong instrumental soloists (Levinson, 1999; Simon, 1974). As Miller's initial band did not have a differentiating strength, it was quite forgettable and failed to resonate with listeners, musicians, financial backers or promoters.

Building on this failure, Miller now understood the necessity of differentiating his band's sound from other groups. He used key contacts who he had met over the years to secure financial backing up front in order to put together a new group that was musically more precise and harmonious in style. This second band had its own unique sound that was unlike any group at the time even though it had instrumentation similar to other popular bands (over a dozen musicians performing on bass; drums; an instrument such as piano that could play multiple notes at once; vocals; and between three and six musicians each on trombones, reed instruments and trumpets). The new Glenn Miller Orchestra achieved its signature sound by focusing on the unique reed instrument harmonies of various saxophones coupled with a clarinet on melody, accented by periodic trumpet blasts and augmented by frequently muted trombone lines (Grudens, 2004; Simon, 1974). Such a sound was new and refreshing to audiences and promoters alike and quickly caught on so much that Miller has at times been credited as being an originator of 'pop music'. As there were fewer improvised solos from individual players, the sound was catchy and memorable.

Miller's new band was both a financial and a popular success. For example, it was this group that recorded the hits 'In the Mood', 'Chattanooga Choo-Choo', 'Pennsylvania 6-5000', 'Tuxedo Junction' and 'String of Pearls'. These were some of the most popular songs of the era and are still widely appreciated and recognized by modern audiences (Pener, 1999). Additionally, 'Chattanooga Choo-Choo' became the first ever Gold Record after selling over 1 million copies (Grudens, 2004) and Miller's band was consistently voted as the 'most popular' band by listeners and readers of influential magazines such as *Down Beat* and *Variety* (Grudens, 2004; Levinson, 1999). As a result of these successes, the band was becoming increasingly busy by 1940 with a weekly schedule that often included six sold-out shows, three additional live performances on the radio, and three rehearsals (Simon, 1974). While all of this was occurring, the US was being drawn into the Second World War. Despite the US sentiment of fear and uneasiness, Miller's music was able to calm and entertain Americans afraid of what their future might hold. Thus, he not only innovated the music industry but also became an important patriotic and cultural figure (Grudens, 2004; Simon, 1974).

At the height of his band's popularity, Miller felt an immense responsibility to the country, especially as his music and band's image were increasingly labeled as all-American (Grudens, 2004). Thus, when the US entered the Second World War, Miller disbanded his group, enlisted in the United States Army Air Forces (USAAF) and became its music director. He recruited top-notch musicians to the military band (Lester, 1999), providing an opportunity to breathe new life into USAAF's more traditional and outdated program of marches. Miller sought to boost the morale of the soldiers by providing his own popular, all-American sound (Simon, 1979). Because Miller performed for troops on the front line, he became 'a living symbol of what America meant to them, of what they were fighting for' (Pener, 1999, p. 109). Sadly, before Christmas of 1944, just as Miller was to realize his dream of performing for troops in France, his plane disappeared over the English Channel (Lester, 1999). Figure 13.1 presents a snapshot timeline of Glenn Miller's life.

Despite his disappearance, Miller's band continued performing the all-American songs that made him famous (Lester, 1999; Grudens, 2004). Even today, his legacy lives on in the band which carries his name, in his recognizable songs and in many other musical groups influenced by his style (Grudens, 2004; Vale and Wallace, 1998).

Based on the narrative presented above, Miller is an excellent example of an 'extreme' leader because his situation falls outside the norm of daily experience. Furthermore, according to Hannah et al. (2009), 'extreme' leaders exist in contexts exhibited by temporal transitions between stability and chaos; highly probable and devastating consequences; the proximity of parties to the consequences; and a combination of psychological, physical or material threat. Miller was an extreme leader because he experienced such a context. As noted above, Miller was a change agent of the music industry, thereby moving it from stability to chaos and back to stability in terms of influencing popular music. Moreover, because of the war, the US was experiencing a state of chaos with potentially devastating consequences. Though US civilians and troops varied in their proximity to battle, most Americans experienced very probable and devastating threats to their way of life. Though more specifics of Miller's 'extreme' context will be elaborated on later in this chapter, it is important to understand that Miller was an 'extreme' leader prior to further analyzing his leadership. In essence, Miller was an 'extreme' leader because he negotiated such an uncertain context and led an organization to innovate popular music, led the military in a fresh direction, and ultimately led the US toward hope and enjoyment.

This short summary provides a glimpse into Glenn Miller's leadership by highlighting areas of effectiveness and success. As effectiveness and success (though briefly noted and explained above) are both potentially subjective in nature, we now articulate our criteria for judging Miller's success.

MILLER'S SUCCESS AND EFFECTIVENESS

For the purposes of this chapter, we identify Miller as an effective and successful 'extreme' leader, and in this section we elaborate on what

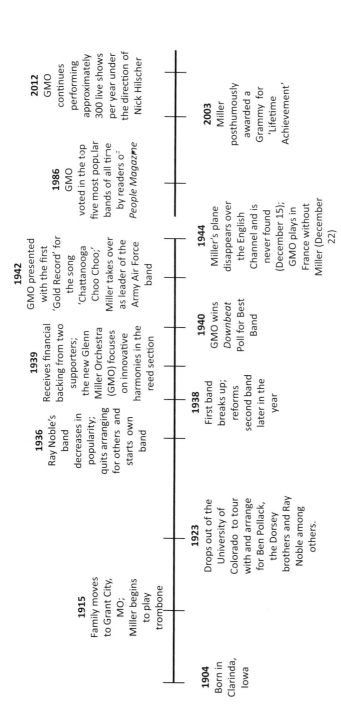

1904
Born in Clarinda, Iowa

1915
Family moves to Grant City, MO; Miller begins to play trombone

1923
Drops out of the University of Colorado to tour with and arrange for Ben Pollack, the Dorsey brothers and Ray Noble among others.

1936
Ray Noble's band decreases in popularity; quits arranging for others and starts own band

1938
First band breaks up; reforms second band later in the year

1939
Receives financial backing from two supporters; the new Glenn Miller Orchestra (GMO) focuses on innovative harmonies in the reed section

1940
GMO wins *Downbeat* Poll for Best Band

1942
GMO presented with the first 'Gold Record' for the song 'Chattanooga Choo Choo;' Miller takes over as leader of the Army Air Force band

1944
Miller's plane disappears over the English Channel and is never found (December 15); GMO plays in France without Miller (December 22)

1986
GMO voted in the top five most popular bands of all time by readers of *People Magazine*

2003
Miller posthumously awarded a Grammy for 'Lifetime Achievement'

2012
GMO continues performing approximately 300 live shows per year under the direction of Nick Hilscher

Figure 13.1   Glenn Miller time line, 1904 to present

169

traits and behaviors made him effective and how these led to specific success criteria. We consider him to be successful as a leader on the basis of his band's popularity, being considered a role model to Americans, the sustainability of his music and band, and the fact that he was a change agent of the music industry and the military. Examples of each of these factors clearly highlight the fact that Miller was quite successful.

With regard to popularity, we have noted earlier that the Glenn Miller Orchestra was voted as the favorite band of listeners in various readers' and listeners' polls. Furthermore, his albums were top sellers, having earned the first-ever gold record for selling 1.2 million copies of the song 'Chattanooga Choo-Choo' (Grudens, 2004; Simon, 1974). Miller understood the complex context in which his band operated in order to take the failed experience of leading his first band, learning from the challenges that it presented and ultimately leading his band to become one of the most popular musical groups of all time.

Miller was also a role model because he set an example for his musicians and for the American public. As an illustration, understanding that he had an issue with band members who arrived to performances drunk in his first band, he set an example early on in his successful band by never drinking in front of other band members. Furthermore, to help portray an all-American clean-cut image, Miller was always clean-shaven with a pressed suit and a conservative haircut. By appearing this way, Miller set expectations for his musicians' manner of appearance. Additionally, Miller understood that in order for the US to be successful in the 'extreme' context of the Second World War, citizens needed to be patriotic toward their country. He was a role model for how to be patriotic by enlisting in the military even though he was a celebrity at the height of his fame. Furthermore, Miller was very public about donating proceeds of his music to the armed services and encouraged others to contribute financially as well (Simon, 1974).

Sustainability is another key criterion of success evidenced by Miller. With regard to sustainability, Miller built an organization that was able to perform immediately after his disappearance without his physical presence on stage (Simon, 1974). Furthermore, Miller's band has had longevity as it continues to perform nearly 300 shows a year (Grudens, 2004; Lester, 1999). Additionally, his band's music is still appreciated by listeners and continues to be an influence on more modern music groups (Grudens, 2004; Vale and Wallace, 1998). His music's longevity was further proved when Miller won the Lifetime Achievement Grammy award in 2003 (grammy.org, n.d.).

Last, Miller was also a successful leader because he was a change agent. Understanding the complex environment of the music industry,

Miller found a way to compete with other popular bands by differentiating his sound. Doing so helped him to be considered one of the first 'pop' musicians. Furthermore, Miller changed the way that the USAAF military band operated by replacing stodgy marches with his popular music, thereby inspiring the US troops overseas (Simon, 1974). All four of these measures of success were met in an 'extreme' context characterized by temporal transitions between stability and chaos; highly probable and devastating consequences; parties with varying proximity to the consequences; and a combination of psychological, physical or material threats (Hannah et al., 2009) as introduced in the previous section. Table 13.1 summarizes these examples of Miller's success.

Table 13.1   Miller as an effective and successful leader

Success criteria	Examples
Popularity	Glenn Miller Orchestra was voted as the favorite band in a *Variety* poll of listeners of 20 radio stations (1939)
	Glenn Miller Orchestra was voted as 'favorite musical group' by readers of *Downbeat Magazine* (1940)
	Glenn Miller Orchestra's 'Chattanooga Choo-Choo' was the first ever certified 'Gold Record' for selling over 1.2 million copies (1942)
Role model	Maintained well-groomed physical appearance (pressed suit, neat haircut, clean-shaven) that he demanded of his band members
	Never drank alcohol while serving as band leader and encouraged his band members to also not partake
	Enlisted in USAAF and inspired others to do so as well
Sustainability	Glenn Miller Orchestra continues to perform to this day
	Glenn Miller's music is still widely played by other musical groups and recognized by listeners of many different ages
	Glenn Miller won the Lifetime Achievement Grammy Award (2003)
Change agent	Deviated his band's sound by focusing on a cohesive reed section playing harmonies instead of individual improvised soloists
	Considered one of the first 'pop' musicians due to emphasis on catchy melodies
	Innovated USAAF military band repertoire by bringing in popular music instead of outdated marches

With these four criteria in mind, Miller possessed seven specific traits and behaviors that allowed him to be successful within his 'extreme' environment. As we will note later, it is the complex interplay between these seven characteristics and Miller's environment that truly allowed him to be successful. Therefore, all of these are examples of 'extreme' leadership because they contributed toward his success in an 'extreme' environment. Miller exhibited the following traits and behaviors that were effective (Grudens, 2004; Simon, 1974):

1.   Persistence: for example, though his first band failed, Miller did not give up but developed a new band that redefined popular music. Additionally when Miller met resistance within the 'extreme' context of the USAAF band, he pushed his ideas forward in order to boost the morale of troops and contribute toward his success factors as we have noted.

2.   Sought relevant knowledge: for example, Miller used the 'extreme' context of the music industry to understand both what listeners wanted to hear and how other bands were not meeting their needs.

3.   Created a niche: for example, Miller used his relevant knowledge to create a product that would resonate with audiences and ultimately the American psyche that was being threatened by the context of the Second World War.

4.   Focused on strengths, not weaknesses: for example, rather than focus on soloing (which he was not strong at) as other bands did, Miller focused on creating innovative harmonies that featured his entire band – doing so resonated with listeners as is evident in the above success criteria.

5.   Laid infrastructure for his organization's success: for example Miller found initial funding for his successful band, hired more suitable musicians and provided them with precise arrangements that negated the use of solo improvisations (which decreased the potential negative effects of member turnover) – doing so allowed the band to perform for a long time and allowed for the creation of his new innovative sound.

6.   Never demanded of others that which he would not do himself: for example, Miller followed all rules and regulations that he placed upon the band, thus contributing to his role model status.

7.   Actions were visionary: for example, Miller communicated his all-American vision and sound to his musicians well, and planned for ways to continue to innovate his band once the war ended which allowed everyone to understand the purpose and image of the group.

Table 13.2 provides examples for these seven specific behaviors which encompass Miller's leadership style and contributed to the four measures of success. When examining these examples, it is important to recall that they allowed for success only within Miller's own unique context, which is why we consider them to be contributors to Miller as an 'extreme' leader (and not necessarily other leaders more generally).

Table 13.2   Miller's traits and behaviors that contributed to success

Traits and behaviors	Examples
Persistence	Despite initial failure as a band leader, and later meeting resistance from the USAAF for repertoire changes, Miller continued to push forward.
Sought relevant knowledge	Miller understood that listeners and dancers wanted to hear music that was easy to dance to, but also catchy and melodic. He knew that other bands were not meeting this need.
Created a niche	Miller used his relevant knowledge to create melodic and catchy, danceable rhythms. He fostered an all-American image for himself and band which resonated well with audiences.
Focused on strengths, not weaknesses	Miller knew he could not be a star solo trombone performer, so he focused on innovative harmonies rather than featured solos.
Laid infrastructure for organization's success	Miller laid his band's infrastructure by finding initial funding, hiring less experienced musicians who could be easily molded to fit the band's culture and providing his musicians with precise musical arrangements which increased member substitutability.
Never demanded of others that which he would not do himself	Often hardest on himself, Miller followed all rules and regulations that he set upon his band.
Actions were visionary	Miller's vision of a band focused on reed section harmonies instead of improvisation; this was unique for its time. Additionally, he was planning for ways to continue to innovate his band once the war was over.

As noted, these behaviors alone would not have been enough to elevate Miller to 'extreme' leadership without the complex interplay of his context. In the next section, we consider this complex interplay by analyzing Miller's behavior and leadership style using Transformational Leadership and Complexity Leadership Theory.

EXTREME LEADERSHIP

Miller was an effective and successful leader and his style mirrors some aspects of Transformational Leadership. However, as shall be delineated, key components of Transformational Leadership are missing from Miller's style which suggests that there may be a useful alternate perspective in examining 'extreme' contexts through Complexity Leadership Theory. With both theories, we advocate considering the complex interplay of context and traits and behaviors when analyzing how a leader is successful. Because Miller was successful in what we consider to be an 'extreme' environment, we leverage both of these theories to further show the nature of Miller's 'extreme' leadership.

TRANSFORMATIONAL LEADERSHIP

Transformational Leadership (Burns, 1978) is one of the most widely utilized theories in current leadership research (Hiller et al., 2011). It is concerned with improving the performance of followers by developing them to their full potential through idealized influence, intellectual stimulation, individualized consideration and inspirational motivation (Avolio, 1999; Bass and Avolio, 1990; Northouse, 2010). As such, Transformational Leadership is said to occur when leaders broaden and elevate the interests of employees, when they generate awareness and acceptance of purpose and mission, and when they stir employees to look beyond their own self-interests for the betterment of a group (Bass, 1990).

The strongest connection between Miller and this theory is within the two components of idealized influence and inspirational motivation. Idealized influence suggests that transformational leaders are able to influence their followers by becoming someone followers aspire to be (a role model) (House, 1977). Miller, as noted above, served as a role model to the American public, to members of the armed forces and to his band.

Additionally, Miller's leadership style aligns with inspirational motivation which exhibits having and communicating a clear vision. Bennis and Nanus (1985) defined effective leaders as those who had a clear vision, were social architects, developed trust and had knowledge of their strengths and weaknesses. Similarly, Kouzes and Posner (2007) suggest that establishing and communicating a clear vision is a main leadership criterion. Miller excelled in this area. As discussed, using relevant knowledge and building off past failures, Miller provided a clear vision for how his band should sound and how to boost the morale of soldiers on the front line.

Miller's leadership style was not as closely aligned with the other two components of Transformational Leadership: intellectual stimulation and individualized consideration. Intellectual stimulation suggests that leaders challenge their followers to innovate and question norms (Northouse, 2010). Although he questioned norms, Miller focused much of his energies on creating formal processes and enforcing strict codes of conduct. For example, his innovative musical arrangements focused on the blend of instruments working together. That is, a musician who could play a particular instrument and read music could be substituted for another (Simon, 1974). While innovative at a musical level, it did not allow for deviation or innovation from Miller's musicians.

The fourth component, individualized consideration, is related to developing followers' potential (Northouse, 2010). Biographical accounts suggest that Miller was not concerned with helping others reach their potential. For example, although he hired younger less experienced musicians, mentoring them was not his intent. Instead, he desired to reduce costs and work with musicians with smaller egos (Simon, 1974).

Though these '4 I's' are the basic tenets of Transformational Leadership, Bass and Steidlmeir (1999) also suggest that Transformational Leadership must be grounded in moral foundations. These authors suggest that transformational leaders exhibit strong moral character rooted in ethical values. In line with this, Miller had a clear set of values and ethics, most notably a strong sense of patriotism which guided much of his moral character, vision, decision-making and actions. Thus, Miller fits some criteria of a transformational leader despite not being strong in all four of its major tenets.

Perhaps Miller displayed only a few components of this theory because only certain components were important to the complex 'extreme' environment in which he operated. This notion is consistent with other research related to Transformational Leadership. For example, Pillai and Meindl (1998) state that a leader's level of charisma (which is often associated with the 4 I's of transformational leaders) was a function of contextual factors. Because research on 'extreme' contexts considers contextual factors, Transformational Leadership Theory should consider such research in analyzing leader traits and behaviors. Considering both theories leads to two interesting questions: (1) Are all components of Transformational Leadership important in all contexts? (2) If not, what contexts drive one component versus another? Using the era and context-ual factors surrounding Glenn Miller's leadership, we consider the

complex interaction between leader behaviors and traits with environmental events. Complexity Leadership Theory is a useful tool to help
explore this interaction and to illustrate why Miller is an example of
'extreme' leadership.

COMPLEXITY LEADERSHIP THEORY

Complexity Leadership Theory considers an organization as a complex
adaptive system that mutually influences and is influenced by its open
and ever-changing environment. In such an environment, change agents
are interrelated and interact with organizations so that they move towards
a future outcome (Uhl-Bien et al., 2007). Complexity Theory fits well
with research on 'extreme' contexts because both consider the role that
contexts play in leadership outcomes (as Complexity Theory defines an
environment as being composed of 'context' and 'mechanisms', which
will be further discussed below). While research on 'extreme' contexts
focuses on what makes a particular context different from 'normal'
contexts (Hannah et al., 2009), Complexity Theory complements such
studies by considering the role of context in understanding outcomes.
Furthermore, Complexity Theory considers the difficulty of understanding all aspects of a leader's context. Therefore, it suggests that all
environments are unique because of their complexity and that a leader's
context is also likely 'extreme' (that is, unique) as well. As such, our
approach is that Complexity Theorists discuss 'extreme' contexts when
they talk about environment. Complex (or 'extreme') systems emerge
when the organization is faced with challenges from both the inside and
the outside. As these challenges cannot be treated as separate and distinct
concerns, they force the organization to adapt, explore new possibilities
and make adjustments to their current way of working despite potentially
not knowing the effects of their changes.

Uhl-Bien et al. (2007) suggest that, in helping their organizations to
adapt, leaders have three intertwined roles. The first is administrative,
which is devoted to 'planning and coordinating organizational activities'
(p. 306). Second, the enabling role of leadership focuses on managing the
middle ground between administrative and visionary leadership (p. 306).
Lastly, the role of being visionary is related to motivating followers and
allowing for adaptation. These leadership roles are intertwined because
together they provide for emergent change and adaptability (Uhl-Bien et
al., 2007). Miller exhibited all three of these roles. First, he exhibited the
administrative role through making top-down decisions for his organization as evident in his persistence, seeking relevant knowledge and

finding a niche. Miller also exhibited enabling capabilities by focusing on strengths, laying infrastructure for his orchestra and never demanding of others what he would not do. Additionally, Miller was visionary in the way that he focused his band's sound, innovated the USAAF band and planned to continue with his orchestra once becoming a civilian again.

Although Complexity Leadership Theory recognizes that individual leaders must engage in three roles for an organization to adapt to complexity, it largely ignores how leaders might exhibit certain traits or behaviors that, within their particular environment, allow for successful outcomes at both the leader and organizational levels (Mumford et al., 2002). We argue that the leader is an important component of this theory as they must have the traits, ability and experience to read and adapt to an environment in order to guide the organization (Uhl-Bien et al., 2007). With this in mind, Miller's success and effectiveness were not accidental but due to the combination of 'extreme' contextual components, environment mechanics and his own personal traits and behaviors.

Contextual components are trends or societal climates brought about by the dominant world-view of the time, such as rapidly changing needs and patterns of tension. Note the similarity here to Hannah et al.'s (2009) definition of 'extreme' contexts as having patterns of chaos and complexity. Environmental mechanisms are behaviors of agents that lead to complex outcomes. The interaction of 'extreme' context and environmental mechanisms provides tension, requiring a leader to sift through a complex 'milieu' of constantly shifting or competing ideas as well as uncertainty and ambiguity (Uhl-Bien et al., 2007, p. 307). Current Complexity Leadership Theory thinking appears to assume that a leader will simply know how to attend to the milieu and, working through all three aspects of leadership, create space for adaptation, learning and creativity.

We extend Complexity Leadership Theory by considering Hannah et al.'s (2009) definition of 'extreme' contexts and by suggesting that having the right leader in place is equally important to the milieu; an individual must have the right blend of traits and prior experience to take advantage of the complex patterns and guide the organization. Without the appropriate blend of traits and experience, an individual may not recognize the signals provided by the complex system or have the vision to grasp the need for change. Hunter et al. (2009) suggest that individual leaders respond to complexity in different ways. Thus, if the wrong agent is in place, the contextual signals may not be received. Building on Complexity Theory and 'extreme' contexts, we offer a model of leader effectiveness suggesting that certain leader qualities (for example, self-awareness, vision and leader crucibles; Bennis and Thomas, 2002) must be present before they may successfully lead the organization through the emergent dynamics (see Figure 13.2).

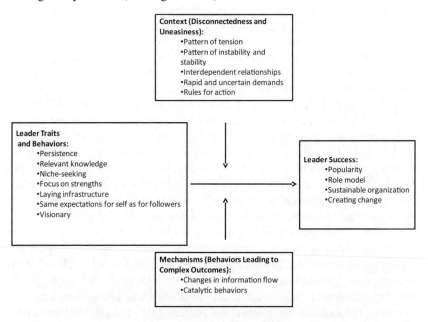

Figure 13.2   Leader-Context Effectiveness Model (with examples from Glenn Miller)

In the Leader-Context Effectiveness Model, while the context and mechanisms of a complex system provide the intrinsically layered tensions necessary for a particular outcome, a leader with the components needed for change also has to be in a position to influence the organization to be successful. This individual must possess the right combination of personality, self-awareness and personal experiences to bring about the change. In Figure 13.2, we show (using Miller as an example) how a leader's traits, behavior and experiences are viewed as equally important to bring about the organizational change.

From this model, it is apparent that Miller had the correct blend of personality, self-awareness and past experiences to become successful within his complex environment comprised in part of an 'extreme' context. Though Complexity Leadership Theory and the study of 'extreme' contexts (Hannah et al., 2009) would suggest that it is impossible to fully describe all of the contextual components at play, it is noteworthy that Miller's 'extreme' context was outside the norm of other leaders. The context of the time was marked by conflict and division, but also opportunity that allowed for Miller to be successful. Therefore, his position within the environment in which he operated was unique. In their studies of Complexity Theory and 'extreme' contexts Uhl-Bien et al. (2007) noted that a context is composed of patterns of tension, patterns of instability and stability, interdependent relationships, rapidly changing demands and rules for action. In noting these components, the question arises as to how a leader can operate in order to be successful (Hannah et al., 2009). Though noted earlier, a few illustrative examples are elaborated on below.

Miller used his behaviors and abilities (for example his persistence to create a unique sound, his inability to solo) to build upon American perceptions of uncertainty and patterns of tensions. As discussed, he realized that his competitors were focused on an individually improvised jazz sound (Grudens, 2004), which may have subconsciously mimicked the disconnectedness and uncertainty of the US. Thus, because of the interaction of the strong desire for unity and certainty in his 'extreme' context and a compelling vision for the future of music, Miller created an organization which recognized solid talent but did not feed and highlight factions. Ultimately, Miller found a way to provide innovative musical phrasing which emphasized an entire section, rather than individual players; this set him apart from competitors and emphasized the group, thus interacting positively with the contextual need for unity. Furthermore, by providing structure to his band in terms of limited improvisation and strict directions on sheet music, Miller's focus on infrastructure interacted positively with the contextual need to minimize ambiguity (perhaps caused by uneasiness related to the war).

A second contextual aspect, rules for action, is also exemplified by Miller's focus on infrastructure as well as his strength of regulating his musicians such as through a strict dress code. Miller operated in a time when proper dress and behavior regulation were emphasized. Due to his personal need for perfection, Miller paid close attention to stage presence, insisting that his musicians be well-groomed, clean-cut and attired similarly. This provided a unique and memorable look of harmony and unity, portraying an all-American image (Simon, 1974). Thus, Miller's vision and prior experience enabled an adaptive change prompted by contextual rules for action. These aspects of Miller's 'extreme' context are summarized in Table 13.3.

It should also be noted that Miller was effective because he was able to read and interact positively with the context described above. He sought relevant knowledge about the environment in which he operated and used this knowledge to develop a niche. Therefore, he was able to lead a

Table 13.3   Contextual aspects of the dynamic system

Contextual aspect	Example
Pattern of tension (tension caused cyclical patterns of behaviors)	Increased ethnic populations from Southern and Eastern Europe clung to Old World culture while attempting to integrate into American society (Jacoby, 2008). Meanwhile, many who had been living in the US for a longer period sought a time when there was less disruption to daily life. They desired harmony and accord and longed for sameness.
Pattern of instability emerging from period of relative stability	After a period of relative stability in their relationships with the white majority, African Americans sought to achieve greater equality in the south. This brought about increased racial attacks and segregation.
Interdependent relationships	The alliance of the US with France and the UK, crafted after the First World War, made the US vulnerable to Hitler's rise to power in 1933.
Rapidly changing environmental demands	With the inevitability of entering the war in Europe, Americans realized the world after the war was unpredictable as no one was assured of its outcome.
Rules for action	The period between 1915 and 1930 emphasized 'regulating behavior and transforming the social fabric' through the use of advertising and guidelines for appropriate behaviors (Green, 1992, p. 9). Related to this, consumerism also began to rise.

Sources: Except where noted, 'Contextual aspects' were elicited from Uhl-Bien et al. (2007), and 'Examples' of these contextual aspects from the dynamic system were elicited from Green (1992).

sustainable organization. However, when considering leader success and effectiveness, it is important to consider both the context and the mechanisms of the environment. Uhl-Bien et al. (2007) consider two mechanisms along with 'extreme' contextual components to be part of a leader's overall environment with which they must interact. These two components are related to change: both the change in how information flows as well as the mechanisms that initiate changes to organizations.

Of these two mechanisms mentioned, changes to information flow was perhaps the most visible. Miller's ability to reach a broad audience (thereby allowing him to become more popular, a role model and a change agent in the music industry) was facilitated by the ability of the radio to reach more listeners. Radio's delivery mechanism shattered poverty lines and diversified the acquisition of information (for example, Miller's music) across the nation. Additionally, success in this delivery mechanism drove the need for repeatable hummable music (Miller's initial vision). Thus, Miller leaned on personal traits and experiences to perform unique repeatable hummable harmonies (Grudens, 2004) which gave his band a trademark sound perfect for the radio (Simon, 1974).

On the other hand, Miller also helped to change his context through environmental mechanisms. Miller's own lack of proficiency on the trombone and failed band experience led him to form a band where up-and-coming younger players could easily acquire his vision and sound. He emphasized the use of a regimented repertoire book with sheet music playable by any decent musician, therefore making it easy to substitute or interchange players as needed. Thus Miller, leaning on experience and personal traits, introduced a catalytic behavior change for his industry by allowing for a more efficient process for band member selection and replacement. Table 13.4 outlines the two environmental mechanisms that Miller experienced.

Table 13.4   Mechanisms of the dynamic system

Mechanism	US in 1920–1941
Changes in information flow	Increased production capabilities and rapid consumerism (thanks to the rules for action) meant most households could use the radio as a source of news and connection to outside world (Green, 1992)
Catalytic change to the organization	Popular music supported star instrumentalists often performing free blowing extended improvised jazz solos which created non-repeatable melodies, reliance on individual band members, and less cohesiveness in the minds of listeners (Simon, 1974)

Source: Mechanisms elicited from Uhl-Bien et al. (2007).

LEADERSHIP LESSONS

Using Miller as an example of 'extreme' leadership, we can draw two specific lessons that can be learned. First, context will drive which of the '4 I's' of Transformational Leadership are more important than others. Second, as an extension of Complexity Leadership Theory, an individual's traits, behaviors, self-awareness and experiences will add to the milieu of 'extreme' contexts and mechanisms to allow for leader effectiveness. Therefore, it is impossible to divorce the complex interaction of environment and leader traits and behaviors in order to determine how a leader is successful. As a result, this case study serves as an illustration in considering the interplay between 'extreme' context and the leader, thereby extending theory on 'extreme' leadership.

As noted earlier, Miller's leadership style was low on some dimensions of Transformational Leadership. Specifically, Miller was low on individualized consideration and intellectual stimulation, yet we consider his behavior transformational. We suggest that the environment in which he operated did not require individual consideration and intellectual stimulation. For example, by not offering to help others reach their full potential or to help them to think creatively, Miller created a hugely successful product for listeners. Additionally, doing so helped him play to his strengths by emphasizing the importance of infrastructure. It would appear, then, that a leader who is able to interact positively within a context is more important than possessing all four 'I's' of Transformational Leadership.

This is applicable in many business situations. For example, a manager who feels that they are not good at setting a compelling vision (inspirational motivation) might still be effective within a particular environment. Specifically, if their context were one in which employees already had a clear uniting vision set by their team or organization, this component of Transformational Leadership would not be important. Additionally, their strength of getting their employees to think creatively (intellectual stimulation) could help their team to achieve organizational goals efficiently. This is but one hypothetical example where not all the '4 I's' of Transformational Leadership are important because the environment dictates which are the most crucial. This proposition holds true for a variety of situations, jobs and industries. However, to appropriately comprehend which aspects are most crucial, business leaders should understand (to the extent possible) the nature of the environment in which they operate, including (but not limited to) employee strengths, the competitive landscape and broader societal trends.

We also propose that Complexity Leadership Theory and research on 'extreme' contexts may be extended by recognizing the intricate interplay between the individual leader, context and environmental mechanisms which allow for the effectiveness and overall success of a leader. We argue that an individual's traits, skills and experience are co-mingled with an individual's environment because all work to create space for that leader to succeed. In reaction to this connection, they are able to exhibit precisely the right behaviors and characteristics necessary for the creativity and adaptation. Thus, environmental complexity may have a much greater impact on a leader's ultimate success than what is sometimes assumed.

In the example presented above, the manager who feels that they are not strong at communicating a strong vision, but can encourage thinking outside of the box, does so perhaps instinctively. It is for this reason that, in an environment where creating a vision is not required, they feel comfortable. However, just as Miller would most likely not be able to lead a band successfully in a different context, so too the manager would be likely to feel uncomfortable in an environment that would require them to craft a vision. That is, they would feel uncomfortable if they were unable to adapt to that particular environment or to interact with their environment in such a way that they changed it. Regardless of industry or work context, leaders will always have strengths and weaknesses, so it is important for them to find a certain level of fit with what the environment requires of them or adapt the environment to better suit their skills.

Taken together, these lessons suggest that those aspects of a leader which allow for success and effectiveness may not operate in the same manner for all leaders, even those with similar traits, skills and experiences. This is because context and environment may be vastly different for all leaders. Because Complexity Leadership Theory suggests the importance of both internal and external forces, leaders must consider industry, societal, geographical and organizational characteristics among others when considering how to achieve a particular outcome. Similarly, an effective leader in one complex system may not be as effective in other contexts. As evidence of this, Hunter et al. (2009) have explored different types of leadership behavior and found that effectiveness is contingent on many variables such as the level of complexity that exists.

One final caution should be noted when examining leader effectiveness. Often, it is very difficult to truly understand the nature of a leader's context and mechanisms and the complex interplay of how they affect each other. Therefore, it may very well be that understanding how one fits within a context (whether it be an organization's culture, industry or even the broader trends of a nation) is the most crucial component to becoming a successful leader. Though difficult for many leaders to do, once their leader–environment fit is determined, leaders can then seek to influence their organization through emphasizing certain aspects of their individual characteristics.

CONCLUSION

As highlighted by Miller, the role of context is important for leader effectiveness. While many may try to emulate Miller's seven successful characteristics, we argue that doing so may not guarantee leader effectiveness. Contextual situations, industry and societal mechanisms will vary from Miller's experiences and may be equally complex in their own unique way.

This chapter has introduced the Leader-Context Effectiveness Model in order to clearly show readers how components of 'extreme' contexts and environmental mechanisms complexly relate to a leader's traits and behaviors. Doing so extends leadership theory by highlighting the importance of a leader's fit with the environment. Furthermore, this case teaches two important lessons: (1) the nature of the 'extreme' context drives which leader traits and behaviors are most important; and (2) leader characteristics need to be considered within the milieu of an environment. Both of these lessons are extensions of leadership theory and can be applied to almost any business context. Through Miller's example, a leader needs to fit within a particular environment or adapt the environment in order to fit their traits and behaviors. While much work needs to be done in order to better understand how leaders can gain an understanding of precisely how to fit with their environment, this case study makes it clear that only when a leader has some level of 'fit' within an environment will they have successful outcomes. Therefore, the concept of leader–environment fit has implications for recruiting employees for leadership roles as well as for training current leaders to better understand crucial components of their environment and to encourage them to seek out ways in which they might capitalize on their strengths to be successful.

While Miller is an example of an 'extreme' leader with the characteristics that allowed for success in his environment, he is not the only leader who we could have considered, as these leadership lessons apply to many known leaders. However, we selected Miller after reading biographical accounts of his life written by people who knew him first hand and found his leadership to be an excellent illustrative example for our purposes. One cannot know about Miller's life without pondering how he was able to be so wildly successful in his industry (and a patriotic hero in the minds of Americans of the time) yet was only a mediocre trombone player. Upon further analysis, through reading multiple accounts of his life, we were able to clearly see that Miller was successful because his traits and behaviors were needed within his 'extreme' context. While first-hand interviews and conversations with people who knew Miller would have strengthened this chapter methodologically, the number of people still living who knew Miller personally are likely few. Furthermore, because we triangulated published perspectives of Miller's life and leadership through multiple accounts, we are confident in the appropriateness of our analysis.

While we have noted that Miller is one clear example of the importance of leader–environment fit, the challenges that he experienced are not unique for other leaders. Specifically, the challenge for individuals who aspire to leadership is to know their own strengths, ideals and characteristics as well as Miller did. This self-awareness will enable them to act to the best of their ability within a particular context which may be 'extreme', complex and ever-changing.

REFERENCES

Avolio, Bruce J. (1999). *Full Leadership Development: Building the Vital Forces in Organizations*. Thousand Oaks, CA: Sage.

Bass, B.M. (1990). From transactional to transformational leadership: learning to share the vision. *Organizational Dynamics*, 18, 19–31.

Bass, Bernard M. and Bruce J. Avolio (1990). *Transformational Leadership Development: Manual for the Multifactor Leadership Questionnaire*. Palo Alto, CA: Consulting Psychologist Press.

Bass, B.M. and P. Steidlmeier (1999). Ethics, character, and authentic transformational leadership. *Leadership Quarterly*, 10, 181–217.

Bennis, Warren G. and Burt Nanus (1985). *Leaders: The Strategies for Taking Charge*. New York: HarperCollins Publishers.

Bennis, W.G. and R.J. Thomas (2002). Crucibles of leadership. *Harvard Business Review*, 80, 39–45.

Burns, James M. (1978). *Leadership*. New York: Harper and Row.

Grammy.org (n.d.). Lifetime Achievement Awards. http://www.grammy.org/recording-academy/awards/lifetime-awards.

Green, Harvey (1992). *The Uncertainty of Everyday Life: 1915–1945*. New York: HarperCollins Publishers.

Grudens, Richard (2004). *Chatanooga Choo Choo: The Life and Times of the World Famous Glenn Miller Orchestra*, Stonybrook, NY: Celebrity Profiles Publishing Company.

Hannah, S.T., M. Uhl-Bien, B.J. Avolio and F.L. Cavarretta (2009). A framework for examining leadership in extreme contexts. *Leadership Quarterly*, 20, 897–919.

Hiller, N.J., L.A. DeChurch, T. Murase and D. Doty (2011). Searching for outcomes of leadership: a 25-year review. *Journal of Management*, 37, 1137–77.

House, R.J. (1977). A 1976 theory of charismatic leadership. In J.G. Hunt and L.L. Larson (eds), *Leadership: The Cutting Edge*. Carbondale, IL: Southern Illinois University Press, pp. 189–207.

Hunter, S.T., K.E. Bedell-Avers and M.D. Mumford (2009). Impact of situational framing and complexity on charismatic, ideological and pragmatic leaders: investigation using a computer simulation. *Leadership Quarterly*, 20, 383–404.

Jacoby, Susan (2008). *The Age of American Unreason*, New York: Vintage Books/ Random House.

Kouzes, James M. and Barry Z. Posner (2007). *The Leadership Challenge*, 4th edn. San Francisco, CA: Jossey-Bass.

Lester, J. (1999). Glenn Miller. In Steve Knopper (ed.), *MusicHound Swing: The Essential Album Guide*. Farmington Hills, MI: Visible Ink Press, pp. 216–19.

Levinson, Peter J. (1999). *Trumpet Blues: The Life of Harry James*. New York: Oxford University Press.

Mumford, M.D., G.M. Scott, B. Gaddis and J.M. Strange (2002). Leading creative people: orchestrating expertise and relationships. *Leadership Quarterly*, 13, 705–50.

Northouse, Peter G. (2010). *Leadership: Theory and Practice*. Thousand Oaks, CA: Sage.

Pener, Degen (1999). *The Swing Book*. Boston, MA: Back Bay Books.

Pillai, R. and J.R. Meindl (1998). Context and charisma: a 'meso' level examination of the relationship of organic structure, collectivism, and crisis to charismatic leadership. *Journal of Management*, 24, 643–71.

Simon, George T. (1974). *Glenn Miller and his Orchestra*. New York: Da Capo Press.

Uhl-Bien, M., R. Marion and B. McKelvey (2007). Complexity leadership theory: shifting leadership from the industrial age to the knowledge era. *Leadership Quarterly*, 18, 290–318.

Vale, V. and Marian Wallace (1998). *Swing! The New Retro Renaissance*. San Francisco, CA: V/Search Publications.

Walker, Leo (1964). *The Wonderful Era of the Great Dance Band*. Garden City, NY: Doubleday

14. Extreme leadership as creative leadership: reflections on Francis Ford Coppola in *The Godfather*

Charalampos Mainemelis and Olga Epitropaki

INTRODUCTION

How do extreme leadership situations arise? According to one view, they are triggered by environmental factors that have nothing or little to do with the leader. The term 'extreme' in that case refers to some form of external adversity, such as environmental perils (for example, physical disasters, financial crises) or other external threats deeply embedded in the context of specific types of organizations (for example, the military, law enforcement, crisis response units and so on). In such settings, the role of leadership is mainly viewed as reactive to the extreme contextual conditions. Leaders respond to externally induced crises and attempt to handle them in the most effective way possible (for example, Hannah et al., 2009). According to a second view, extreme leadership situations are triggered by leader behaviors that have nothing or little to do with the external environment. The term 'extreme' in that case refers to severe group dynamics directly caused by the actions of the leader. Past research has linked leader-induced extreme situations to dysfunctional leader behaviors such as abusive (Aryee et al., 2007), toxic (Lipman-Blumen, 2005) and destructive leadership (Einarsen et al., 2007).

In this chapter we offer a third view which focuses on extreme leadership situations that arise from the leader–context interaction, rather than from the environment or from the leader alone. Unlike the first view, we focus on extreme leadership situations that are internal to the organization and social in nature; and unlike the second view, we suggest that leader-induced extreme situations are not always dysfunctional but can lead to superior creative performance. We illustrate this third type of extreme leadership with a case study of the film director Francis Ford

Coppola and the making of the film *The Godfather*, which was produced by Paramount Pictures in 1972. We select *The Godfather* because its monumental success (in artistic acclaim, financial performance and lasting cultural impact) emerged from a collaborative film-making process that is still remembered today as one of the most extreme, chaotic and tenuous in the history of Hollywood (see Browne, 2000). Furthermore, Coppola's personal behavior during the film's production serves as an exemplar of an extreme leader who is at once creative, visionary, risk-seeking, stubborn, aggressive, deviant, deceiving and even abusive.

We first present the case study, and then we draw on extant leadership and creativity theories in order to analyze the emergence and effectiveness of extreme leadership in the *Godfather* case and, more generally, in collective creative endeavors.

THE UNLIKELY MAKING OF A CINEMATIC CULT

The Historical Context

In the 1960s the auteur movement sought to establish cinema as an art (versus a craft or product) and the director as an artist (versus a machine operator) (Mainemelis et al., 2008). Positioning itself against historical determinism, the auteur movement posited that it is the director's distinctive individual stamp that distinguishes the artistic value of a film (Sarris, 1962, 1968). A parallel development at that time was that ticket admissions started to decline in the early 1960s and reached a then historic low by 1971. According to Peter Bart, then Paramount's vice-president of production, 'The movie industry was more on its ass than any time in its history, literally almost wiped off the face of the earth' (in Biskind, 1998, p. 20).

Up to that time directors were older men who worked with limited creative freedom. In the late 1960s the studios opened their doors to a generation of young directors in an attempt to save Hollywood. Director John Boorman recalls that 'There was a complete loss of nerve by the American studios at that point. They were so confused and so uncertain as to what to do, they were quite willing to cede power to the directors' (in Biskind, 1998, p. 22). As soon as the young directors walked into the studio system, however, they found themselves fighting a fierce battle against the old establishment. According to Steven Spielberg:

> It was not like the older generation volunteered the baton. The younger generation had to wrest it away from them. There was a great deal of

prejudice if you were a kid and ambitious. When I made my first professional TV show, *Night Gallery*, I had everybody on the set against me. The average age of the crew was sixty years old. When they saw me walk on the stage, looking younger that I really was, like a baby, everybody turned their backs on me, just walked away. I got the sense that I represented this threat to everyone's job. (quoted in Biskind, 1998, p. 20)

In the early 1970s, Coppola's *The Godfather* (1972) and Spielberg's *Jaws* (1975) were hailed as the first blockbusters in history. The phenomenal financial success of these films, in conjunction with the rising influence of the auteur movement, revitalized Hollywood, shifted power among the professional roles in it (Baker and Faulkner, 1991), and bestowed upon the role of the director supreme power and prestige (Allen and Lincoln, 2004; Hicks and Petrova, 2006). As studios started to look at the blockbuster as a formula for high profits (Mezias and Mezias, 2000), some directors were able to 'cash' their box office success by gaining more power and creative freedom. The movies made during that era did not merely reach unprecedented creative heights and massive financial returns; they also brought battalions of young people to the movie theaters and elevated the status of film-making as an art form in US society (Sontag, 1996). Peter Gruber, ex-head of Sony Pictures, has described that period of Hollywood as follows: 'It was like the ground was in flames and tulips were coming up at the same time' (quoted in Biskind, 1998, p. 14).

The Events

In 1968 Paramount acquired the movie rights of Mario Puzzo's novel *The Godfather*, but it was reluctant to produce it because other gangster movies had just flopped, including Paramount's *Brotherhood*. The studio reconsidered only after Puzzo's novel started ascending the bestseller list and Universal Studios offered Paramount $1 million to purchase the option (Biskind, 1998). Robert Evans, Paramount's head of production, commissioned Puzzo to write a script that diverged in many ways from the book. After several directors turned down the offer to direct the film (including Bogdanovich, Brooks, Costa-Gavras, Leone, Pechinpah, Schaffner and Yates), Evans's vice-president Peter Bart suggested Coppola, who had made a name as a scriptwriter and had also directed smaller films (Sragow, 1997). In his memoirs, Evans (1994, p. 220) recalls his initial reaction: 'That's your esoteric bullshit coming out. The guy made three pictures: *You're a Big Boy Now*, artsy-fartsy, no business, *Finian's Rainbow*, a top Broadway musical he made into a disaster, and *Rain People*, which everyone rained on.'

Bart managed to persuade Evans, but Coppola rejected the offer because he considered it a low-quality commercial movie. Coppola envisioned himself as a writer-director who would maintain complete control of his creative work, and he believed that 'The way to come to power is not always to challenge the establishment, but first to make a place in it and then challenge and double-cross the establishment' (in Pye and Myles, 1979, p. 83). According to George Lucas, 'Francis could sell ice to Eskimos. He has charisma beyond logic. I can now see what kind of man the great Caesars of history were, their magnetism' (in Bock, 1979, p. 9). Coppola (1994) has described how in the early 1960s he made a movie, when producer Roger Corman:

> gave me a check for $20 000 ... and I went to Ireland. When I was in Ireland ... this guy offered me to buy the English rights for $20 000. So I had now $40 000. Roger, of course, expected to get his $20 000 back, still make the movie for the 20 with the English rights, and get the film for free. But I sort of just duped him. I took both checks and I put it in the bank ... Then I made the movie for $40 000, which was this little black-and-white horror film called *Dementia 13*.

Director John Milius remembers that, when Coppola was making *Finian's Rainbow* at Warner Brother Studios in 1967: 'Francis had this closet in the producer's building. He was stealing film stock and equipment and putting it in there. He said, "Someday when they finally throw me out of here, we'll have enough and we make another film"' (quoted in Biskind, 1998, p. 38).

In 1969 Coppola, Lucas and others founded American Zoetrope in San Francisco. Marcia Lucas recalls that 'Francis left LA because he didn't want to be a small fish in a big pond. I think he wanted to be a big fish in a small pond' (in Biskind, 1998, p. 91). When Coppola rejected Paramount's offer, Zoetrope had started accumulating debt and Coppola was also unable to pay back his substantial personal debts to Warner, Corman and other people. Bart kept on pressing Coppola and, eventually, Lucas persuaded him that they desperately needed Paramount's money.

Coppola accepted under the condition that he would rewrite the script, which he did in collaboration with Puzzo. He first removed all 'sleazy commercial elements', including hippies, an Italian-American singer's dipsomania, and a girl with an oversized vagina. Next, he infused the story with personal experiences from his own Italian-American family. He then got the idea that this was a family story as much as a crime story, where the Mob was just a metaphor for American capitalism (Sragow, 1997). Later the *New Yorker*'s Pauline Kael would call the book 'trash' and others would give Coppola full credit for turning a gangster plot into a bold allegory (Murray, 1975). Puzzo has said that 'To this day, I can't even remember what's mine and what's Francis. I feel it's Francis's picture' (in Sragow, 1997). According to Coppola:

> It wasn't trash ... if the two movies are strong, it's because of what Mario originally put in his book that was strong and valid ... I have great respect for Mario. He created the story, he created the characters, even in Part II which I wrote more of than Part I. But all the key elements go back to his book. (Quoted in Murray, 1975)

After persuading the studio what the story 'is really about', Coppola fought to increase the budget and shoot the film in New York in a 1940s setting. Paramount wanted to shoot the film in Los Angeles in a contemporary (1970s) setting in order to keep the budget below $2 million. Coppola hired New York-based crew members, hoping that the studio would rather shoot the movie in New York (a very expensive location) instead of paying an equal amount of money to fly the entire crew to Los Angeles (Shanken, 2003). The huge sales of Puzzo's book at that time also influenced the studio's decisions, and what got started as a $2 million gangster movie that was set in the 1970s and was to be filmed in Los Angeles was transformed by Coppola into a $6.2 million grand allegory set in the 1940s and filmed in New York (Lewis, 2000).

Coppola then clashed with Evans about casting. The common practice in Hollywood was that extras were professional actors, but Coppola spent several hours in the streets of New York screening barbers, bakers and other non-actors who looked and talked like genuine Italian-Americans. Coppola also insisted stubbornly that the leading roles should be played by Marlon Brando (Don Corleone) and Al Pacino (Michael), but Evans rejected both. 'Bob Evans was a handsome guy, a tall guy, so he tended to see Michael as someone more like himself. He was suggesting Ryan O'Neal and Bob Redford and I was suggesting Pacino. I wanted someone more like me' (Coppola, in Sragow, 1997). While in retrospect Coppola's intuition was remarkably spot on, Evans's judgment was far from unreasonable: Al Pacino was a young theatrical actor who had never made a movie before, and Brando was overweight, had a terrible reputation as a troublemaker, and his last films were disasters. When a deadlock ensued, Coppola was summoned to a meeting where, in front of executives and lawyers, Stanley Jaffe told him: 'As president of Paramount Pictures, I assure you that Marlon Brando will never appear in this motion picture and, furthermore, as president of the company, I will no longer allow you to discuss it' (quoted in Murray, 1975).

Coppola's reaction was to quickly collapse on the floor in a heap, pretending an epileptic fit. He got up only after Jaffe told him that he could have Brando under the condition that he would agree to a screen test. Coppola did not dare to ask Brando to do a screen test, but he signed him anyway (Lewis, 2000). According to Bart, although Coppola got the actors that he wanted – Brando, Pacino, Duvall and Keaton – he had wasted so much energy in fighting with Evans that he did not have the time to think about locations and other aspects of the movie.

Coppola began shooting on 29 March 1971. A week later he was already falling behind schedule and losing control of the tough New York crew, who were used to working with strong and decisive directors like Kazan, Lumet and Penn (Biskind, 1998). In an industry where status and symbolic capital are key (Jones, 1996), Coppola was a 30-year-old recent film graduate whose credibility had been undermined in the pre-production period by his clashes with Evans and the studio. Steven Kesten, first assistant director, recalled (in Biskind, 1998, p. 155): 'Francis's credentials at that point, as a director, were zip. He was at the bottom of the abyss. Running a set means you gotta be the guy that makes it go forward. And it just wasn't happening. Francis was always having to be nudged along.'

Coppola has always felt that, if a film finishes exactly as it was initially planned, it is unlikely to be a good film. But his tendency to improvise and delegate, in conjunction with his belief that film-making is a fluid and unfolding creative process, brought chaos to the *Godfather* set. Coppola kept on rewriting the script at night and spending half of the morning rehearsing rather than shooting scenes, while the crew was sitting around waiting. Actors whose roles had been eliminated would appear on the set, and crew members were faced with new or continually shifting demands. One day Al Pacino walked by mistake into an unlit room in the Corleone house. Coppola loudly assured the crew that his actors have the freedom to walk wherever they want to. Cinematographer Gordon Willis asked for a few minutes in order to relight, but Coppola insisted that he wanted to shoot right away. Willis stormed out of the set, Coppola ordered Willis's cameraman to shoot, and when the latter refused, Coppola retreated into his office screaming 'why won't they let me make my movie?' (quoted in Biskind, 1998 p. 157). Willis recalls:

> It was hard for Francis because everybody was trying to pull his pants off. He was not well schooled in that kind of moviemaking. He had only done some kind of on-the-road running-around kind of stuff … I was like Hitler. If anybody was doing the right thing to get this movie made from day to day, it was me. I like to lay out a thing and make it work, with discipline. Francis's

attitude is more like, 'I'll set my clothes on fire – if I can make it to the other side of the room it'll be spectacular.' You can't shoot a whole movie hoping for happy accidents. What you get is one big accident. (Quoted in Sragow, 1997)

There were daily rumors that the film was a disaster and Coppola was going to get fired. One day Coppola disappeared from the set and was later found wandering in a toy store. Martin Scorsese recalls visiting Coppola on the set of the film's funeral scene: 'Francis just sat down on one of the tombstones and started crying' (in Rensin, 1991). Things got worse when the New York Mob started shutting access to key filming locations. Dean Tavoularis, production designer, notes that 'We looked high and low; somebody would follow us; we'd strike a deal for a location and suddenly it would unravel.' Evans (1994) recalls receiving such messages as, 'To kill the snake you cut off its head', and, 'If you want your son to live longer than two weeks, get out of town.'

The studio was disappointed with everything about the movie, but Coppola (in Shanken, 2003, p. 86) kept on frustrating them; for example, for the needs of a scene he flew from Chicago some tomatoes 'at a cost of $3000 or so much a tomato'. Peter Bart recalls trying to keep Coppola on the job when other studio executives wanted to replace him with Elia Kazan:

> At a pivotal meeting in Bob Evans' office, I brought in a prominent Hollywood figure; he asserted that he had talked to Kazan and found him to be senile, and was sufficiently persuasive that the idea of hiring him was thrown out. I'm not proud of this – I knew that Gadge was not senile – but at every studio there comes a crunch time when you have to be devious. (Quoted in Sragow, 1997)

At some point a group of crew members, led by the film's first editor Aram Avakian, tried to get Coppola replaced, but Coppola (in Shanken, 2003, p. 84) reacted quickly:

> Now I had a group in my own movie that was conspiring to get rid of me. My own friends! They figured I was lost … But I've been told that film studios never fire a director on a weekday, because if a director gets fired on a weekday, then the studio loses two days in the transition. They'll always wait till the weekend. They'll fire him after Friday, then the new director comes in and he'll be ready for Monday. So I took a real chance. I went in – and I knew who all the conspirators were; there were about 16 of them – I fired them all on Wednesday. They were like, 'What do you mean we're fired?' I said, 'I'm the director. Fired. You're out.'

While Coppola's quirky and delegative style was a major source of conflict, it allowed him to elicit superb creative contributions from his crew. When he first met with Brando to discuss his role, Brando put shoe polish on his hair and Kleenex tissues in his mouth, improvising on the spot the Don Corleone character. Later, when Coppola told Brando that he did not know how to shoot the scene where Don Corleone plays with a kid and dies, Brando said 'This is how I play with kids' and put some orange peels in his mouth, only to hear Coppola saying that he would not like to shoot the scene in any other way. Gordon Willis, whose novel, dark and devilish-looking images influenced movies for decades, has stated that 'I just did what I felt like doing' (in Biskind, 1998, p. 155). Veteran editor William Reynolds considered the opening scene (which intercuts Connie Corleone's wedding party with the Don granting favors in his office) one of the sublime challenges of his career: 'Francis knew he had to stage a real Italian wedding and he did it superbly, but there wasn't any plan as far as the script was concerned about going back and forth. We did it; I did it' (in Sragow, 1997). Several other aspects of the film that later received high critical acclaim were Coppola's personal choices: from Nino Rotta's music to young actors Pacino and De Niro.

Back in 1971, however, no one, including Coppola, was confident about the film:

> *The Godfather* was a very underappreciated movie when we were making it. They didn't like the cast. They didn't like the way I was shooting it. I was always on the verge of getting fired. So it was an extremely nightmarish experience. I had two little kids and the third one was born during [the making of the film]. We lived in a little apartment, and I was basically frightened they didn't like it. They had as much as said that, so when it was all over I wasn't at all confident that it was going to be successful, and that I'd ever get another job. (Coppola, 1994)

The Aftermath

Coppola finished shooting in September 1971. For Paramount it was imperative that the movie opened for the Christmas season but, due to another fierce and prolonged clash between Coppola and Evans during the editing of the film, it was finally released in April 1972 (Sragow, 1997). *The Godfather* grossed more money more quickly than any other film in history up to that point: $135 million on a budget of $6.2 million. It received dozens of nominations, won three Oscars (Best Picture, Best Actor, Best Screenplay), and Coppola won the Directors Guild Best Director Award.

When Paramount asked Coppola to direct the sequel, he initially refused by saying that he hated Paramount. He later accepted on four conditions: Paramount would finance his film *The Conversation* knowing that it was not a commercial film; given that he did not trust Paramount, he would first shoot *The Conversation* and only then shoot the sequel; he would be paid $1 million for the sequel (up from $175 000 in *The Godfather*, Part I); and Evans and other executives whom he named would not be involved in the film. Paramount agreed and Coppola (in Shanken, 2003) later said that he directed *The Godfather Part II* as he wanted to, without any interference from the studio. As a result, the making of the sequel was not marked by the tensions experienced in the first *Godfather* movie. In 1974 *The Godfather Part II* won six Oscars, including Best Director (Philips, 2004; Philips and Hill, 2004). In 1990 Coppola completed the trilogy by directing *The Godfather Part III*. Today the American Film Institute ranks *The Godfather* (Part I) as the second-greatest film of all time, second only to Orson Welles's *Citizen Kane*.

THE EXTREME LEADERSHIP OF FRANCIS FORD COPPOLA

To analyze the events of the case study we draw on three theoretical perspectives. In order to understand Coppola's individual behavior as an extreme leader, we utilize the charismatic leadership approach as he exhibits several behaviors linked to attributions of charisma (Conger and Kanungo, 1997; Epitropaki and Martin, 2004; Murphy and Ensher, 2008). He is a leader with clear artistic vision, who is not afraid to take risks, both personal (such as being on the verge of getting fired throughout the movie) and work-related (such as his casting Brando and Pacino for the leading roles). He engages in unconventional behaviors (such as faking an epileptic fit or firing the 16 people conspiring against him) and constantly challenges the status quo and the authority of studio executives in order to make his artistic vision a reality. He scans the environment for threats and opportunities, deliberately creates trouble and destabilizes the (temporary) organization of his film-set to bring the change he has envisioned.

Furthermore, in order to explain the radical creativity and outstanding performance that were the outcomes of his extreme leadership we utilize the complexity leadership theory (Uhl-Bien et al., 2007) and the theory of creative deviance (Mainemelis, 2010). Complexity leadership theory 'recognizes that leadership is too complex to be described as only the act of an individual or individuals; rather it is a complex interplay of many interactive forces' (Uhl-Bien et al., 2007, p. 314). It views leadership as 'emergent, interactive, dynamic' (p. 299) and clearly embedded in the context of the interactions among interdependent agents. *The Godfather's* film-set is a good example of a complex adaptive system (CAS) where multiple individuals (Coppola, the studio executives, the scriptwriters, the crew-members and the actors) dynamically interact to produce creativity and learning. Complexity leadership theory further proposes an inter-connected relationship among three types of leadership: (1) administrative leadership, that represents the actions of those in formal managerial positions who provide structure and coordinate organizational processes; (2) enabling leadership, that fosters the conditions for innovation and change and (3) adaptive leadership, that emerges as a collaborative change movement from the interactions among the actors in the network. In the *Godfather* case, the studio executives clearly exercise strong administrative leadership in the particular network, whereas Coppola acts as an enabler for adaptive leadership to emerge throughout the network. He plays a critical role in destabilizing the complex adaptive system of the film-set by disrupting existing patterns of behaviors, thereby pushing the system towards chaos.

Creative deviance theory (Mainemelis, 2010) is also an important theory in this context as it posits that the social structure of an organization plays a pivotal role in creativity-related non-conformist behaviors, such as those that violate supervisors' orders and other organizational norms. Organizations that place a high value on creativity are more likely to induce and later tolerate creative deviance behaviors, especially when the latter appear to hold some promise for resulting in a breakthrough outcome. Both complexity leadership theory and creative deviance theory, therefore, acknowledge internal organizational tension as an important parameter for creativity and learning. Drawing on the case study, we argue that an artist-turned-leader induces extreme collaborative tensions with complex systems agents (such as the studio executives, the scriptwriter, the crew members, the actors and so on; see Figure 14.1 for a complete mapping of the collaborative tensions) which in a context of a traditional organization might lead the system to collapse. However, in the particular context (temporary organization, focused on innovation and creativity) and with the artist-leader who fully embodies all the tensions associated with the creative pursuit (charismatic, true to his 'calling', authentic) such an extreme and tenuous form of leadership has led to radical creativity and superior performance. We argue that when the artist-leader 'survives' the extreme situation, the success of the final product increases his idiosyncrasy credits (Hollander,

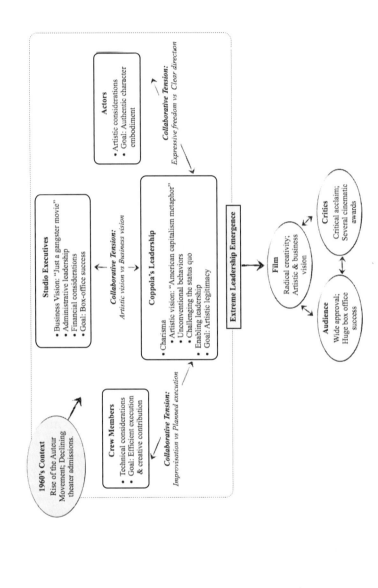

Figure 14.1   Extreme Leadership Emergence in a network of collaborative tensions induced by the leader

1958); allows him or her to build on the success and claim greater creative freedom (as evidenced in the two *Godfather* sequels); and even shapes the professional field's perception that the magnitude of creativity is directly linked to the degree to which artist-leaders (from film directors to top chefs) drive themselves and their teams to the extremes.

EXTREME LEADERSHIP LESSONS

There are several lessons about extreme leadership that we can draw from the *Godfather* case study. Besides its unique and idiosyncratic elements, the making of *The Godfather* exemplifies extreme leadership within a context where: (1) the leader is a creative artist pursuing a cherished artistic vision that is deeply personal but cannot be realized without the collaboration of a creative team; (2) the team is composed of creative professionals who want to leave their own creative stamp on the final product; (3) the success of the final product depends on its creativity, a fact that infuses the collaborative process with uncertainty, ambiguity and unpredictability; and (4) the temporary collaborative process unfolds within a larger and permanent organizational structure that has to balance creativity with other organizational goals and imperatives (Lampel et al., 2000).

Our analysis has showed that in such an extreme leadership context, the leader acting as the troublemaker who induces crises and creates chaos does not necessarily cause the organization to collapse. On the contrary, the leader's unconventional, challenging behaviors can set in motion a process of deep organizational transformation characterized by double-loop learning (Argyris and Schön, 1978) and radical creativity. Our analysis also highlighted the process of extreme leadership emergence from the collaborative tensions between multiple actors in a complex adaptive system and the enabling role of the leader-artist in the particular context. The extreme leader Coppola not only fostered internal tensions, but he also judiciously injected tension in the system and allowed for adaptive outcomes to emerge (such as learning, innovation and high performance).

CONCLUSION

We have presented a case study of the film *The Godfather*, directed by Francis Ford Coppola and produced by Paramount Studios. By utilizing two existing theoretical frameworks on leadership, that is, the charismatic leadership theory (Conger and Kanungo, 1998) and the complexity leadership theory (Uhl-Bien et al., 2007), as well the creative deviance theory (Mainemelis, 2010), we attempted to cast light on how Coppola as an artist-leader working in a complex but temporary organizational system (a film-making project) enabled learning and unique creation emergence through his extreme leadership. Our analysis suggests that: (1) when artists-turned-leaders are given the license to pursue a personal vision in complex creative projects, extreme collaborative tensions are likely to emerge; (2) although rarely pleasant, such socially tenuous leadership can lead to positive organizational outcomes; and thereafter (3) it can gain cultural legitimacy as an acceptable leadership style in creative 'temporary organizations' (Bechky, 2006).

REFERENCES

Allen, M.L. and A.E. Lincoln (2004). Critical discourse and the cultural consecration of American films. *Social Forces*, 82, 871–94.

Argyris, C. and D.A. Schön (1978). *Organizational Learning: A Theory of Action Perspective*. Reading, MA: Addison-Wesley.

Aryee, S., Z.X. Chen, L. Sun and Y.A. Debrah (2007). Antecedents and outcomes of abusive supervision: test of a trickle-down model. *Journal of Applied Psychology*, 92, 191–201.

Baker, W.E. and R.R. Faulkner (1991). Role as resource in the Hollywood film industry. *American Journal of Sociology*, 97, 279–309.

Bechky, B.A. (2006). Gaffers, gofers, and grips: role-based coordination in temporary organizations. *Organization Science*, 17, 3–21.

Biskind, P. (1998). *Easy Riders, Raging Bulls*. London: Bloombsury.

Bock, A. (1979). George Lucas: An interview. *Take One*, 6.

Browne, N. (ed.) (2000). *Francis Ford Coppola's The Godfather Trilogy*. Cambridge: Cambridge University Press.

Conger, J. and R. Kanungo (1998). *Charismatic Leadership in Organizations*. Thousand Oaks, CA: SAGE.

Coppola, F.F. (1994). Interview. Academy of Achievement, Washington, D.C. http://www.achievement.org/autodoc/page/cop0int-1.

Einarsen, S., M.S. Aaslnad and A. Skogstad (2007). Destructive leadership behavior: a definition and conceptual model. *Leadership Quarterly*, 18, 207–16.

Epitropaki, O. and R. Martin (2004). Implicit leadership theories in applied settings: factor structure, generalizability and stability over time. *Journal of Applied Psychology*, 89 (2), 293–310.

Evans, R. (1994). *The Kid Stays in the Picture*. Beverly Hills, CA: Phoenix Books.

Hannah, S., M. Uhl-Bien, B. Avolio and F. Cavarretta (2009). A framework for examining leadership in extreme contexts. *Leadership Quarterly*, 20, 897–919.

Hicks, A. and V. Petrova (2006). Auteur discourse and the cultural consecration of American films. *Poetics*, 34, 180–203.

Hollander, E.P. (1958). Conformity, status, and idiosyncrasy credit. *Psychological Review*, 65, 117–27.

Jones, C. (1996). Careers in project networks: the case of the film industry. In M.B. Arthur and D.M. Rousseau (eds), *The Boundaryless Career: A New Employment Principle for a New Organizational Era*. New York: Oxford University Press, pp. 58–75.

Lampel, J., T. Lant and J. Shamsie (2000). Balancing act: learning from organizing practices in cultural industries. *Organization Science*, 11, 263–9.

Lewis, J. (2000). If history has taught us anything ... Francis Ford Coppola, Paramount Studios, and the Godfather Parts I, II, and III. In N. Browne (ed.), *Francis Ford Coppola's the Godfather Trilogy*. Cambridge: Cambridge University Press, pp. 23–56.

Lipman-Blumen, J. (2005). The allure of toxic leaders: why followers rarely escape their clutches. *Ivey Business Journal*, 69 (3), 1–40.

Mainemelis, C. (2010). Stealing fire: creative deviance in the evolution of new ideas. *Academy of Management Review*, 35, 558–78.

Mainemelis, C., S.M. Nolas and S. Tsirogianni (2008). Auteurs as microcosms: identity play and career creativity in Hollywood, 1967–2007. Paper presented at the EGOS Colloquium, Amsterdam.

Mezias, J.M. and S.J. Mezias (2000). Resource partitioning, the founding of specialist firms, and innovation. *Organization Science*, 11, 306–22.

Murphy, S.E. and E.A. Ensher (2008). A qualitative analysis of charismatic leadership in creative teams: the case of television directors. *Leadership Quarterly*, 19, 335–52.

Murray, W. (1975). *Playboy* interview: Francis Ford Coppola. *Playboy*, July.

Phillips, G.D. (2004). *Godfather: The Intimate Francis Ford Coppola*. Lexington, KY: University Press of Kentucky.

Phillips, G.D. and R. Hill (eds) (2004). *Francis Ford Coppola Interviews*. Jackson, MS: University Press of Mississippi.

Pye, M. and L. Myles (1979). *The Movie Brats: How the Film Generation Took Over Hollywood*. New York: Holt, Rinehart and Winston.

Rensin, D. (1991). Interview with Scorsese. *Playboy*, 38 (4), 57–72, 161.

Sarris, A. (1962). Notes on the auteur theory in 1962. *Film Culture*, 27, 1–8.

Sarris, A. (1968). *The American Cinema: Directors and Directions, 1929–1968*. New York: Dutton and Co.

Shanken, M. (2003). The Godfather speaks. *Cigar Aficionado*, September.

Sontag, S. (1996). The decay of cinema. *New York Times*, February 25.

Sragow, M. (1997). Godfatherhood. *New Yorker*, March 24.

Uhl-Bien, M., R. Marion and B. McKelvey (2007). Complexity leadership theory: shifting leadership from the industrial age to the knowledge era. *Leadership Quarterly*, 18, 298–318.

15. Lost in a fog? Power comes from values

Andrea Hornett, Peggy Daniels Lee and James G. Perkins

INTRODUCTION

Leaders need and use power. In extreme crises, leaders can feel powerless. This case is an example of power in leadership during an extreme crisis, when the leader is 'flying blind'.

One summer day, Andi and Jim met for lunch but it wasn't casual or usual. Jim's US-based company was in crisis: 'The coil market has gone crazy. Tyco's Mallinckrodt Division (TMD) has closed their plant in Mexico and stopped shipping product. We're going nuts trying to serve our existing customers and meet the new demand from their customers. We've got the plant on double shift and we're shipping twice the volume we had two months ago. What's going to happen next? A few weeks ago, TMD came to us and asked us to produce product for them. Should we do it?'

Jim was in trouble and Andi was alarmed. What should Jim do?

An extreme situation is defined as one that falls outside the norm; that is, the situation falls outside the scope of daily experience (Hurley-Hanson and Giannantonio, 2012). When TMD, with 65 percent share of the US market, announced that it would not be shipping any computed tomography (CT) lines,[1] the situation was extreme. For Custom Medical Specialties, Inc. (CMS), with less than 5 percent US market share, this was not merely a disruption, it was a veritable tsunami.

Jim was flummoxed and trying not to panic. He told Andi that he felt like he was 'flying in fog without instrumentation'. 'What should I do?' Jim asked. 'How long can our employees operate in a crisis mode without messing up? May I come to your Strategic Management class and ask them what they think?'

Andi said yes but knew that absent information or examples to instruct them, CMS would not be alone in that dark fog. Jim arrived early in the fall semester and told the students the history of the crisis. He promised to come back in a month for their analyses of the situation.

COILS CRISIS SITUATION

In the late spring of 2005, TMD approached CMS to find out if they were amenable to and capable of manufacturing CT lines for distribution by TMD. TMD's lines were popping out during procedures and spilling dye. TMD engineers inspected CMS's facility and promptly approved CMS as a vendor for their CT lines. TMD issued CMS a purchase order for as many lines as CMS could produce on a monthly basis, looking for upwards of 500 000 lines (5000–10 000 cases) per month.

At the time, CMS was shipping 400 cases a month, double their levels from the first quarter of the year. Their plant, located in a one-traffic-light town in the southern United States, was the town's sole employer of any size under the direction of Jack, Jim's partner. There was additional physical space at the site for possible expansion but a long-term investment was not feasible if TMD started to produce and ship its own lines again.

The sales force, all women in various locations in the US, called customers on the phone and sent free samples to prospective buyers. They could offer low prices because CMS had the lowest overheads in the industry. Every few months, Jim would mail postcard flyers to hospitals and imaging centers and hold a contest to reward the sales rep who brought in the most new customers ('newbies').

In mid-July 2005, TMD finally notified all of its customers that TMD would not be able to supply CT lines to them and directed TMD's sales reps in the US to have their customers contact Medrad, Coeur or CMS to purchase lines (see Table 15.1). Customers legitimately broke their purchasing contracts as TMD was unable to perform. Bristol-Myers-Squibb, a major global pharmaceutical company, wrote to its customers alerting them to the crisis.

Table 15.1   The CT coils industry 2005

Company / history / identity	Role in this crisis
TMD: Tyco's Mallinckrodt Division, multi-billion-dollar corporation. Specializes in respiratory care, imaging products and prescription pharmaceuticals. (Note: The division was a company founded in the 1800s and acquired by Tyco prior to 2005. It has since been a divestiture from Tyco.) Six locations, employing nearly 2500 of its more than 12 000 employees worldwide. TMD was an industry leader in imaging and was positioned as a solutions partner, providing a full line of contrast media and delivery systems, radiopharmaceuticals, and urology imaging systems for the diagnosis and treatment of disease in many imaging procedures.	Dominant player. Caused the crisis. Products for hospitals, freestanding imaging centers and radio-pharmacies. Expertise: contrast agents. Coils' abnormal failure rate; CT lines would disconnect from patient's injection sites and leak contrast dye into the treatment area in examination rooms, causing procedures to be delayed while new CT coil assemblies were inserted. Failures reduced examination room availability and wreaked havoc on hospital and physician schedules. CT scans were delayed or rescheduled.
Medrad, Inc. Winner of the Malcolm Baldridge National Quality Award for manufacturing. Founded in the 1960s with the invention of the first powered angiographic injector. Also, first injector technology for computed tomography (CT) and magnetic resonance (MR) imaging. Medrad's products were sold to hospitals and medical imaging centers in over 85 countries with direct sales and service in ten European countries and representation by distributor operations in 35 European countries. Its European headquarters are in Maastricht, The Netherlands. Annual sales surpassed $411 million in 2005, with a workforce of more than 1500 people based in 15 locations around the world. Total revenues in 2004 were $343 million.	Medrad's expertise was in injector technology. In 2005, Medrad, Inc. served 31 percent of the CT coils market. The only company of sufficient size to 'replace' TMD.

Table 15.1 continued

Company / history / identity	Role in this crisis
Coeur. State-of-the-art designer and contract manufacturer for the medical and commercial marketplace. Its own proprietary line plus full complement of services ranging from design, molding, tubing extrusion, assembly and packaging of medical devices.	Coeur made CT and angiographic syringes that fit a wide variety of power injectors, including Medrad, Inc. injectors.
CMS: Custom Medical Specialties, Inc. Four years old and a small ($4 million annual revenue) supplier of disposable medical products, experiencing double-digit growth through new product development and growing sales.	The firm manufactured and sold a variety of products in the disposable medical supplies market but the CT coils, focus of the current crisis, constituted about a third of CMS's annual revenues. Because CMS only made coils, it could focus on the main problem in the crisis: insufficient coils to meet demand.

CMS TAKES ACTION BASED ON VALUES

CMS prepared to sell more CT lines and added a second shift at the plant, increased its workforce from 40 to 50, and ordered additional equipment to facilitate coiling the lines, the most labor-intensive step in production. CMS added additional office personnel at the plant to help handle the huge influx of orders from frustrated TMD customers attempting to buy lines. CMS's sales representatives contacted each customer to discuss the present lines supply situation with them, to assure them of CMS's intention to accommodate their existing and future needs, and to strengthen and build strong relationships with all. They reinforced their value for a customer relationship by saying, 'TMD has put us all in the same boat together.'

CMS provided all existing customers with their normal, monthly line requirements, sometimes shipping a month's supply in weekly increments to reduce the pressure on production. Then, CMS allocated whatever quantities it could provide to new customers to help them through this period, always concerned for the patients who needed the scans.

By the end of September, CMS production had tripled and new equipment had arrived. How much more could CMS produce and ship? Their maximum production capacity appeared to be 2000 cases per month but no one could calculate the actual strain on the business or the opportunity cost to the company's other product lines for being absorbed in this crisis.

VALUES IN ACTION – EXAMPLES FROM THE CRISIS

CMS's strategy grew out of values, which were: 'family, faith, then, work'. These values infused all decisions made by the executive team. For example, when a salesperson, working on commission, had a difficult pregnancy, the company paid her anyway. Another time, a major hospital in Texas called in a panic. They had no lines at all and would have to cancel procedures. CMS had leftover coils from production runs that were used as samples. CMS shipped these 'orphan coils' via next day air to Texas at no charge, as a goodwill gesture. First and foremost, CMS thought about the patients and their families and what rescheduling or canceling procedures would mean to them.

Jim told Andi's students this background and asked them to help him predict what the competition would do and what he should do. The students studied the industry to prepare themselves for Jim's second visit to class.

CT LINES AND THE INDUSTRY

Medical device manufacturing requires US Food and Drug Administration (FDA) approval in response to filing a 510K form. Because the CT line transports the dye but does not enter the patient, the FDA is not involved in regulating the lines per se; however, manufacturers must follow good manufacturing practices.

The market for CT lines is a segment of the overall market for disposable medical supplies, and in 2005 the market for CT lines was growing. The market had increased almost 50 percent from 2002 to 2005 to about 40 million units per year for individually packaged sterile lines that were used with hand-filled injection syringes. During this disruption crisis year, nearly 24 million CT procedures were potentially vulnerable due to the industry-wide shortage of CT lines caused by TMD exiting the market.

THE COMPETITION

The major players in the CT lines market were Tyco's Mallinckrodt Division (TMD), Medrad, Inc. and Coeur (Table 15.1). Their customers are primarily large purchasing groups of affiliated healthcare providers, the Veterans Administration (VA), and numerous individual hospitals and imaging centers. All competitors, except CMS, provided volume discounts because that was standard practice in the medical supply industry. Table 15.2 compares the competition and CMS in the individually packaged sterile CT coil market. Figure 15.1 presents a Porter's Six Forces analysis of the CT coils industry.

Table 15.2   Competitive market shares and prices in 2005

Company	Market share (%)	Estimated number of coils	Price point
TMD – Tyco's Mallinckrodt Division	65	26 000 000	$1.55–$1.95
Medrad, Inc.	31	12 400 000	$2.65
Coeur	<3	1 200 000	$2.00
Custom Medical Specialties (CMS)	<1	400 000	$1.35*
Total	100	40 000 000	

Note: * it is common practice to give price discounts to high-volume buyers. CMS never did this; it was one price for all buyers.

In addition to their examination of the industry, Andi's students considered the questions that were plaguing Jim about this crisis. For example, should he try to produce 10 000 cases as TMD requested? Could his production facility change that much? How could CMS simultaneously serve existing and new customers? What might the impact be on the rest of the business? What was the right price? How should the sales force be compensated? Was TMD going to re-enter the market? Some of his concerns were already addressed since the crisis did not unfold in accordance with the students' semester schedule. However, Jim was also seeking reassurance that he was doing the right thing.

Andi's students told Jim: 'Not only is TMD coming back but you better pray they do. Our Porter's analysis [Figure 15.1] indicates that structure of the industry is such that losing a player as big as TMD could

Figure 15.1   Porter's Six Forces analysis, CT coils industry

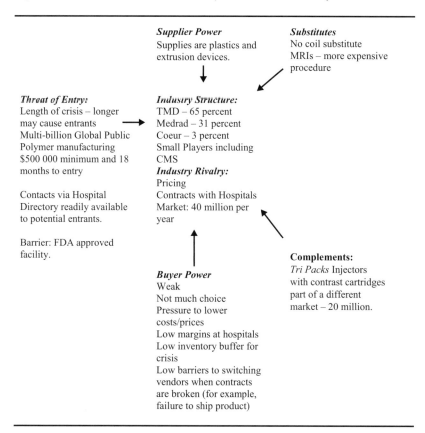

Supplier Power
Supplies are plastics and
extrusion devices.

Substitutes
No coil substitute
MRIs – more expensive
procedure

Threat of Entry:
Length of crisis – longer
may cause entrants
Multi-billion Global Public
Polymer manufacturing
$500 000 minimum and 18
months to entry

Contacts via Hospital
Directory readily available
to potential entrants.

Barrier: FDA approved
facility.

Industry Structure:
TMD – 65 percent
Medrad – 31 percent
Coeur – 3 percent
Small Players including
CMS
Industry Rivalry:
Pricing
Contracts with Hospitals
Market: 40 million per
year

Buyer Power
Weak
Not much choice
Pressure to lower
costs/prices
Low margins at hospitals
Low inventory buffer for
crisis
Low barriers to switching
vendors when contracts
are broken (for example,
failure to ship product)

Complements:
Tri Packs Injectors
with contrast cartridges
part of a different
market – 20 million.

be so destabilizing there could be a price war for market share plus new
entrants and substitutes. Your little company might not survive such
extreme change.'

EXPERIENCE CLARIFIES

The students' prediction came true four months later. TMD resumed
shipments without comment in the spring of 2006. CMS's market share
stabilized that year at more than double its initial level and Jim learned
the answers to his questions:

1. CMS did not even try to meet TMD's request for 10 000 cases a month. Jim would have had to increase his market share thirtyfold to fully meet TMD's request. Coeur is not much larger than CMS; so, it was doubtful that either firm could replace the loss of TMD from the market in the short term.
2. CMS gave first priority to existing customers and accommodated new customers when it could. By shipping weekly instead of monthly, CMS smoothed out the peaks in the production cycle and eased product storage issues for customers.
3. CMS did not change prices during the crisis and it maintained one price for all. In accordance with the profit maximization theory of the firm, this 'left money on the table' and was not wise policy. However, before the crisis, hardly anyone had heard of CMS. Once TMD notified its sales force, CMS was visible. When new customers contacted CMS, they experienced care and integrity. For a small entrepreneurial venture, this is building a brand, a reputation for integrity, not 'leaving money on the table'. Further, it protected relationships with existing customers and made making sales easier for the sales force.
4. CMS did not change its sales compensation practices, even though one could argue that the sales people had received a windfall. Jim adhered to his values and they were 'family'.
5. Jack hired additional workers at the plant and installed an additional piece of equipment in the production line. They worked overtime and had reached their limits by fall.
6. TMD put its plant in Mexico back on line and started shipping product. It was doubtful all along that it could simply walk away from a commitment in Mexico.

CONCLUSION

Lessons learned? Jim says: 'When you're in a fog, you have to rely on your values to get through.' For Jim, the essence of leadership during this crisis had more to do with faith than facts. Where he could manage, he did. Where he could not, he asked for cooperation. In drawing lessons from this case of leadership in an extreme situation, we explore the role of power in leadership.

Control What You Can

The key challenge for Jim was to manage what he could. He did maintain his own customer base during the crisis and he did this by having the sales force phone all customers, explain the situation and negotiate more frequent but smaller shipments. Also, Jim did not raise prices and did not take advantage of the desperate situation. As a result CMS, a virtually unknown company, earned a good reputation and acquired goodwill.

In 2012, a very similar disruption in supply occurred in a different product category but involving the same actors as this case. This time, the situation seemed less extreme because Jim and CMS remembered what to do.

Leadership Power

CMS's values are: 'family, faith, then, work'. Jim relied on instinct and a consistent expression of values while having faith that the situation would turn out alright. He felt powerless in that he had no information or experience models to rely on – that is an essential aspect of an extreme crisis. However, he did guide the organization through the crisis and he did maintain the cooperation of both the employees and the customers.

What was the nature of power in this example of leadership in an extreme situation? Table 15.3 presents selected theories of power for consideration. Some theories assume the ability to coerce (for example, a powerful leader can make others do things); some consider a reciprocal dynamic (leader–follower); or, more broadly, an interdependency (for example, Boje et al., 1996). This case illustrates how Jim created a sense of interdependency not only with the employees but also with the customers and potential customers ('we're all in the same boat'). They were all 'family' now.

Theories of Power

Jim had authority as the co-owner of the business but felt he had no legitimacy when he could not see how to navigate the organization through the crisis. By creating a common 'enemy' – the dysfunctional non-shipping TMD – he united the various constituencies (plant personnel, sales force and customers, both existing and potential). This is one of Bion's (1961) theories: group unity through a shared 'enemy'. This is power.

Table 15.3   Some theories of power in the organizational theory literature

Theorist	Nature of power
	Coercive:
Blau (1969; see also Milgram, 1974)	The ability of persons or groups to impose their will on others
Weber (in Duke, 1976, citing Parsons's interpretation)	Power (*macht*) is the probability that one actor within a social relationship will be in a position to carry out their own will despite resistance, regardless of the basis on which this probability rests.
March (in Riker, 1969)	The ability to restrict outcomes.
Parsons (in Bell et al., 1969) (Note: this is one of his ideas; there are others.)	The capacity of persons or collectives to get things done effectively, in particular when their goals are obstructed by some kind of human resistance or opposition. Power is the means of acquiring control of the factors in effectiveness. (A zero-sum game does not hold for systems of a sufficient level of complexity.)
Simon (in Cartwright, 1959) (see also Pfeffer, 1981)	For the assertion 'A has power over B', we can substitute the assertion 'A's behavior causes B's behavior'.
	Resource-dependent:
Hickson and McCullough (in Salaman and Thompson, 1980)	Power is the capacity to use resources – for example, wealth, status or expert knowledge – to affect others.
Mohrman (in Mohrman et al., 1995)	Power is both the authority to make decisions and the opportunity to influence decisions made elsewhere that impact one's work.
	Reciprocal / reciprocating:
Follett (1949 [1987]; in Metcalf and Urwick, 1940 and in Bowen and Boone, 1987)	The ability to make things happen, to be a causal agent, to initiate change (p. 99).
Boje et al. (1996; see also Clegg, 1989; Boulding, 1989)	This postmodern theory of organizational power demonstrates that we are empowered only through the action of others – through social supplementarity. This suggests that textbook theories locating power in individual discretion or the structural properties of organization should be abandoned. Relational theory suggests that managers do not control the fate of their decrees. Instead, power is a matter of social interdependence; it is affected through the coordination of actions around specified definitions (p. 58).

Theorist	Nature of power
Latour (1986)	Paradox of power: when an actor simply has power nothing happens and they are powerless; when, on the other hand, an actor exerts power it is others who perform the action. It appears that power is not something one can possess – indeed it must be treated as a consequence rather than as a cause of action (Latour, 1986, p. 264). *Other:*
French and Raven (in Cartwright, 1959)	Five bases of power: reward, coercive, referent, legitimate and expert.
Perrow (in Salaman and Thompson, 1980)	There are four views on power: 1. There are elites on top. 2. Negotiated power is bargained (March and Olsen, 1979). 3. Co-operative systems (Barnard, 1938 [1968]). 4. Natural systems – actors play roles; power wielders are enacting roles.

Power is a key element of leadership (McClelland, 1955, 1975, 1987). Accordingly, some of the famous names in organization theory have addressed the subject of power (Table 15.3). Cartwright (1969) says: 'One of the earliest and most influential of the revisionists was Barnard (1938 [1968]), who advanced a distinction between the "authority of position" and the "authority of leadership"' (p. 126). Table 15.3 poses distinctions among coercive, reciprocal and resource-based power.

Summary

TMD's 'leadership' in the crisis best fits with the coercive types of power. In contrast, CMS successfully employed a reciprocal and recipro-cating approach with its current and potential customers. Jim's leadership in the crisis created unity among customers, CMS employees and patients needing CT scans.

This is only one case, bounded in time and in a particular industry. However, it appears that coercive power would work best when a leader is certain about what to do and can afford to do it. Otherwise, leaders will want to create and manage group identity (Schein, 1985 [1993]) as they engage others to take action.

NOTE

1. Computed tomography (CT) is a diagnostic procedure that enables physicians to identify blockages or growths by injecting a contrast dye into the patient's veins and

then scanning the patient's body or specific areas: abdomen, chest, head, sinuses, spine and the colon in both adults and children. CT lines are used to convey contrast media under pressure into a patient in either a hospital or a freestanding imaging center. A CT line is often coiled so that it can stretch out as the patient is moved through an imaging machine.

REFERENCES

Barnard, C.A. (1938 [1968]). *The Functions of the Executive*. Cambridge, MS: Harvard University Press.

Bell, R., D.V. Edwards and R.H. Wagner (1969). *A Reader in Theory and Research*. New York: Free Press.

Bion, W.R. (1961). *Experiences in Groups and Other Papers*. New York: Basic Books.

Boje, D.M., R.P. Gephart and T.J. Thatchenkery (1996). *Postmodern Management and Organization Theory*. Thousand Oaks, CA: Sage.

Boulding, K.E. (1989). *Three Faces of Power*. Newbury Park, CA: Sage.

Bowen, Donald D. and Louis E. Boone (1987). *The Great Writings in Management and Organizational Behavior*. New York: Random House.

Cartwright, D. (ed.) (1959). *Studies in Social Power*. Ann Arbor, MI: Research Center for Group Dynamics, Institute for Social Research, University of Michigan.

Cartwright, D. (1969). Influence, leadership, control. In R. Bell, D.V. Edwards and R.H. Wagner (eds). *Political Power: A Reader in Theory and Research*. New York: Free Press, pp. 123–65.

Clegg, S. (1989). *Frameworks of Power*. Newbury Park, CA: Sage.

Duke, J.T. (1976). *Conflict and Power in Social Life*. Provo, UT: Brigham Young University Press.

Follett, M.P. (1949 [1987]). The essentials of leadership. In L.E. Boone and D.D. Bowen. *The Great Writings in Management and Organizational Behavior*. New York: McGraw-Hill, pp. 49–61.

Follett, M.P. (1987). *Freedom and Coordination: Lectures in Business Organizations*. New York: Garland.

Hurley-Hanson, A.E and C.M. Giannantonio (2012). Going to extremes: leadership lessons from outside the norm. Symposium, AOM, Boston, MA.

Latour, B. (1986). The powers of association. In J. Law (ed.). *Power, Action and Belief: A New Sociology of Knowledge?* London: Routledge and Kegan Paul, pp. 264–80.

March, James G. and Johan P. Olsen (1979). *Ambiguity and Choice in Organizations*. Bergen: Universitetsforlaget.

McClelland, D.C. (1955). *Studies in Motivation*. New York: Appleton-Century-Crofts.

McClelland, D.C. (1975). *Power: The Inner Experience*. New York: Irvington Publishers, John Wiley and Sons.

McClelland, D.C. (1987). *Human Motivation*. New York: Cambridge University Press.

Metcalf, H.C. and L. Urwick (eds) (1940). *Dynamic Administration: The Collected Papers of Mary Parker Follett*. New York: Harper Brothers.

Milgram, S. (1974). *Obedience to Authority: An Experimental View*. New York: Harper and Row.

Mohrman, S.A., S.G. Cohen and A.M. Mohrman (1995). *Designing Team-Based Organizations*. San Francisco, CA: Jossey-Bass.

Mohrman, Allan M. Jr., Susan Albers Mohrman, Gerald E. Ledford Jr., Thomas G. Cummings and Edward E. Lawler III (1989). *Large-Scale Organizational Change*. San Francisco, CA: Jossey Bass.

Pfeffer, J. (1981). *Power in Organizations*. Marshfield, MA: Pitman Publishing.

Riker, W.H. (1969). Some ambiguities in the notion of power. In R. Bell, D.V. Edwards and R.H. Wagner (eds). *Political Power: A Reader in Theory and Research*. New York: Free Press, pp. 110–19.

Salaman, G. and K. Thompson (eds) (1980). *Control and Ideology in Organizations*. Cambridge, MA: MIT.

Schein, E.H. (1985 [1993]). *Organizational Culture and Leadership*. San Francisco, CA: Jossey Bass.

16. Jeanne's story: a leader and her team's journey through crisis

Connie S. Fuller

INTRODUCTION

In the late 1990s, I was hired by a telecom manufacturing company as an internal organization development consultant to work with their self-directed work teams. For seven years I worked closely with an organization that initially grew, but then began to shrink from over 1500 employees to about 300 as product demand declined. In the end, the facility was closed. But before the closure, some amazing things happened. It was at this facility that I met Jeanne, whose story I want to share with you. Jeanne is one of many impressive people I met at the plant, but Jeanne's story is special. She overcame not only a business challenge, but a personal challenge as well. She did it with determination and grace. She gave the gift of personal growth to her employees, and she caused them to be steadfast in their commitment to the job and to the company under the worst of circumstances. She demonstrated true leadership under extreme conditions of personal and professional loss. Jeanne was an extreme leader.

BACKGROUND

Acme Manufacturing Company (a pseudonym) was jointly owned by two telecommunications giants. It made hardware for the telecommunications industry, specifically hard line telephone switching stations. Switching stations were used to connect calls across the country and around the world. It was a huge and dynamic business. At the time of this story, Acme's hardware manufacturing took place in a small town in central Illinois, where it was the major employer.

In 1992, Acme completed a downsizing of its manufacturing capacity from a high in the 1980s of approximately 18 000 employees at a

1.8 million-square-foot facility in a large metropolitan city to a fraction of that number in rural central Illinois. There had been a steady decline in annual line count demand (the number of new lines added to each switching station each year), which was projected to continue until the switching stations built and installed by Acme Manufacturing were fully deployed. No new switches were expected to be built at that point, so only maintenance and repair parts would be needed. While business related to the switch was expected to continue for some time, the business was viewed as a 'harvest' business with a limited lifespan. Remaining manufacturing could be done in the smaller, rural facility at a greatly reduced cost. As a result, the larger facility was sold and a limited number of managers, engineers and union associates made the transition to central Illinois. Thus began a period of discontinuous change (Nadler, 1998) that would impact the facility for the next 12 years.

Acme's management recognized that methods used successfully in a large facility would not be appropriate for management of the smaller facility, and that methodologies previously used at the small facility would not be appropriate for Acme's future role in the industry. The management team agreed that downsizing offered an ideal opportunity to bring state-of-the-art manufacturing practices to the small facility. Steps were put in place to restructure not only the size of the organization, but its entire scope of manufacturing practices as well.

Specific goals were established for manufacturing lead times, inventory days of supply, and quality and yield goals. The primary products to be manufactured in this facility were frames and loose parts (printed circuit board assemblies and loose cables) for use in Acme's core product, telephone switching stations. Acme's focus was on components of the switching station itself in order to support switches already in the field.

Support for human resources in the facility was particularly important because it had been determined that the site would incorporate self-directed work teams to accomplish its manufacturing objectives, thereby removing several layers of management and significantly reducing costs. The facility would be similar to a 'greenfield site' (Ketchum and Trist, 1992) in that it would be using processes that would be new to all involved. As a greenfield site, the likelihood of success with a team structure was significantly better than if a team structure were to be imposed on an ongoing operation. Teams were to be used not only for associates on the manufacturing floor, but also for non-union employees working in manufacturing support functions (purchasing, shipping, human resources, etc.) within the facility. The facility was a union shop. Team activity within boundaries of the labor contract had the full involvement and support of the union from the beginning. Though designated as 'self-directed', work teams were never intended to be fully self-managed. Boundaries were determined by contract restrictions, and were renegotiated with each contract renewal. Areas specifically forbidden by contract for employees to manage included hiring, firing and disciplinary action. Work rules also restricted some movement of employees between job classes, though restrictions were more lenient than those found in many union operations. Decision boundaries were expanded as teams developed the capacity to make more of the day-to-day operational decisions. Each team had a coach instead of a supervisor; the coach handled decisions the team was not allowed to handle by contract, or by not yet having acquired the skill to handle.

Throughout 1992 and 1993, training in operating as teams was ongoing. In 1994, teams were rolled out to all manufacturing and non-manufacturing areas in the facility. Internal facilitators trained coaches; coaches, in turn, trained their teams. Team development was designed to take a team through four phases, each with specific requirements. As a team entered a new phase, it was expected to continue to meet the requirements of all previous phases, as well as learn how to meet requirements of the new phase. All teams started in Phase 1 and were expected to progress from phase 1 to phase 4, paralleling Tuckman's (1965) stages of group development. A phase 4 team was considered to be high performing. This method of operation was expected to carry the team through its continuing decline to a point of status quo in supporting aging switches in the field (http://www.telephonetribute.com/historical_information.html).

An unexpected impact on Acme Manufacturing was the introduction and expanding appeal of the Internet. Almost overnight, the decline in line demand that had caused Acme's restructuring reversed its downward trend. Demand for lines and line capacity virtually exploded as homes and businesses across the country tried to support Internet connections on their PCs. Telephone companies, in turn, demanded an expansion of features and capabilities on their switches. Acme's switch, viewed as a harvest business in 1992, found itself suddenly alive and growing three years later.

By 1997, employment at the manufacturing facility in central Illinois had tripled; the plant was operating three shifts, 24 hours a day, five and sometimes seven days a week. Three years after full start-up, there were over 40 self-directed work teams. Fewer than half were beyond phase 2 of their development. Those that had progressed into phases 3 and 4 were primarily non-manufacturing teams. Jeanne's team in shipping and receiving was an exception; it had progressed into phase 3 and was quickly approaching phase 4. Management felt even more strongly than before that having a team-based organization was appropriate for effective and efficient operation of the plant. However, the size of the operation had, by 1997, far exceeded original expectations. Rapid growth had introduced factors that had not been considered under the 'near-greenfield' scenario that existed when teams were first conceptualized for this facility. Recalled and new employees knew nothing about teams. Many were hesitant to risk future security by speaking out, even when invited to do so. Coaches who had been successful with, or at least had more experience with, traditional approaches to management began to revert to more traditional behaviors to manage new employees and increased production. Team development was facing a crisis. Additionally, the newly hired population of factory workers was significantly more Hispanic than the existing workforce and somewhat younger than many current and recalled Acme employees. The potential for cultural conflict was ripe.

These elements are critical in understanding the dynamics of the teams that Jeanne ultimately led. The organization as a whole was in the midst of significant business and social change. Jeanne's teams did not develop under ideal conditions. Rather, team development came about in the midst of unpredictable, unstable and often unforgiving conditions of everyday life on the manufacturing floor.

LEADERSHIP UNDER FIRE

As a result of her success with the shipping and receiving team, Jeanne was put in charge of a new team in the cables area following a major restructuring of their processes. This was one of the busiest product areas of the plant after the business boom of 1997. The population in Jeanne's first cables team started at 39. Large groups have a greater tendency to break into subgroups, which in turn can affect ongoing communication (Katz et al., 2005). Jeanne knew that team size was a potential issue (Hollingshead et al., 2005) and purposefully created opportunities for small-group activity so that each team member would have the ability to be heard. Her approach was simple, yet profound; and it was fun. As noted by Hughes (2005), acts of courage are often exhibited by conveying serious lessons through humor.

Jeanne's team met weekly for one hour to discuss work processes, work issues, work performance and to participate in team development. The size of the team mandated that it meet in the facility's auditorium rather than in a typical team meeting room. Jeanne began each meeting with a game, usually a simulation of some kind of TV game show such as *Who Wants to be a Millionaire?* Team members were placed into teams of three or four. They then competed to answer questions that Jeanne had prepared ahead of time. Picture the scenario: Jeanne was on stage, team members were in small teams in the auditorium, questions would be asked, and whichever team got the correct answer first won a certain number of points. Points were accumulated, and the team winning the most points for the session got the prize, usually something nominal such as candy or toys.

Jordan-Evans and Kaye (2012) in their article 'Are we having fun yet?' remind us that a fun-filled workplace builds enthusiasm which leads to increased productivity, positive attitudes, strong loyalty and even longevity. They go on to say that fun does not have to be excessively planned, but that it can be spontaneous and simple. While preparation of these weekly games took a considerable amount of Jeanne's time and energy, what the games accomplished was exactly what team members and the circumstances required. The games taught workers that they could have fun and still accomplish goals. The games showed workers that it was okay to take a few minutes away from work to do something fun and seemingly non-work-related. The greatest benefit, however, was that the associates learned they could work with anyone on the team, whether they liked them or not. One of the rules of Jeanne's games was that, at the end of the session, the team with the most points could choose to stay together or they could disband into new teams for the following week. All other teams had to disband and form new teams. It did not take long before everyone on the team of 39 had worked with everyone else on the team through games. Then, when they were moved around on the manufacturing floor to work where they were needed, there were no in-group and out-group problems (Graen and Uhl-Bien, 1991). Social subgroups remained, but work-related subgrouping disappeared. Associates were asked to work together effectively, and they did. This happened as a result of Jeanne's leadership in teaching them, in a fun way, how to do it and how to do it well. It also positioned Jeanne as an authentic leader, one who develops positive and trusting leader–follower relationships through humor and transparency (Hughes, 2005).

Development of Jeanne's teams also incorporated another basic philosophy of Jeanne's leadership, that if people know what you expect and they know how to do it, they will perform to your expectations. It is known that the influence of others' beliefs will influence how an individual responds (Madon et al., 2011). Jeanne made it clear that she expected members of her teams to work together to get the job done, whether they liked one another or not, and that they were to treat one another with courtesy and respect. Jeanne's transparency modeled how she wanted team members to treat each other by treating them that way herself. She treated them with respect and believed that they would give their best to the team. That belief became a self-fulfilling prophecy.

Members of Jeanne's team quickly became experienced in effective team behavior and structure, experienced with the product, and anxious to get the team to a high-performing state. This was also true for Jeanne who, from past experience, knew the team structure would be beneficial to both employees and the business of the cables department. Members of her team knew that she was fair, treated her people well, taught them what they needed to know, gave them the information they needed to be fully empowered, would troubleshoot if they ran into a problem and, most of all, would hold them to high levels of performance on both quantity and quality of work. In this way, Jeanne further demonstrated her authentic leadership (George, 2007). George describes authentic leadership as comprising five dimensions: purpose, values, relationships, self-discipline and heart, which lead to passion, behavior, connectedness, consistency and compassion. Jeanne instilled the same level of self-knowledge and self-regulation in her team as she practiced herself. In the process, she created meaningful work-related relationships (Kerfoot, 2010).

A significant change for Jeanne's team at one point was the presence of a few members who were not perceived to be doing their share of the workload. There were strong opinions that the coach should be address-ing these situations more aggressively, with little understanding of the union contract and other organizational practices that made addressing poor performers difficult. Jeanne worked with these members to hold them individually accountable for their work processes instead of allow-ing them to become social loafers on the team. Gradually their perform-ance improved, or they chose to leave. This is a testament to Jeanne's lack of hubris (Petie and Bollaert, 2012). Jeanne remained authentic to who she was and what she saw as important – treating people with respect and getting the job done. Her goal was to empower and develop, to encourage critical thought and decision-making, to focus employees on the goal, and to recognize the humanity in each and every person.

It was at about this time that Jeanne came face to face with a personal challenge; Jeanne was diagnosed with breast cancer. It was, as is often the case, unexpected. It was certainly unwelcomed. In addition to giving attention to her work and team, Jeanne was now mandated to give attention to herself. She also had a choice: to pretend that her illness was no big deal, or to embrace her vulnerability and engage the support of her team. Women leaders tend to handle vulnerability differently from men (Eagli and Carli, 2007), and Jeanne was no exception. As tends to be typical of female leaders, Jeanne communicated openly and honestly with her team, making it as safe for them to express their concerns and emotions as she was to express her own (Fine, 2007).

She told her team, all at one time during a team meeting, about the diagnosis. She advised them that she would be out for a while for surgery and that another coach would be taking over in her absence. She cried. So did the members of her team, men and women alike. Whatever problems had manifested themselves in the team took second place to Jeanne's news. The team pulled together to make sure that they continued the work ethic Jeanne had helped instill in them. Jeanne assured them she would be back and that she expected no less, that she knew they could and would continue their excellent work. She counted on the self-efficacy (Bandura, 1997) she had built in the team to carry it through this unexpected circumstance, and it did.

In the handling of her illness, Jeanne modeled transformational leadership (Kouzes and Posner, 2002) at its finest. She was vulnerable, yet strong. She had developed them to their full potential, and let them know she expected them to perform at that level in her absence. She was effective at motivating her team members to act in the good of the organization without her presence.

In extremis leadership is defined as ensuring that followers have purpose, motivation and direction in conditions of physical danger (Kolditz and Brazil, 2005). Jeanne's followers faced the danger of losing their success, commitment to the team, job satisfaction and high levels of performance without their leader. Contrary to conventional wisdom, Jeanne did not revert to legitimate and coercive power to influence her teams during this crisis (Hughes et al., 1993). She maintained her referent power and the strength of her relationships to hold team members to previous levels of high performance. They responded positively.

Jeanne's presentation as a leader indicates that she is primarily androgynous, showing equal levels of both task and relationship characteristics (Korabik and Ayman, 2007). In such leaders, be they male or female, it is the environmental context that dictates which behaviors, task or relationship, will be used. Jeanne was clearly drawing on both sets of behaviors to manage her team through this crisis. Exemplary leaders set an example for their followers by following through on their commitments, fulfilling promises and leading with their hearts. In this most dire set of circumstances, Jeanne proved that she was, indeed, an exemplary leader.

As a result of her team's success, Jeanne was moved to become coach of two different cables teams that were struggling when she returned to work. The coach who had filled in for Jeanne while she was gone continued on as coach for Jeanne's first team. A fourth team was disbanded and scattered among the remaining three teams. At this point, Jeanne's span of control swelled to over 60 people. The practices she had instituted with her first team continued to serve her well with her new teams and they, too, developed to levels of high performance.

Over the next few years, product demand once again declined with the growth of wireless protocols eliminating the need for Acme's telephone switch. As the plant population steadily declined, Jeanne's teams continued to be committed to the organization, continued to go where the work took them, and continued to provide excellent products for Acme's customers until the facility finally closed for good in December 2004.

The success of Jeanne's teams through unexpected growth, new approaches to management, a personal leadership crisis and, ultimately, organizational decline, makes it clear that successful teams are dependent on effective leadership (Fuller, 2001). Team member confidence in the viability of the team is a direct reflection of the coach's belief in the viability of the team, as demonstrated in both words and action. Jeanne's leadership style allowed a critical mass of team members to have interaction with their coach at a professional and at a personal level, fostering job satisfaction and sustained levels of high performance. Jeanne's directness, openness, commitment to the success of followers, willingness to acknowledge her own limitations, transparency and commitment to be held accountable were a testament to the authentic and transformational leadership she sustained throughout both personal and organizational crises (Avolio et al., 2004)

LESSONS LEARNED

Leadership lessons from Jeanne's example are noteworthy:

- Leaders must be confident, but not arrogant, about their own abilities and be willing to do whatever is needed to help their teams grow and develop.
- Leaders must be humble and never feel they are above their followers. Without followers, there can be no leaders.
- In-groups and out-groups, whether they are between leaders and followers or between the workers themselves, will destroy a team.
- Leaders must lead by example, and they must lead from the floor – not from behind their desks or their office doors. Relationships are the key to leader effectiveness.

- People will rise to a leader's expectations of them only if leaders give them clear guidance about what those expectations are, and the tools (including information) that they need to achieve them.
- Good leadership is a mosaic of practices that come together in just the right way to meet the ever-evolving needs of the situation and of the people involved. Good leadership in a crisis situation is ultimately heart, common sense and courage.

EPILOGUE

When the Acme facility closed, their team experience helped many of Acme's former employees secure new jobs in the surrounding communities. Jeanne retired, but not for long. She eventually took a part-time job at a local grocery store where she continues to supervise and train younger workers. She is still doing what she loves most, just in a different setting and with different people. There has been no recurrence of her cancer. In her spare time, she is an avid golfer. Jeanne is happy, healthy and living a peaceful life.

REFERENCES

Avoilo, Bruce J., William L. Gardner, Fred O. Walumbwa, Fred Luthans and Douglas R. May (2004). Unlocking the mask: a look at the process by which authentic leaders impact follower attitudes and behaviors. *Leadership Quarterly*, 15, 801–23.

Bandura, A. (1997). *Self-efficacy: The Exercise of Control*. New York: W.H. Freeman and Company.

Eagly, A.H. and L.L. Carli (2007). *Through the Labyrinth: The Truth About How Women Become Leaders*. Boston, MA: Harvard Business School Press, Center for Public Leadership.

Fine, M.G. (2007). Women, collaboration, and social change: an ethics-based model of leadership. In J.L. Chin, B. Lott, J.K. Rice and J. Sanchez-Hucles (eds), *Women and Leadership: Transforming Visions and Diverse Voices*. Malden, MA: Blackwell Publishing, pp. 177–91.

Fuller, C. (2001). Antecedents to high performance breakthrough in permanent self-managed teams. Dissertation, Benedictine University, USA.

George, B. (2007). *True North: Discover Your Authentic Leadership*. San Francisco, CA: Jossey-Bass.

Graen, G.B. and M. Uhl-Bien (1991). The transformation of professionals into self-managing and partially self-designing contributions: toward a theory of leadership making. *Journal of Management Systems*, 3 (3), 33–48.

Hollingshead, A.B., G.M. Wittenbaum, P.B. Paulus, R.Y. Hirokawa, D.G. Ancona, R.S. Peterson, K.A. Jehn and K. Yoon (2005) A look at groups from the functional perspective. In M.S. Poole and A.B. Hollingshead (eds), *Theories of Small Groups: Interdisciplinary Perspectives*. Thousand Oaks, CA: Sage Publications, pp. 21–62.

Hughes, L.W. (2005). Developing transparent relationships through humor in the authentic leader–follower relationship. In W.L. Gardner, B.J. Avolio and F.O. Walumbwa (eds), *Authentic Leadership Theory and Practice: Origins, Effects and Development*. San Diego, CA: Elsevier, pp. 83–106.

Hughes, R.L., R.C. Ginnett and G.J. Curphy (1993). *Leadership: Enhancing the Lessons of Experience*. Homewood, IL: Irwin.

Jordan-Evans, S. and B. Kaye (2012). Are we having fun yet? *Leadership Excellence*, April, p. 11.

Katz, N., D. Lazer, H. Arrow and N. Contractor (2005).The network perspective on small groups: theory and research. In M.S. Poole and A.B. Hollingshead (eds), *Theories of Small Groups: Interdisciplinary Perspectives*. Thousand Oaks, CA: Sage Publications, pp. 277–312.

Kerfoot, K.M. (2010). Leaders, self-confidence, and hubris: what's the difference? *Nursing Economics*, 28 (5), 350–59.

Ketchum, L.D. and E. Trist (1992). *All Teams Are Not Created Equal: How Employee Empowerment Really Works*. Thousand Oaks, CA: Sage Publications.

Kolditz, T.A. and D.M. Brazil (2005) Authentic leadership in in extremis settings: a concept for extraordinary leaders in exceptional situations. In W.L. Gardner, B.J. Avolio and F.O. Walumbwa (eds), *Authentic Leadership Theory and Practice: Origins, Effects and Development*. San Diego, CA: Elsevier, pp. 345–56.

Kouzes, J.M. and B.Z. Posner (2002). *The Leadership Challenge*, 3rd edn. San Francisco, CA: Jossey-Bass.

Korabik, K. and R. Ayman (2007). Gender and leadership in the corporate world: a multiperspective model. In J.L. Chin, B. Lott, J.K. Rice and J. Sanchez-Hucles (eds), *Women and Leadership: Transforming Visions and Diverse Voices*. Malden, MA: Blackwell Publishing, pp. 106–24.

Madon, S., J. Willard, M. Guyll and K.C. Scherr (2011). Self-fulfilling prophecies: mechanisms, power, and links to social problems. *Social and Personality Psychology Compass*, 5 (8), 578–90. DOI: 10.1111/j.1751-9004.2011.00375.x.

Nadler, D.A. (1998). *Champions of Change: How CEOs and Their Companies are Mastering the Skills of Radical Change*. Jossey-Bass Business and Management Series. New York: John Wiley and Sons.

Petie, V. and H. Bollaert (2012). Flying too close to the sun? Hubris among CEOs and how to prevent it. *Journal of Business Ethics*, 108, 265–83.

Tuckman, Bruce W. (1965). Developmental sequence in small groups. *Psychological Bulletin*, 63 (6), 384–99.

17. The Sandy Hook Elementary School shootings

Amy E. Hurley-Hanson and Cristina M. Giannantonio

Unfortunately, extreme situations occur in places we can only hope they would not. The Sandy Hook Elementary School shooting that occurred on 14 December 2012 was an extreme situation. In less than five minutes, a person walked into a school and killed 20 children and six adults. The student victims were eight boys and 12 girls, between six and seven years of age (Reuters, 2012a). The events that occurred that day were well outside the norm of daily activities for the principals, teachers and aides that worked at Sandy Hook in Newtown, CT. We include this tragic event because it illustrates the wide spectrum of extreme situations where inspirational and authentic leadership may emerge. By analyzing the selfless behaviors displayed in this extreme situation, leadership lessons may be learned from those who were thrust into an extreme situation and ran towards it to do what they could to save lives.

THE EVENTS OF DECEMBER 14

It was approximately five minutes from when the shooter entered the building until he shot himself. It was 40 minutes from when the shooting began until the survivors were led out of the building. To those living this nightmare it seemed like an eternity. The shootings at Sandy Hook Elementary School in Newtown, CT illustrate the leadership behaviors of ordinary citizens who found themselves in an extreme situation. The administrators and teachers who lost their lives trying to stop the shooter and protect the children will be remembered as heroes. Each of these individuals were leaders in this extreme situation. The actions of several other individuals who acted as leaders in an effort to save the lives of the schoolchildren are also described in this case.

224

SANDY HOOK ELEMENTARY SCHOOL

Sandy Hook Elementary School educated close to 700 students. The principal of the school was Dawn Hochsprung. Prior to the shootings on 14 December 2012, the principal and the school district had often discussed 'What if a shooting occurred at our school?' scenarios. Especially after the shootings at Columbine High School in Colorado, 'What if?' scenarios were given serious consideration. Earlier in the year the principal had a new security system installed at the school. All the doors were locked at 9.30 a.m. every day. Before being admitted into the building, visitors had to be seen on camera before the doors were unlocked and they were buzzed into the school.

On 14 December 2012, a gunman grabbed three firearms and headed to Sandy Hook Elementary School. The gunman shot the locked doors in order to gain entrance into the building. The principal, Dawn Hochsprung, school psychologist Mary Sherlack, school therapist Diane Day, vice-principal Natalie Hammond, reading consultant Becky Virgalla, and other faculty members were in a meeting in the administrative offices of the school. When Hochsprung heard the shots, she, Sherlack and Hammond jumped out of their seats and ran into the hall. As she ran into the hall, Hochsprung may have turned on the school intercom so that others could hear that this was a real situation and not a drill. Hochsprung told the others to hide in the principal's office as she ran out to confront the shooter in the hallway. The three women were heard to scream 'Shooter! Stay put!' letting their colleagues know about the danger (Virgalla, 2012). Hochsprung and Sherlack tried to attack him and they tried to take the gun away from him. He shot and killed them both (Levitz, 2012). Hammond was also shot but she made her way back to the offices and survived. The efforts of Hochsprung, Sherlack and Hammond may have given the teachers a few extra minutes to try to lead the children to safety.

The gunman then ran through the school, going into classrooms and shooting teachers and students. Teacher Victoria Leigh Soto led some of her students into a closet at the back of the classroom while others were hiding under their desks (Altimari et al., 2013). As the shooter entered her classroom she told him the children had been sent to the gym (Weisskopf, 2013). When the shooter walked towards the closet he noticed the children under the desk and began shooting them (Williams, 2012; Rayment, 2012; *NBC News*, 2012). The shooter shot at the children as they tried to run for safety. Soto put herself between her students and the shooter; she was fatally shot. Police found the five children who had been hidden in the closet unharmed when they entered the classroom. Eleven children from Soto's class survived.

Laura Rousseau had been a long-term substitute at the school and had recently learned that she was to be permanently hired at the school. She was gunned down along with 14 of her students. Rachel D'Avino who worked with the special needs children at the school was fatally shot. She died trying to protect her students (Oritz, 2012). In the same classroom Anne Marie Murphy was shot dead. She was a teacher's aide who also worked with special needs students. Her body was found over the body of a six-year-old student who she had tried to save by covering his body with hers (Ramos, 2012; Cleary, 2012a).

Teacher Kaitlin Roig thought she was hearing automatic gunfire. She locked her classroom door and led her 14 students into a bathroom and moved a bookcase in front of the door to keep out the shooter. She kept telling the students that she loved them and told them to pray or think happy thoughts. Even when the shooting was over she would not let the police near her students until they slid their badges under the door. Even then she insisted they get a key and unlock the door, which they did (Emmert, 2012; Cleary 2012b). She and her 14 students survived.

Music teacher Maryrose Kristopik also took her students to a classroom closet (Roberts, 2012). The shooter arrived moments later, pounding and yelling 'Let me in'. The students and Kristopik stayed quiet (Sabillon, 2012). They survived. As soon as she heard gunshots, teacher Laura Feinstein, a reading specialist, led two students into her classroom and locked the door. She hid the students in the classroom under the desks and attempted to call 911 but had no reception (WTOP, 2012). They could hear multiple gunshots. Eventually the police spoke over the intercom and said 'You're safe. We're here.' She hid with the children for approximately 40 minutes, until law enforcement came to lead them out of the room. They survived (Winter, 2012).

Custodian Rick Thorne saw the gunman in the hall. He began to run through the halls screaming 'A gunman is coming!' He tried to make sure all of the classroom doors were locked (Christoffersen, 2012). He survived. Two third-graders were heading to the office with their classroom attendance report. Teacher Abbey Clements pulled them into her classroom as the shooting began. They survived (Nikitchyuk, 2012).

School library staff members Yvonne Cech and Maryann Jacob hid 18 children in a part of the library the school used for lockdown in practice drills. Upon discovering that one of the doors would not lock, they moved the children into a storage room and barricaded the door with a filing cabinet. They survived (*BBC News*, 2012; *New York Times*, 2012; Barron, 2012).

The shooting stopped between 9.46 and 9.49 a.m. One hundred fifty-four rounds were fired from the shooter's rifle. The shooter fled from the police into Soto's classroom and then killed himself (MSNBC, 2013; Altimari et al., 2013; *New Haven Register*, 2012; Goldstein and Rashbaum, 2012; *CBS News*, 2012; Candiotti and Ford, 2012). All of the shooting had occurred in less than five minutes (Emmert, 2012). Immediately the police locked down the school and began evacuating the survivors (Macleans, 2012).

Following the events of 14 December, this extreme situation would require additional leadership efforts to help the survivors deal with multiple issues of adjustment and logistical questions. How could these young children go back to school? Where would they go back to school? Who would lead the school? Several individuals assumed leadership roles to help the school deal with these issues. An empty school, Chalk Hill Middle School in Monroe, CT, was decided upon as the site for the school for the surviving children. For three weeks preparations were made to make the school comfortable for the surviving children and teachers. Desks were brought over from Sandy Hook. The artwork on the classroom walls at Sandy Hook was moved to the new school. The school was temporarily renamed Sandy Hook. Donna Page, who had earlier retired as principal of Sandy Hook Elementary School, returned to the position to lead the school back to some sense of normalcy. The students returned to school at this new site on 3 January 2013 (Reuters, 2012b; *News-Times*, 2012; *BBC News*, 2013), their lives forever changed by the events of 14 December.

LEADERSHIP THEORIES

As stated on the National Center for Education Statistics website, 'Violent deaths at schools are rare but tragic events with far-reaching effects on the school population and surrounding community.' The Indicators of School Crime and Safety Report (2011) defines a school associated violent death as 'a homicide, suicide, or legal intervention (involving a law enforcement officer), in which the fatal injury occurred on the campus of a functioning elementary or secondary school in the United States'. Sandy Hook Elementary School is now classified as the most deadly school shooting in a United States public school (Bratu, 2012).

In the fall of 2012, close to 50 million students were expected to enroll in public elementary and secondary schools, with 70 percent enrolled in elementary schools. Another 5 million students were expected to attend private school (Institute of Education Sciences, 2012). Expenditures at public schools for 2012–2013 were estimated at \$571 billion. The numbers of teachers estimated to be employed in the public school systems in the fall of 2012 was estimated at over 3 million in full-time-equivalent teachers (Institute of Education Sciences, 2012). When administrators, staff, aides and service personnel are added to these numbers, it is obvious that this is a large number of employees who may potentially experience a violent episode at their place of work.

Of course, school settings are not typical places of work. Along with employees, schools are also comprised of students whose safety is entrusted to the principals, teachers and staff who work in those schools. In fact, an early study looking at educational leaders identified 21 types of educational leaders (Harding, 1949). Two of these types that are relevant to this case are 'child protector' and 'optimist'. It is obvious that the educators at Sandy Hook Elementary School stepped immediately into the role of child protectors. These acts of leading included hiding children in storage areas, broom closets and bathrooms, yanking children out of hallways to hide them in their room, putting their bodies between the children and the shooter to protect the children, and in the case of the unarmed principal, attacking the shooter and trying to get the gun away from him.

The teachers who survived the shootings were optimists in the face of a horrific situation. Optimism is a frequent theme throughout most leadership theories (Seligman and Csikszentmihalyi, 2000). The extreme situation of a shooter entering an elementary school takes very qualified leaders to demonstrate optimism. Many of the teachers recounted how they kept telling the students that they would be 'OK', and many discussed how they would be ready for Christmas in 11 days. Over the years, empirical evidence has supported that positive states such as optimism and hope will lead to positive outcomes for leaders (Stajkovic and Luthans, 1998). However, these two states tend to be spontaneous and are often induced by situational factors. In the extreme situation of a shooter in their school, many of the educators appeared able to demonstrate optimism and this may have led to positive outcomes for some of those on the school grounds.

Hope is a bit different from optimism. Snyder's (2000, p. 21) theory defines hopes 'as a positive motivational state that is based on both a sense of being capable of being successful and of having a pathway to success. If the pathways become blocked, the hope process allows these blockages to be perceived as challenging and learning opportunities'. The optimism of the educators at Sandy Hook may have led them to being hopeful that they could keep the children alive and that they could find a pathway to safety and overcome the blocked paths the shooter had created. The behaviors of the teachers suggest that they appeared to remain hopeful even though they assessed their chances of survival as being very slim. Hope and optimism were two important traits that may partially explain the leadership behaviors exhibited by several teachers and administrators at Sandy Hook Elementary School.

Early leadership theories first looked at the traits of leaders. They felt that by studying the traits of great leaders these traits could be identified and categorized and would help to identify new leaders. While often controversial, there are three traits that empirical research has shown to be part of effective leadership. The three common traits found are intelligence, initiative and self-confidence. At Sandy Hook Elementary School these educators were very intelligent. Someone, probably the principal, turned on the intercom system so the rest of the school would know there was a shooter in the building. The other educators realized they would not be able to get children out of the building, so they needed to find places to shelter them.

Examples of initiative were rampant throughout the case. Teachers found hiding places for their students, they found ways to barricade the doors against the shooter, they pulled students out of the hallways, they found ways to keep five- and six-year-old children quiet and still in confined spaces, and they maintained their composure as they invented lies to tell the shooter about the location of the students.

Self-confidence was shown by all the educators in this case. Three administrators ran straight to the shooter to confront him. If they were having any doubts about their survival, as would be expected in this type of situation, most of the teachers displayed extreme levels of self-confidence to their students. They told their students that they would need to wait for the good guys, that they would be OK, and that everything would be all right (Emmert, 2012; Cleary, 2012b).

The self-confidence that the teachers displayed may be explained by the theory of self-managing individuals and leaders (Bandura, 1977). Within this theory leaders create self-managing individuals. At Sandy Hook Elementary School there were no examples of followers waiting to be told what to do. The teachers described in this case self-managed themselves, and sprang into action with the goal of saving the children.

In *Theories of Educational Leadership and Management*, Tony Bush (2003), identifies three dimensions as the basis of educational leadership. These three dimensions are influence, values and vision. Many definitions of leadership specify that there must be a process of influence (Yukl, 2002). Clearly, at Sandy Hook, the principal had a great deal of influence with the other educators, students and parents. Cuban (1988,

p. 193) describes the influence process as leadership referring to people 'who bend the motivation and actions of others to achieve certain goals; it implies taking initiatives and risk'. The principal clearly was this kind of leader. When others talk of her day-to-day leadership in the years before the shootings occurred, we hear how she motivated others and was a wonderful influence on the teachers and students. On the day of the shooting she risked her life to save the students by attacking the shooter and trying to disarm him.

Values are also an important component of educational leadership. Many theories of leadership find that effective leadership needs to be grounded in firm personal and professional values (Wasserberg, 2000). Day et al.'s (2001) research on effective schools found that effective educational leaders were able to articulate their professional, personal and educational values for their schools. The values at Sandy Hook Elementary School seem very much grounded in keeping the children safe. For example, a new alarm and entry system had recently been put into place at the school. Considerations were made about 'What if?' shooting scenarios. The selfless actions of so many of the teachers suggests that they immediately implemented their personal values of keeping the children safe.

Vision is also regarded as an important component of effective leadership. Besides having a vision for the school, leaders must be able to articulate the vision clearly to their followers and be able to motivate them to believe in the vision (Bennis and Nanus, 1985). In education, it is very important that a principal has a vision specific to their school and not an overall educational vision for the system. Clearly Hochsprung was a principal beloved by the parents and teachers in Sandy Hook. She was able to articulate her vision for the school and its students. When her vision was clouded by the shooter, she refocused and quickly communicated her new vision of saving the children to the other teachers and staff.

Servant leadership (Greenleaf, 1977) is often associated with educational leaders. In servant leadership the needs of the others are the highest priority. Leaders have to share power and help their followers to grow. One theory emerging from servant leadership that is applicable to the Sandy Hook case is self-sacrificial leaders (Choi and Mai-Dalton, 1999). This theory posits that effective self-sacrificial leaders give up or postpone what is best for themselves in order to help their followers. Studies found that employees felt they would be more likely to be self-sacrificial leaders if their own leaders displayed self-sacrificial behavior (Yorges et al., 1999). From the moment the two administrators sacrificed themselves to save the children, the rest of the school responded in kind. Hochsprung and Sherlack clearly displayed self-sacrificial leadership behavior, although probably far beyond how the theorists imagined their theory being utilized.

LEADERSHIP LESSONS

While it may still be too early to fully extract all of the leadership lessons that can be learned from the incident at Sandy Hook Elementary School, there are several important leadership lessons that can be drawn from the actions of Sandy Hook administrators, teachers and staff.

Leadership Lesson 1: Danger Does Not Always Come from Outside

The danger to Sandy Hook Elementary School did not come from a person or an event outside of the school environment. The shooter had been a former student. There was no apparent reason for anyone at the school to think that he might return to the school and kill them until they saw him with a gun in his hands. While this is an extreme situation, it is suggested that organizations do not ignore internal turbulence in an effort to search their external environment for threats.

Leadership Lesson 2: Crisis Response Plans are Critical

The educators at Sandy Hook Elementary School had completed training programs about extreme events in their environment including bomb threats and shooters. This training may have played an important part in the crisis response actions of the principal and several of the teachers. When shots were first heard in the school, the principal confronted the shooter and is likely to have turned on the intercom system to alert others. After she was shot and killed, the other teachers mobilized into action. They did not collapse and lose hope and they appeared to have intuitively remembered some of their crisis response training. They removed the students from the hallways, they hid students, they barricaded classrooms, bathrooms and storage closets, and they isolated the section of the school where the shooter was. They were able to take deliberate actions to save the children under a very dangerous and extreme situation. Organizations are urged to review and update their current crisis response plans and to immediately design and implement plans if none are in place (Hurley-Hanson and Giannantonio, 2009).

Leadership Lesson 3: Sustain Hope and Stay Realistic

Enduring an event as extreme as the school shooting at Sandy Hook Elementary School seemed like an eternity for both those inside the building and those waiting outside for news of their loved ones. Research suggests that people who experience a tragic event will go back and try to find that one moment when their faith and hope were rewarded or they realized that there was no more need for hope (Houlahan, 2012). In reliving tragedies, people look for that one last moment before all hope was lost and their lives changed forever. When the shootings at Sandy Hook were over, and the people on the inside were escorted out of the school, their hope to survive and save the children was rewarded. However, as they walked by the bodies of those who were killed, they realized that not all of their hopes had been realized. These reactions were experienced by those who survived the shootings, their relatives waiting on the outside, and the first responders who were sent to deal with extreme events.

First responders arrive at extreme situations with the very real hope and optimism that they can do something to de-escalate the situation and save people. In Newtown, CT, the emergency medical technicians who arrived on site to help save lives were told that their expertise was not needed inside the school or anywhere else on the school grounds. They realized that all hope was lost when the Newtown EMT captain 'ordered them to stand down, and that there was no one left to help, no one left alive' (Houlahan, 2012).

What does this mean for organizations? It is important that organizational leaders balance the need to sustain hope and stay realistic. The importance of remaining optimistic and sustaining hope when managing problems and dealing with difficult situations cannot be overstated. Leaders are cautioned to stay realistic and avoid escalation of commitment when evidence presents itself that an implemented strategy is no longer effective.

Leadership Lesson 4: A Split-Second Decision May Determine the Rest of Your Life

In most extreme situations split-second decisions may make the difference between whether a person survives or dies. At Sandy Hook Elementary School numerous decisions about what to do were made in a split second. The actions taken by the teachers who survived reflect employees reacting to crisis situations with little or no warning. Employees who are prepared for crisis situations may be better trained to quickly make decisions and take actions in extreme situations. Training needs to include helping to improve the intuitive thinking and decision-making of employees, so that their intuitiveness will kick in when they are faced with a split-second decision. Hopefully, most employees will not be making split-second decisions that determine whether they live or die, but they may be making decisions regarding the fate of a product, an account or even a company. At Sandy Hook Elementary School the administrators and educators all were faced with a split-second decision of what to do. Some such as Hochsprung and Sherlack lost their lives because of their decision to act. They almost surely knew this would be the outcome. However, they felt the risk was worth taking if they could avoid any more bloodshed. Others had to make quick decisions such as where to hide the children or whether they should try to run. Each decision-maker relied on their intuition and previous training to guide them as to which decision would save the children. They all made split-second decisions that sealed their fate in this extreme situation.

CONCLUSION

At the heart of much leadership research is trying to predict how leaders will behave in different situations. The events at Sandy Hook Elementary School were clearly an example of an extreme situation. When they went to work on 14 December 2012 the administrators, teachers and staff did not expect to be faced with an extreme situation. What caused these leaders to react the way they did? Their selfless actions saved dozens of lives that day. What happened at Sandy Hook reminds us that each of us may be called to be a leader in today's extreme work and life environments. Maybe we have to work on being self-leaders since it appears we might need to lead when we least expect it. And that uncertainty is perhaps the most extreme situation we will ever have to face.

REFERENCES

Altimari, D., Edmund H. Mahony and Jon Lender (2013). Newtown shootings: Adam Lanza researched mass murderers, sources say. Available at http://articles.courant.com/2013-03-13/news/hc-newtown-lanza-mass-murderers-20130313_1_adam-lanza-nancy-lanza-mary-scherlach (accessed 14 March 2013).

Barron, J. (2012). Children were all shot multiple times with a semiautomatic, officials say. Available at http://www.nytimes.com/2012/12/16/nyregion/gunman-kills-20-children-at-school-in-connecticut-28-dead-in-all.html?_r=1& (accessed 17 December 2012).

BBC News (2012). Newtown school massacre victims identified. Available at http://www.bbc.co.uk/news/world-us-canada-20744701 (accessed 16 December 2012).

BBC News (2013). Newtown shooting: Sandy Hook students back to school. Available at http://www.bbc.co.uk/news/world-us-canada-20896341 (accessed 3 January 2013).

Bandura, A. (1977). Self-efficacy: towards a unify theory of behavioral change. *Psychological Review*, 84, 191–215.

Bratu, B. (2012). Connecticut school shooting is second worst in US history. Available at http://usnews.nbcnews.com/_news/2012/12/14/15909827-connecticut-school-shooting-is-second-worst-in-us-history?lite (accessed 17 December 2012).

Bennis, W.G. and B. Nanus (1985). *Leaders: The Strategies for Taking Charge*. New York: Harper and Row.

Bush, T. (2003). *Theories of Educational Leadership and Management*, 3rd edn. Thousand Oaks, CA: SAGE Publications.

Candiotti, Susan and Dana Ford (2012). Families hold funerals as school resumes for some Newtown students. Available at http://www.cnn.com/2012/12/18/us/connecticut-school-shooting/index.html (accessed 18 December 2012).

CBS News (2012). Investigators probe life of mass-murderer Adam Lanza. Available at http://www.cbsnews.com/8301-201_162-57559442/investigators-probe-life-of-mass-murderer-adam-lanza (accessed 28 December 2012).

Choi, Y. and R.R. Mai-Dalton (1999). The model of followers' responses to self-sacrificial leadership: an empirical test. *Leadership Quarterly*, 10, 397–421.

Christoffersen, John (2012). 20 children, 6 adults killed at Connecticut school. Available at http://abclocal.go.com/wpvi/story?section=news/national_world&id=8920117 (accessed 15 December 2012).

Cleary, Tom (2012a). Dylan Hockley died in Anne Marie Murphy's arms. Available at http://www.ctpost.com/news/article/Dylan-Hockley-died-in-Anne-Marie-Murphy-s-arms-4122828.php (accessed 18 December 2012).

Cleary, Tom (2012b). 'Hero teacher' rushed students to bathroom to keep students safe. Available at http://blog.ctnews.com/newtownshooting/2012/12/14/hero-teacher-rushed-students-to-bathroom-to-keep-students-safe (accessed 15 December 2012).

Cuban, L. (1988). *The Managerial Imperative and the Practice of Leadership in Schools*. Albany, NY: State University of New York Press.

Day, E., A. Harris and M. Hadfield (2001). Challenging the orthodoxy of effective school leadership. *International Journal of Leadership in Education*, 4 (1), 39–56.

Emmert, Don (2012). Conn. elementary school shooting: 20 children, seven adults killed. Available at http://www.masoncountydailynews.com (accessed 18 December 2012).

Goldstein, Joseph and William Rashbaum (2012). 27 killed in Connecticut shooting, including 20 children. Available at http://www.nytimes.com/2012/12/15/nyregion/shooting-reported-at-connecticut-elementary-school.html (accessed 14 December 2012).

Greenleaf, R.K. (1977). *Servant Leadership*. Indianapolis, IN: Robert K. Greenleaf Center.

Harding, L.W. (1949). Twenty-one varieties of educational leadership. *Educational Leadership*, 6, 299–302.

Houlahan, P. (2012). Sandy Hook EMT and former Whittier resident reflects on massacre. Available at http://www.dailynews.com/ci_22247188/sandy-hook-emt-and-former-whittier-resident-reflects (accessed 23 December 2012).

Hurley-Hanson, A.E. and C.M. Giannantonio (2009). Crisis response plans post 9/11: current status and future directions. *Academy of Strategic Management Journal*, 8, 23–36.

Indicators of School Crime and Safety Report (2011). Available at http://nces.ed.gov/ programs/crimeindicators/crimeindicators2011/index.asp.

Institute of Education Sciences (2012). Available at http://ies.ed.gov/.

Levitz, Jennifer (2012). Sandy Hook locals face new reality. Available at http:// online.wsj.com/article/SB10001424127887323297104578181583018831100.html (accessed 19 December 2012).

Macleans (2012). Twenty children dead in mass shooting at Connecticut elementary school. Available at http://www2.macleans.ca/2012/12/14/18-children-dead-in-connecticut-school-shooting/ (accessed 28 December 2012).

MSNBC (2013). Inside Newtown shooter Adam Lanza's home. Available at http:// tv.msnbc.com/2013/03/28/inside-newtown-shooter-adam-lanzas-home (accessed 28 March 2013).

NBC News (2012). Lives saved by teachers, custodian and even children in Connecticut school shooting. Available at http://usnews.nbcnews.com/_news/2012/12/15/ 15927932-lives-saved-by-teachers-custodian-and-even-children-in-connecticut-school-shooting?lite (accessed 18 December 2012).

New Haven Register (2012). Newtown school shooting: transcript of police, fire radio dispatch. Available at http://nhregister.com/articles/2012/12/14/news/doc50cc089 7adc1a203744261.txt?viewmode=2 (accessed 17 December 2012).

New York Times (2012). Who would do this to our poor little babies? Available at http://www.nytimes.com/2012/12/15/nyregion/witnesses-recall-deadly-shooting-sandy-hook-newtown-connecticut.html (accessed 16 December 2012).

News-Times (2012). Sandy Hook students to move to Monroe school. Available at http://www.newstimes.com/local/article/Sandy-Hook-students-to-move-to-Monroe-school-4122271.php (accessed 16 December 2012).

Nikitchyuk, Andre (2012). Breaking the silence! Father of surviving Sandy Hook student admits turning a blind eye to gun violence can no longer be an option. Available at http://www.nydailynews.com/new-york/father-surviving-sandy-hook-student-admits-turning-blind-eye-gun-violence-longer-option-article-1.1222370? localLinksEnabled=false (accessed 18 December 2012).

Oritz, Erik (2012). Newtown school shooting snuffs out promising lives of teachers, students. Available at http://www.nydailynews.com/news/national/conn-shooting-takes-young-teacher-aide-life-article-1.1221839?localLinksEnabled=false (accessed 18 December 2012).

Ramos, Victor Manuel (2012). Sandy Hook educators died trying to save the children. Available at http://www.newsday.com/news/nation/sandy-hook-educators-died-trying-to-save-the-children-1.4338161 (accessed 26 December 2012).

Rayment, Sean (2012). Teachers sacrificed themselves to save their pupils. Available at http://www.telegraph.co.uk/news/worldnews/northamerica/usa/9746935/ Teachers-sacrificed-themselves-to-save-their-pupils.html accessed 15 December 2012).

Reuters (2012a). Children in Connecticut rampage were six, seven; shot multiple times. Available at http://uk.reuters.com/article/2012/12/15/uk-usa-shooting-connecticut-idUKBRE8BD0Z220121215 (accessed 15 December 2012).

Reuters (2012b). Connecticut survivors to attend school in neighboring town. Available at http://www.reuters.com/article/2012/12/16/us-usa-shooting-connecticut-school-idUSBRE8BF0B520121216 (accessed 16 December 2012).

Roberts, Christine (2012). Teacher's words of comfort to class during Newtown rampage: 'I love you all very much … it's going to be OK'. Available at http://www.nydailynews.com/news/national/sandy-hook-teacher-speaks-ordeal-article-1.1222727 (accessed 18 December, 2012).

Sabillon, Nicholas (2012). Sandy Hook student, recalls killer pounding on his classroom door. Available at http://www.huffingtonpost.com/2012/12/18/nicholas-sabillon-sandy-hook-student_n_2322261.html?utm_hp_ref=crime (accessed 19 December 2012).

Seligman, M.E.P. and M. Csikszentmihalyi (2000). Positive psychology: an introduction. *American Psychologist*, 55, 5–14.

Snyder, C.R. (2000). *Handbook of Hope*. San Diego, CA: Academic Press.

Stajkovic, A.D. and F. Luthans (1998). Self-sufficiency and work-related performance: a meta-analysis. *Psychological Bulletin*, 124, 240–61.

Virgalla, Becky (2012). Newtown shooting survivor, says Principal, others saved her in Sandy Hook rampage. Available at http://www.huffingtonpost.com/2012/12/24/becky-virgalla-_n_2357284.html (accessed 28 March 2013).

Wasserberg, M. (2000). Creating the vision and making it happen. In H. Tomlinson, H. Gunter and P. Smith (eds), *Living Headship*. London: Paul Chapman Publishing.

Weisskopf, Arlene (2013). *Face the Nation* (Producer). 21 April. New York: CBS.

Williams, Matt (2012). Victoria Soto: Sandy Hook teacher who wanted to mold young minds. Available at http://www.guardian.co.uk/world/2012/dec/15/sandy-hook-teacher-victoria-soto (accessed 16 December 2012).

Winter, Michael (2012). Tales of Sandy Hook heroism, young and old. Available at http://www.usatoday.com/story/news/nation/2012/12/14/newtown-connecticut-sandy-hook-school-shooting-heroism/1770555 (accessed 26 December 2012).

WTOP (2012). 'Absolutely heartbreaking': Sandy Hook teacher's terrifying experience. Available at http://www.wtop.com/1272/3157532/Teacher-Shots-and-shots-and-shots (accessed 16 December 2012).

Yorges, S.L., H.M. Weiss and O.J. Strickland (1999). The effect of leader outcomes on influence, attributions, and perceptions of charisma. *Journal of Applied Psychology*, 84, 428–36.

Yukl, G. (2002). *Leadership in Organizations*, 5th edn. Upper Saddle River, NJ: Prentice Hall.

Index

Academy of Management (AOM)
    xi–xii, xvii
Acme Manufacturing Company
    (pseudonym)
    downsizing of 214–16
    employee roster of 216–17, 222
Aguilar, René, role in Chilean miner
    rescue 124
American Film Institute 195
Amundsen, Roald xiv, 19, 21, 26
    Antarctic Expedition (1910–12) 3–6,
        16–17, 20, 23–5, 28, 33
    Northwest Passage Expedition
        (1903–6) 37, 42
    team used by 28, 31
Antarctica xiii, 9, 47, 50, 52–3
    Bay of Whales 16, 23
    Beardmore Glacier 21–2
    Cape Evans 16, 22–3
    Elephant Island 7
    environmental/geographical
        characteristics of 20, 24, 47–9,
        59
    Great Ice Barrier 27
    Northwest Passage xiv, 4, 19, 34,
        37–8, 40, 42, 44
    One Ton Depot 22, 27, 29–30
    South Georgia Island 7
    South Pole 3–6, 8, 11, 15–17, 19–23,
        33, 36, 38, 103
Aramark, role in Chilean miner rescue
    125
Arctic
    North West Passage 37–8
    North Pole 34, 38–41
Australia 47

Bart, Peter 193
    Paramount Pictures Vice-President of
        Production 188, 190
Bjaaland, Olva 28
Boorman, John 188
Bowers, Henry 28
Bowman, Mark
    background of 142, 145–6
    use of LMX 153–5
Brando, Marlon 191–2, 194
Brash, Andrew 73–5
British Antarctica Survey, stations
    operated by 47
British Petroleum (BP), Deepwater
    Horizon Oil Disaster 156
Burundi 109–10
Bush, Tony, *Theories of Educational
    Leadership and Management* 229

Cambodia 110
Capparell, Stephanie, *Shackleton's
    Way: Leadership Lessons from the
    Great Antarctic Explorer* 10
Cech, Yvonne, librarian at Sandy Hook
    Elementary School 226
Center Rock, role in Chilean miner
    rescue 125
Chile
    Copiapó 117, 121, 123
    Santiago 117, 121
Chilean miner rescue (2010) xv,
    117–20, 122, 125–9, 131, 135–9
    drilling of boreholes during 122, 125,
        133
    international organisations involved
        in 125–6

key personnel involved in 124–5
media observation of 120–21
skillset of miners in 132–3, 137
China 65
borders of 84
Clements, Abbey, teacher at Sandy
    Hook Elementary School 226
complex adaptive system (CAS),
    examples of 196
Complexity Leadership Theory 165,
    173–4, 176–9, 182–3, 195–6, 199
    concept of 176, 183
    Leader-Context Effectiveness Model
        178, 184
computed tomography (CT) lines
    201–2, 206
    procedures 205
    sale of 202, 204
Cook, Frederick 3
Cook, James, model of maritime
    exploration 38–9
Coppola, Francis Ford xv, 190–92
    as example of successful 'extreme
        leader' 195–6, 198
    Godfather, The (1972) 187–96, 198–9
    Godfather Part II, The (1974) 195,
        198–9
    Finian's Rainbow 190
Crean, Tom 7, 9–10
creative deviance theory, concept of 196
Custom Medical Specialties (CMS)
    201–2, 205–6, 208–9
    market share of 207
    personnel of xv–xvi, 211
    sale of CT lines 202, 204

D'Avino Rachel, death of 226
decision conflict model, concept of 19
Democratic Republic of Congo (DRC)
    109
    malaria infection rates in 112–13
    Ministry of Health 111
    Moba Territory 113
De Niro, Robert 194
Duvall, Robert 192

El Teniente, personnel of 124
Evans, Edgar 28

health problems suffered by 28–9
Evans, Robert 190–91
    Paramount Pictures head of
        Production 189
expedition objectives 21–2
    prioritisation 22
extreme situation management 35

Feinstein, Laura, reading specialist at
    Sandy Hook Elementary School
    226
France 38, 168
Franklin, Sir John 39–40, 42, 44
    Royal Navy Northwest Passage
        Expedition (1845–8) 34, 37–8
Fuchs, Sir Vivian and the
    Commonwealth Trans-Antarctic
    Expedition (1955–8) 53

de Gerlache, Adrien and the Belgian
    Antarctica Expedition (1897) 3
Germany, Third Reich (1933–45) 166
Glenn Miller Orchestra, record sales
    figures for 167, 170
Golborne, Laurence 117–18, 120–24
    Chilean mining minister 117
    organized leadership of 126–7
Google Inc. 11
Greenland xiv, 40–41, 96, 98–9, 101,
    103
    coast of 39
    crossing routes 97
grounded theory 37
Gruber, Peter 189

Haiti 110
Hall, Lincoln, rescue of 74–7, 81
Hammond, Natalie, vice-principal of
    Sandy Hook Elementary School
    225
Hanssen, Hilmer 28
hastily formed networks (HFNs)
    concept of 153
    swift trust in 153
Hauge, Harald 103
    background of 97–8
Hewlett-Packard (HP), partnership with
    LTFHC 111

Hitler, Adolf, rise to power (1933) 166
Hochsprung, Dawn, principal of Sandy
    Hook Elementary School 225
Honduras 110
Hurley, Frank 9

IBM, personnel of 98
India 110
International Association of Chiefs of
    Police (IACP) 14
    curriculum of 142
    personnel of 142

Jacob, Maryann, librarian at Sandy
    Hook Elementary School 226
Jaffe, Stanley 191
Jofré, Gerardo, chairman of Codelco
    124
Johansen, Hjalmar 24

K2
    Bottleneck 85–7
    environmental characteristics of
        84–5, 90
    expeditions on 84–8, 90
    fatalities on 84, 88
    nocturnal descents on 88
    Traverse 85–6, 93
Kazan, Elia 192–3
Keaton, Diane 192
Klinke, Christopher 87
Kranz, Eugene, Apollo 13 flight director
    118
Kristopik, Maryrose, teacher at Sandy
    Hook Elementary School 226

Lake Tanganyika Floating Health Clinic
    (LTFHC) 111–12
    founding of (2009) 110
    Katanga Kicks Malaria 2010 (KKM)
        113
    partnership with HP 111
    personnel of 111
    upgrade of Kirnado Health Center
        113–14
Lansing, Sir Alfred 13
leader inheritance, 'Great Man' theory
    49

leadership 11–13, 16, 18, 20, 32, 44,
        49, 55–6, 62–3, 79–80, 88–9,
        91–2, 98–9, 101–3, 145, 152,
        221–2, 229
    communication 50–51, 57–8
    distributed 91
    emotional awareness/characteristics
        52–4
    environmental fit 57
    executive 156–7
    extreme 168, 170–74, 182–5, 187,
        195–6, 198–9, 220, 224–5, 232
    goal commitment 136–7
    impact of personality 32
    integration 147–8
    internal/external coordination 137–8
    multi-tiered 117–19, 126–9
    organized 126–7
    pack courage 11
    pack curiosity 11
    pack nourishment 11–12
    pack optimism 12
    personality 51–5
    project manager 69–70
    responsibility 80, 98
    risk awareness 80–81, 100
    role of 'body' in 92
    role of extreme situations upon 33,
        65, 77–80, 94, 134–6, 138–9
    rotation 99
    self-sacrificial 230–31
    shared 89–90, 93–4
    sovereign 126–7
    style of thinking 55–6, 58, 99–100
    team 126–7, 131–4, 136–7, 141,
        143–4
    transformational 220
    trust 50, 57, 80, 99
leadership-motivated excellence
    (LMX) 142–3, 151
    application of 151–5
Lehman, Amy 107, 109–11,
        113–15
    background of 110
    founder of LTFHC 110
Lesotho 107
Lie, Morten, background of 98
Lucas, George 190

malaria
  fatalities from 112–13
  long-lasting insecticide treated bed
      nets (LLINs) 113
management situation 36
  traditional concept of 35
Markham, Sir Clements 25
Mazur, Dan
  Mount Everest expedition (2006)
      73–9, 81
  rescue of Lincoln Hall 74–7, 81
Mercy Ships 110
Mexico 201, 208
Milius, John 190
Miller, Glenn 165, 179–80, 183–4
  as example of 'Complexity
      Leadership Theory' 176–9, 182
  as example of successful 'extreme
      leader' 168, 170–74, 182, 184–5
  as example of Transformational
      Leadership Theory 174–6, 182
  background of 166–7
  military service of 167–8, 177
Morrell, Margot, *Shackleton's Way:
  Leadership Lessons from the
  Great Antarctic Explorer* 10
Mount Everest 73
  'Death Zone' 72
  environmental characteristics of 72–3
  expeditions on 73–8, 81, 84, 96
  fatalities on 79, 83–4
Murphy, Anne Marie, death of 226

Nansen, Fridtjof 26, 39, 41, 43–4
  Norwegian North Polar Expedition
      (1893–6) 34–5, 38, 40
  team used by 42
National Aeronautics and Space
      Administration (NASA) 125
  Apollo 13 incident (1970) 118, 128
  personnel of 118
  role in Chilean miner rescue 125–6
National Center for Education Statistics
      227
National Copper Corporation of Chile
      (Codelco), personnel of 124
Nepal 76
New Zealand 55

non-governmental organizations
      (NGOs) 110
North Atlantic Treaty Organization
      (NATO), personnel of 98
Norway 19, 38, 40, 97–8, 102
  Oslo 101, 103
  Royal Navy 98
Norwegian Defense Headquarters 98

Oates, Lawrence 5, 26–8, 30
  health problems suffered by 28–9
organizations 141–2
  internal development 214
  sustainable 180
Osborne, Myles 73–5

Pacino, Al 191, 194
Page, Donna 227
Pakistan, borders of 84
Paramount Pictures 198–9
  personnel of 188–91
Peary, Robert 3
Perkin, Dennis, *Leading at the Edge:
  Leadership Lessons from the
  Extraordinary Saga of
  Shackleton's Antarctic Expedition*
      10
Piñera, Sebastian 121, 123–5
  President of Chile 117–18
  sovereign leadership of 126–7
polar stations
  restrictive characteristics of 54
  staff of 47–55, 58–9
police 141–2
  application of LMX 151–5
  Crisis Negotiation Team 147, 149
  dog handling (K9) team 146–8
  interdependence among 149
  operational management 146–50
  Special Weapons and Tactics (SWAT)
      Team 144–5, 147, 149
  trust dynamics 142–3
post-traumatic stress (PTS) 155
  'prevention training' 145
  recognition of 143
preparation 40–41
  adaptation opportunities 40–41
  use of scientific knowledge 41–2

professional military education (PME) 156

Project Darwin (2009) xiv, 36, 62–3, 66, 68–70
    as example of 'successful leadership failure' 67–8
    expedition phase 63–4
    funding of 66
    personnel of 65–6
    preparatory phase 63
    post-expedition phase 63

Project HOPE 110

Puzzo, Mario, *Godfather, The* 190–91

Roig, Kaitlin, teacher at Sandy Hook Elementary School 226

Royal Geographical Society 18–19, 21

Sandy Hook Elementary School shooting (2012) xxii, xvi, xvii, 224-36

Schramm, role in Chilean miner rescue 125

Scorsese, Martin 193

Scott, Robert Falcon xiv, 15, 21–2
    Antarctic base camp 22–4
    death of (1912) 5, 16
    Discovery Expedition 4–5, 18
    team used by 28
    Terra Nova Expedition (1912) 3–4, 16, 18, 21–3, 25–6, 28, 30–31, 33

Second World War (1939–45) xv, 165, 167, 170, 172
    Pearl Harbor attack (1941) 166

Shackleton, Sir Ernest 5, 8
    HMS *Endurance* expedition (1914–15) xi, xiii–xiv, 3, 6–13, 36
    Nimrod expedition (1907–9) 16, 20, 24
    planning conducted by 9

Sherlack, Mary, school psychologist of Sandy Hook Elementary School 225

Sherpa, Jangbu 73–5

Skog, Cecile, Norwegian K2 expedition 87

Sony Pictures, personnel of 189

Soto, Victoria Leigh
    death of 225, 227
    teacher at Sandy Hook Elementary School 225–7

Sougarret, André 125
    role in Chilean miner rescue 124–5

spectral leader 91
    concept of 89–90
    emergence of 93

Spielberg, Steven 188–9
    Jaws (1975) 189

Stokkan, Bård 98

sub-Saharan Africa (SSA) 107–8, 111
    population of 108

successful leadership failure, concept of 67–8

supply depots
    examples of 27
    location of 26–7
    number of 27
    relocation of 30

Tanzania xv, 109–10
    Health Services Development Program (PHSDP) 108
    Kipili 114
    Kirando 114
    Lake Tanganyika 107, 109–11
    Ministry of Health and Social Welfare (MoHSW) 108
    Rukwa region 113–14

team development 215–20

team management/selection 27–8, 36–7, 78–9
    fitness issues 28–9
    skill sets 28

Tenerife air disaster (1977) 31

Thorne, Rick, custodian at Sandy Hook Elementary School 226

Tierra del Fuego
    Cape Horn 66
    Cordillera Darwin 62–4, 67

timing, poor 23–4

Tollefsen, Ivar Erik, background of 98

Transformational Leadership Theory 165, 173–4, 182
    concept of 174–6

transport methods
    depot-laying 24
    dog-hauling 25–6, 28
    man-hauling 25
    multiple 24–5
    pony 24, 28
trust
    role of risk in 152
    swift trust 153
Tyco's Mallinckrodt Division (TMD)
        201, 206–8, 211
    inability to supply CT lines 201–2,
        204, 209

United Kingdom 98
    London 6
    military of 28–9
    Royal Navy 18, 28–9, 38–9, 41–2
United Nations
    Children's Fund (UNICEF) 113
    Millennium Development Goals 108,
        113
United States of America 47, 142, 155,
        179, 201
    9/11 attacks xi, 143
    Air Force (USAF/USAAF) 143,
        167–8, 171–2, 177
    Alaska 65
    Boston Marathon bombing (2013) xi
    Chicago 193
    Columbine High School massacre
        (1999) 225
    education system of 227–8
    Food and Drug Administration (FDA)
        205
    Los Angeles 191
    Marine Corps 143

Military Academy at West Point 142
    military of 143, 171
    Navy of 143
    New York 191–2
        Veterans Administration (VA) 206
    see also Sandy Hook Elementary
        School shooting
Universal Studios 190
UPS, role in Chilean miner rescue 125
Urzúa, Luis 118
    shift foreman in Chilean miner rescue
        118, 132
    team leadership of 126–7, 133–4,
        136–7

Van Rooijen, Wilco 86
    Norit K2 expedition 87, 90
vigilant decision processes 19
Virgalla, Becky, reading consultant of
        Sandy Hook Elementary School
        225

Warner Brother Studios 190
Weber, Max 8
Welles, Orson, *Citizen Kane* (1941) 195
Wilson, Edward 18, 28
Wisting, Oscar 28
World Health Organization (WHO) 114
    anti-malaria program 113
    minimum standard of health worker
        ratios 108–9
    World Health Report 2006 107
Worsley, Frank 7, 9–10

Yahoo!, Inc. 11

Zambia 109–10